TRANSIENT LITERACIES IN ACTION

COMPOSING WITH THE
MOBILE SURROUND

T0308868

#WRITING

Series Editor: Cheryl E. Ball

Series Associate Editors: Tessa Brown, Stephen McElroy, and
  Sarah Warren-Riley

The #writing series publishes open-access digital and low-cost print editions of monographs that address issues in digital rhetoric, new media studies, digital humanities, techno-pedagogy, and similar areas of interest.

The WAC Clearinghouse, Colorado State University Open Press, and the University Press of Colorado are collaborating so that books in this series are widely available through free digital distribution and in a low-cost print edition. The publishers and the series editor are committed to the principle that knowledge should freely circulate. We see the opportunities that new technologies have for further democratizing knowledge. And we see that to share the power of writing is to share the means for all to articulate their needs, interest, and learning into the great experiment of literacy.

OTHER BOOKS IN THE SERIES

bonnie lenore kyburz. *Cruel Auteurism: Affective Digital Mediations toward Film-Composition* (2019)

Derek N. Mueller, *Network Sense: Methods for Visualizing a Discipline* (2017)

TRANSIENT LITERACIES IN ACTION

COMPOSING WITH THE
MOBILE SURROUND

By Stacey Pigg

The WAC Clearinghouse
wac.colostate.edu
Fort Collins, Colorado

University Press of Colorado
upcolorado.com
Louisville, Colorado

The WAC Clearinghouse, Fort Collins, Colorado 80523

University Press of Colorado, Louisville, Colorado 80027

ISBN 978-1-64215-101-5 (PDF) | 978-1-64215-102-2 (ePub) | 978-1-64642-144-2 (pbk.)

DOI: 10.37514/WRI-B.2020.1015

Produced in the United States of America

Library of Congress Cataloging-in-Publication Data

Names: Pigg, Stacey, author.
Title: Transient literacies in action : composing with the mobile surround / By Stacey Pigg.
Description: Fort Collins, Colorado : The WAC Clearinghouse; University Press of Colorado, [2020] | Series: #writing | Includes bibliographical references.
Identifiers: LCCN 2020033057 (print) | LCCN 2020033058 (ebook) | ISBN 9781646421442 (paperback) | ISBN 9781642151015 (pdf) | ISBN 9781642151022 (epub)
Subjects: LCSH: Computers and literacy. | Composition (Language arts) | Writing. | Authors—Effect of technological innovations on. | Mobile communication systems in education.
Classification: LCC LC149.5 .P54 2020 (print) | LCC LC149.5 (ebook) | DDC 371.33—dc23
LC record available at https://lccn.loc.gov/2020033057
LC ebook record available at https://lccn.loc.gov/2020033058

Copyeditors: Don Donahue
Designer: Mike Palmquist
Cover by Cheryl E. Ball; Original cover design by Than Saffel
Series Editor: Cheryl E. Ball
Series Associate Editors: Tessa Brown, Stephen McElroy, and Sarah Warren-Riley

The WAC Clearinghouse supports teachers of writing across the disciplines. Hosted by Colorado State University, and supported by the Colorado State University Open Press, it brings together scholarly journals and book series as well as resources for teachers who use writing in their courses. This book is available in digital formats for free download at wac.colostate.edu.

Founded in 1965, the University Press of Colorado is a nonprofit cooperative publishing enterprise supported, in part, by Adams State University, Colorado State University, Fort Lewis College, Metropolitan State University of Denver, University of Colorado, University of Northern Colorado, University of Wyoming, Utah State University, and Western Colorado University. For more information, visit upcolorado.com.

Contents

Acknowledgments

At least three different cities shaped this book, and each had a coffee place or two that became woven into it. I mark the beginning of this project in Lansing, Michigan, when I started walking from my house to the Gone Wired Café almost daily to read and write for class. The coffee shop was a block or so away from the bus stop nearest my home, and three blocks away from my house. I was a fixture there, as much as anyone who participated in my research. It wasn't just Gone Wired though. There was Biggby if I wanted a change of pace, or Espresso Royale if I wanted to find grad school friends. My laptop was clunky, but it allowed me to be in any of those places. My phone was a flip phone, but I still texted with it.

My dissertation committee of Malea Powell, Bill Hart-Davidson, Dànielle DeVoss, and John Monberg helped me think about why it might be important to study not only mobile composing, but also how habits of mind and body co-produced with mobile devices and their ecologies shaped what social interactions and places were possible. Across my big Dell laptop and several Moleskine notebooks, I puzzled through how to describe what I saw in the café and leaned on the amazing community of scholars at Michigan State at the time. Staci Perryman-Clark, Collin Craig, Qwo-Li Driskill, Jeff Grabill, Angela Haas, Kendall Leon, Terese Monberg, Jim Ridolfo, Donnie Sackey, Jennifer Sano-Franchini, Robyn Tasaka, and Douglas Walls are a just a few of the people beyond my dissertation committee who helped me figure out what I was saying, and who supported me by collaborating on other projects that shaped my thinking.

When I moved to Orlando for my first job at the University of Central Florida in 2011, I wanted to better understand whether and how the social arrangements I'd identified in my coffee shop study intersected with on-campus social learning environments. By this time, cell phones and laptops were everywhere, tablets were becoming more integrated, and the large, diverse student population at UCF was on the constant lookout for places to use them for study and online socializing. Encouragement from colleagues like Melody Bowdon, Laura Gonzales, Gabriela Raquel Rios, Angela Rounsaville, Blake Scott, and Douglas Walls pushed me to keep researching and to transition toward thinking about how my project could be a book. Melody, Chuck Dzuiban and others at UCF had been thinking through issues of space design for a long time, and I learned from teaching, researching, and discussing learning spaces alongside them.

At UCF, I also received an internal research support grant to research composers in the Technology Commons, as well as a National Endowment for the Humanities Summer Stipend that made it possible to complete my phase of research in the Technology Commons. An undergraduate research assistant, Amy Giroux, was central to data collection and analysis. During my time at UCF, I published two articles that paved the way for this book project and that discuss the same case participants. In *Technical Communication Quarterly* volume 23, issue 2 pages 69–87, I published "Coordinating Constant Invention: Social Media's Role in Distributed Work," which described how one writer used online resources through social media as a foundation for constructing a professional identity. Later in the same year, *College Composition and Communication* published "Emplacing Mobile Composing Habits: A Study of Academic Writing in Networked Social Spaces" in Volume 12, Issue 1, pages 250–275. This article analyzed how two students used shared social spaces as foundations for mobile device use. Chapters 2 and 3 make use of the same case participants' observations to different ends, and so I mention both these articles to acknowledge their influence on this text. During this time, I also learned from the opportunity to present early versions of Chapter 2 and 5 at the University of Texas El Paso and the University of Maine, where students and faculty helped me refine ideas.

When my project moved with me to North Carolina State University in 2015, I reconnected with the phenomenological and materialist lenses that had been foundational to my cultural rhetorics study at Michigan State years earlier. My colleagues in Technical and Professional Communication and Rhetoric at NC State are a privilege to work with and keep me motivated. I also had a fantastic writing group with Ben Lauren and Stuart Blythe, as well as advice from Bill Hart-Davidson for how to frame the manuscript. A graduate research assistant, Stephen Taylor, helped me prepare the book for submission, and the graduate students I've worked with at NC State across the MSTC and CRDM programs are also top notch, which keep me reading, thinking, and caring. I cannot say enough about how much Jim Ridolfo has helped me with the intellectual and affective work of this project over the long haul of my time writing and thinking and rethinking. I also was thrilled for the opportunity to work with Cheryl Ball on this book, and it became stronger thanks to her insight, as well as the open review system of the #writing series. The careful, rigorous, and generative readings that Amy Kimme Hea and Laura Micciche gave my manuscript made me feel lucky to be in our field.

Across these places and moments, my partner Aaron was there. We picked up Bruce the dog, in 2010 at the Ingham County shelter coincidentally right when I was really beginning to get into my dissertation. Ozzy and Eliza joined us in Durham and taught me new ways to care, and also new reasons to not work sometimes, too. Our parents and extended families are really the best, and I wouldn't have been able to write this without them.

TRANSIENT LITERACIES IN ACTION

COMPOSING WITH THE
MOBILE SURROUND

Chapter 1: Introducing Transient Literacies in Action

# #

When everything is all at once, what do we do?

–Anne Wysocki & Johndan Johnson-Eilola, 1999, p. 365

Educators today are concerned not only with how students form sentences and paragraphs but also with how they live among information, technologies, and the material world. That's because many of us who regularly work with students have a felt sense that students' writing, speaking, and learning practices are shifting as a result of changes in what surrounds them. Take for example the educator voices documented in *Digital Nation* (2010), the FRONTLINE documentary on digital culture. As I have discussed in a publication focused on the film's portrayal of student bodies (Pigg, 2015), *Digital Nation* opens with a chapter called "Distracted by Everything" focused on the wired lives of bright, young MIT students. Its beginning scenes depict a student group collaborating together with laptops around a café table. They work in open commons areas among other students, using language that emerges from digital spaces while simultaneously typing on laptops and phones. The professors who provide interview footage for the documentary are depicted much differently, addressing the camera in front of teeming bookcases or university lecterns. Guiding viewers' interpretation, MIT Professor David Jones emphasizes the role he understands students' surroundings to play in their classroom performance: "It's not that the students are dumb, it's not that they're not trying, it's that they aren't trying in a way that's as effective as it could be because they are distracted by everything else." Digital Nation thus positions the places, technologies, and information that comprise "everything else" around students as substantially impacting their academic practices and performances.

There has been no shortage of negative press and water cooler talk about the effects of mobile phones, IM conversations, text messages, social media, and the internet on contemporary students' ways of being in the world. Many of us notice downturned faces toward technologies when students walk through public campus spaces imagined for interaction, and we feel the impact of students' limited attention when we interact in classrooms. Educators might be tempted to ignore the negative connections often drawn among the information environments surrounding students and their

3

learning potential. After all, history shows that crisis claims stemming from the integration of new technologies into everyday life are more complicated than they seem on the surface. Public discourse on literacy crises has often signaled shifting power dynamics around access to literacy or its definitions (Lewis, 2015; Trimbur, 1991). Furthermore, historical arguments blaming new technologies for downturns in intelligence have often relied on determinist assumptions that downplay how humans are capable of regulating their technology use (Rheingold, 2012). To assume that changes enacted by the presence of new technologies in students' worlds are ultimately negative or inescapable is reductive. And, yet, educators also cannot ignore how technologies, information, and locations shape students' learning practices. "Everything else," as Jones referred to it in the quotation above, does matter to how students write, interact, collaborate, and solve problems. In short, surroundings shape how students move and think.

This book will suggest that scholarship in rhetoric and composition can usefully inform the transdisciplinary and public conversations that have developed around how technologies, information, and locations shape students' potential for learning and literacy. Through a recent focus on the relationship between materiality and composing, rhetoric and composition scholars have offered useful concepts and methods for tracing the relationship among students' practices and "everything else" beyond their brains and bodies. By the term "composing" here, I refer to communicative practices that create, curate, or arrange meaning based on the use of "communicative/compositional modes, materials, and practices that may include, but are certainly not limited to, writing or the production of written texts" (Shipka, 2016, p. 254). Rhetoric and composition scholars have long argued that composing practices emerge from more than the cognitive inner workings of a lone writer or even the impact of social influences in communities or societies where composers live and interact. Through inquiries focused on environments, materialities, and infrastructures, rhetoric and composition scholars have illustrated how composing is shaped by forces external to brains and bodies, as technologies, information, and other materials exist as more than simply containers of or backdrops for composing practices. The interplay among composing and "everything else" that surrounds it provides important context for this book, and so I begin with a brief discussion of environments, materialities, and infrastructures to describe the links between composers and their worlds.

Environments, Materialities, and Infrastructures

First, the concept of *environment* has enabled rhetoric and composition scholars to describe how social, man-made, or natural surroundings are intertwined with human activities such as composing. For example, the term "environment" frequently played a role in theories that highlighted the social contexts for writing practice (Cooper, 1986). In this case, "environments" often referred to the totality of situated social factors such as interpersonal, ideological, and organizational relationships that created a context for rhetorical decisions. In this sense, "environments" described social realities that are not immediately visible when writers put pen to paper or fingers to keys but that inform their possibilities for action (Goswami & Odell, 1986). Environments for composing in ecocomposition have also included natural and man-made structures intertwined with locations for writing (e.g., Dobrin & Weisser, 2002; Owens, 2001; Weisser & Dobrin, 2001). For instance, Sid Dobrin and Christian Weisser (2002) described ecocomposition approaches as the "study of the relationships between environments (and by that we mean natural, constructed, and even imagined places) and discourse (speaking, writing, and thinking)" (p. 572). This use of the term "environment" opened the door to exploring the impact of the physical and designed world, in addition to the social world, on the possibilities and realities for discourse.

An intersecting line of inquiry has taken up how *materiality* affects composing practices. Studying composing's materiality has highlighted how reading, writing, and other literate activities take place "in coexistence with ordinary and complex matter" (Micciche, 2014, p. 490). For digital rhetoric scholars, materiality helped explain what Jay David Bolter (2001) called the "writing space," or the historical media systems that constrain and afford written practices and products. A focus on materiality also offered vocabulary for describing characteristics of new media texts themselves (Wysocki, 2004), as well as for describing how the arrangement and presence of information shaped literacy practices (Brooke & Rickert, 2012). As Pamela Takayoshi and Derek Van Ittersum (2018) described, a focus on materiality in studying technologically mediated composing arrived hand-in-hand with a focus on places and embodied experience of them. Importantly, the materials that impact a given digital rhetorical interaction extend beyond media, texts, or other technologies of literacy (Haas, 1996) and into desks, walls, and architectures (Ackerman & Oates, 1996). Places orient people and shape their movements because they "gather things in their midst—where 'things' connote various animate and inanimate entities" and thus perform "'a holding together' of things in particular configurations" (Casey, 1996, pp. 24–25).[1] To put it another

---

1   The terms "place" and "space" have complicated theoretical histories. I use "place" to mean localities that act as experiential interfaces to broader networks of social space (Casey, 2009). I am distinguishing place from space drawing on Henri Lefebrve's (1991) theory of space as an ongoing relational network that reflects and transmits power, as economic histories collide with ongoing human activity. Describing the agentive force of place, philosopher

way, environments and materials work together to influence how humans move through the world. For example, discussing places such as family homes, Nedra Reynolds (2004) emphasized that "places and their built-in constraints" affect the embodied practices of literacy by encouraging "adjustments and compromises" that take place during "the process of accommodating to a place" (p. 14). My own research has built on this foundation to analyze how shared social locations gather materials that shape composing processes, and other scholars have taken up the materiality of composing through a focus on rooms (Rule, 2018) and habitats (Alexis, 2016). Materials and environments that shape composing can exist in ambient realms shaping and enabling practice but transparent to immediate human perception (Rickert, 2013).

At the intersection of environments and materiality, digital rhetoric scholars have further suggested that a focus on *infrastructure* can uncover how arranged structures of materials and values affect conditions for composing. Dànielle DeVoss, Ellen Cushman, and Jeff Grabill (2005) argued that students' rhetorical choices invoke embedded and often transparent organizations of materials and values that include but extend beyond their visible environments. Drawing on Susan Star and Leigh Ruhleder's (1996) theory of infrastructure, DeVoss, Cushman, and Grabill argued that infrastructures are ubiquitous but also dynamic and relational. That is, infrastructures are hailed by activity: writers experience these meaningful and constraining foundations relative to where they are, who they are, and what they are doing. Star and Ruhleder offered the example of a city water system to describe how infrastructures are multiple. For the cook at home, a water system is experienced as something useful for making dinner (often with little thought to its structure), while for the city planner it is "a variable in a complex equation" that can be manipulated and is subject to deterioration (Star & Ruhleder, 1996, p. 113). This relational reading of infrastructure is important for emphasizing how different communities and individuals approach and access material conditions differently (Star & Ruhleder, 1996).

These lines of inquiry focused on environments, materialities, and infrastructures emphasize how "everything else" beyond students' brains and bodies play a significant role in practices like reading and writing, suggesting that human activity cannot be fully understood apart from materials and places that shape it. However, as Van Ittersum and Takayoshi suggest, while the field has generally understood that materiality matters to composing, this theoret-

---

Edward S. Casey highlights how places and the experience of lived bodies are intertwined or "interanimate each other" (Casey, 1996, p. 24). Importantly, for Casey, places create environments where bodies and materials coevolve through mutual influence—an understanding that resonates with ecological theories that emphasize how technologies are given meaning in particular contexts of use (Hawk et al., 2007; Nardi & O'Day, 1999).

ical work has not fully transformed the composing research that attempts to understand writing practices. Furthermore, however useful these foundations are, they do not offer easy explanations for the influence of the technologies I referenced in the opening paragraphs. Networked mobile technologies (laptops, phones, tablets) complicate environments, materials, and infrastructures. By "mobile" here, I am referring to devices that can be easily carried from one place to another, and by "networked" I am referencing the capacity of these technologies to connect and exchange information and resources via either Wi-Fi or cellular networks. These technological systems impact environments where they are used, open the door to new material intrusions and resources, and shift infrastructure uptake in any place where they are switched on. Making sense of how mobile networked devices affect everyday learning and literacy is a complex and transdisciplinary problem being taken up by scholars in information studies, youth and K-12 literacy studies, rhetoric and composition, and beyond. These conversations extend beyond academic journals, as well. As the example that opens this chapter suggests, public media and even small talk among strangers frequently communicate a sense of wonder and dread about what is happening to the generations of children, teens, and younger adults who have grown up with mobile devices.

The Environments for Networked Mobile Computing

Mobile technologies are pervasive among college students, even though we must not make the mistake of thinking that they are integrated equally into all students' lives. With each study released by the Pew Research Center's Internet and American Life Project, we learn about increasing access to smartphones, tablet PCs, and laptops in North America. As of 2013, 91 percent of American adults owned a cell phone and used these handheld devices for information gathering and exchange (Duggan, 2013). Over 50 percent of Americans reported owning a smartphone, and one third of Americans owned a tablet computer, which represented a sharp rise from 3 percent in May 2010 (Zickuhr). Aimee Mapes and Amy Kimme Hea's (2018) longitudinal research at the University of Arizona named laptops as the dominant writing technology supporting students' literacy work and noted the ubiquitous and emotionally fraught use of cell phones for reading and analysis. My research with the Revisualizing Composition workgroup has similarly shown that university students across different institution types, geographical regions, races, and genders report text messaging done on cell phones as their most frequent and valued writing practice, though with reservations about how this writing is valuable (Moore et al., 2016; Pigg et al., 2014). The writing done on mobile technologies often takes place in short incremental bursts throughout a day, often momentarily interrupting other activities (including listening to class-room lectures). As Mapes and Kimme Hea (2018) suggested, many students do not even perceive these brief inscriptions to count as writing.

My particular interest is in how networked, mobile devices complicate the relationship between writers and the environments, materials, and infra-structures that support composing activities. Importantly, students' mobile composing practices often resist categorization by disciplinary or place-based boundaries. As mobile learning scholar Mark Pegrum (2013) noted, "In the desktop era, the internet seemed like a separate place partitioned off from everyday life by monitor screens. Mobile devices, especially our multiplying smart devices, integrate the virtual and the real as we carry the net with us" (p. 3). With networked mobile devices, students not only compose across dif-ferent subject domains but also perform mobile composing as a holistic mode of being that pulls together intimate, social, and professional practices. To draw on the vocabulary I introduced previously, when used with an active Wi-Fi or cellular connection, mobile phones, tablet PCs, and laptops intro-duce materials that have the possibility to transform environments in which they are carried. At the same time, they hail infrastructures in ways that can upset the typical conventions of places where students use them. Mobile com-puting infuses environments where students read, write, and research with new potential through information and social access. As a result, many environ-ments are either being redesigned to support the use of mobile technologies, or technology users are retrofitting environments to meet their computing needs, thereby shifting social norms and behaviors frequently practiced within them. This emerging interconnection among mobile device use and the built and natural environments in which people dwell is an influential part of "everything else" that affects students' learning and literacy potential. Although professors often notice these shifting dynamic changes from the front of their classrooms, mobile devices go everywhere, altering all environ-ments into which they are carried or worn.

Networked mobile computing devices fundamentally impact environ-ments in at least two senses that can shift what composing means and how it is practiced. First, networked mobile devices create the opportunity to use online resources to annotate and transform places in ways that shape how, when, and where people are likely to meet and interact (Rice, 2012; de Souza e Silva, 2006). Think, for example, of how we might plan the vacation route for a cross-state road trip differently if using an online map system that supports social annotations than if using a paper atlas. Observing the links to shops, restaurants, and attractions that line the route and having access to ratings and photos of what we might encounter could be enough to shift our move-ments in directions that we would be unlikely to choose if looking only at a printed map. For instance, we might make an extra turn to stop for a bite to eat at a restaurant that our friends have recommended through a social account instead of at the place most visible on our most direct route. Importantly, digital rhetoric scholars have argued that creating and solidifying new connections among people and materials is a form of writing, influential because of how it shapes others' future action. An action as seemingly insignificant as using a phone and digital networked application to add a "star rating" to a hole-in-the-wall restaurant can shift future participation and movements.

Second, using networked mobile devices shapes environments by combining disparate domains and life spheres onto single screens and then extending those screens into already occupied social places (Levinson, 2006). Mobile technologies create new convergences and overlaps among social communities and domains. This quality of mobile device use means that phones and laptops are often experienced as interruptions to places; they usher in potential connections that might or might not be welcome by the inhabitants of a place (Katz, 2006; de Souza e Silva & Frith, 2012). Consider, for example, how social media and other participatory online sites accessed through mobile devices change the social makeup of a place like a classroom. People using mobile devices operate in social atmospheres that vibrate with the hum of near and distant others available at the push of a button on platforms ranging from Facebook and Twitter to Reddit and 4chan to Tinder and Bumble. Most of us have experienced annoyance when mobile devices lead to converging social spheres, whether it is because a friend cannot turn away from a bleeping cell phone or a restaurant stranger ruins an adjacent table's lunch by loudly broadcasting a private conversation. As mobile computing devices become more pervasive, our "digital reserves," or potential stores of online interaction and information (Knox et. al., 2008), haunt us even when we try to ignore them. Social lives are always burdens of a sort, and wearing or carrying them through space can become heavy. Proliferating information, uneven access, cognitive overload, and the burden of being "always on" are changing the contexts for attention, interaction, and the use of shared places (Hayles, 2008, 2012; McCullough, 2013; Rheingold, 2012; Stone, 2007). When we carry mobile devices, our daily activities take place amidst burgeoning social potential, which can shift even the most traditional learning environments (such as lecture halls) into hubs of far-flung social networks.

The world has always been a complicated place for composing, but the constellation of materials and values invoked by networked mobile device use has invited new participants into composing processes. Networked mobile devices bring worlds that intersect in various ways with the everyday work, academic, and civic demands that are a part of a writing life. It is worth emphasizing that Mapes and Kimme Hea indicate that laptops (presumably networked) are by far the most dominant technology that contemporary students use for academic composing. Thus, the technological assemblages that Mapes and Kimme Hea (2018) described as "mobile device ecologies" are not just foundational to forms of writing traditionally associated with digital composing: social media writing, texting, blogging, or creating profiles for dating apps. Instead, these technological assemblages shape the material foundation for many students' academic and workplace composing as well. When networked mobile devices are used for literacy work, their users must build local knowledge that makes these devices useful technically and socially: places for charging or locations for establishing privacy, just to name a few needs (Erickson et al., 2014; Mark & Su, 2010). At the same time, while writers need practical knowledge to effectively use devices for literacy, networked mobile technologies are not easily contained. That is, completing a school assignment or arguing with family members or getting informed about global, national, and local news are changed not only when they are enacted using mobile technologies and networked access but also when they are enacted *in the presence of* rhetorical ecologies that have been shaped by networked mobile devices. We need to give voice to the composing experiences and collaborations that result from these intersections.

The anxieties that lurk behind statements made about student learning in *Digital Nation* and other public venues suggest that many educators, parents, administrators, and employers worry about how students navigate the literacy environments assembled when they hold these powerful computing devices in their hands. The worries that educators voice about students today resonate with a longer history of questions that digital rhetoric scholars have asked about how to manage the demands of networked, screen-based interaction. For example, Anne Wysocki and Johndan Johnson-Eilola (1999) raised similar issues when they positioned technological literacy as a "spatial relation to information," emphasizing how information exists "not as something that we send from place to place, in books or on paper, over time, but as something we move (and hence think) within" (p. 363). By conceiving of technological literacy as a way of moving inside information, Wysocki and Johnson-Eilola extended technological literacy beyond the traditional skills associated with effectively using devices and interfaces to produce and interpret particular written products. The increasing ubiquity of mobile computing, and the use of mobile media for locative social networking, wayfinding, and identity construction (Frith, 2015; Rice, 2012) has only heightened this sense of information as navigated spatially.

This conception of technological literacy positions what Johnson-Eilola (2005) called the *datacloud* as an immersive surround through which composers move. Questions about how to move through information that feels pervasive, then, are not new in digital rhetoric. I used Wysocki and Johnson-

Eilola's quotation from over twenty years ago to open this chapter: "when everything is all at once, what do we do?" (1999, p. 365). Cast in terms of how networked mobile devices are amplifying this feeling of all-at-once-ness and bringing together unexpected locations, activities, and information, newer versions of this enduring question might be phrased in this way: how is composing experienced when it is surrounded by overlapping mediated social environments assembled on and off networked mobile screens? How do these new materialities affect shared social environments where networked mobile devices are used? What are the effects of these changed environments on students' social interaction and attention practices? As interdisciplinary educators, scholars, parents, and employers concerned about students' literacy and learning practices, what should *we* do to support students learning in landscapes affected by mobile networked technologies?

Introducing Transient Literacies

Transient Literacies in Action joins transdisciplinary and public conversations about the impact of mobile technologies on student life by offering answers to the questions above that are informed by digital rhetoric fieldwork. My approach to digital rhetoric scholarship resituates digital practices (i.e., interactions with applications, platforms, or interfaces) in the context of experienced space, time, and surrounding physical materials. My approach arose from a sense that we needed to better account for the practical, embodied knowledge required to negotiate the information we encounter when composing with mobile, networked technologies in shared social environments. In order to further explain how this book approaches this knowledge, I now introduce *transient literacies*, a term I use to describe a practical knowledge that supports composing with networked mobile devices in everyday life. I follow this definitional work with two short examples from fieldwork that further illustrate the practices I discuss.

Defining Transient Literacies

I use the term transient literacies to describe the arrangement and movement practices that take place when composing with or in the midst of networked mobile devices. The term echoes a phrase that predates the focus on technologically supported mobility that shapes this book. Composition scholar Linda Brodkey (1984) used the term *transient* to shift discourse about composing away from the most common perceptions of solitary, quiet people in confined scenes. Thinking about her own everyday practices, she wrote, "I am struck by how transient are the images of myself as a writer when compared to the seemingly immutable picture of the author limned by the scene in the garret" (1984, p. 396). Imagine Brodkey's garret of composing further expanded by the immediate availability of social connections ushered in by networked mobile devices. Writers who compose with these technologies are open to a range of possibilities for where to navigate both online and offline. *Transience* is further important because the conditions and contexts that surround mobile composers are impermanent and continually reassembled. Thus, composing with networked mobile technologies means interacting with surroundings that are constantly refigured as composers' embodied movements on and off-screen bring them in contact with new architectures, devices, digital and informational reserves, values, attitudes, and social norms. When composing with networked mobile technologies, people absorb the impact of these ever-changing environments and infrastructures. They move while constrained by disparate materials, find and connect information in saturated environments, and negotiate messy, blurred social spheres.

Let me explain why I identify these foundational practices as literacies. My use of the term transient literacies parallels how Douglas Eyman (2015) defined the relationship between digital rhetoric and digital literacies, where digital literacies involve knowledges and skills that are a requirement for digital rhetorical practice. In a similar way, I understand transient literacies as practical and often invisible knowledge that is foundational to composing with mobile device ecologies. Navigating the immersive material and information spaces assembled by networked mobile devices brings along cognitive, social, and spatial challenges. By focusing on literacies, I align this knowledge-in-practice with social approaches that position everyday literacy practices as socially embedded, value laden, and situated rather than cognitively autonomous. Recent rhetoric and composition scholarship on mobile literacies emphasizes the complicated interplay between writers' movements and its systematic regulation through mobility systems that regulate movement. While my work differs from this line of research because of my primary focus on technologies, it shares an interest in how discursive-material constraints affect mobile composing experiences. For example, Wendy Hesford (2006) reviewed how the global turn in composition studies alerted scholars to the differential experience of mobility. Rebecca Lorimer Leonard (2013) extended this idea, offering the oft-cited idea of "the paradox of mobility" to describe how the freedom of movement implied by mobility is always accompanied by restrictions that arise as a result of social context. Brice Nordquist (2017) similarly examined the common assumptions that problematically divorce students' literacy practices from issues of everyday travel and position student learning spaces as bounded and separate from the rest of their lives. By contrast, we know that students compose across context, platforms, and symbol systems working together to constrain their performances, which require fluidity and constant adaptation (Stornaiuolo et al., 2017).

Guided by this scholarship, I discuss transient literacies as practices of everyday analysis and positioning that are foundational to composing with networked mobile technologies and that integrate interactions with materials across screens and physical spaces. Transient literacies involve navigating, generating, and eventually participating in temporary infrastructures that become foundations for composing activities that range from extended academic projects to quick IM texts on the go. Importantly, as I will describe in more detail, the materials that composers encounter are themselves agents in composing and thus transient literacies involve collaboration on multiple levels: negotiating, evolving, and co-constructing surroundings with humans and nonhumans in which it is possible to learn, work, argue, debate, cooperate, and collaborate.

Examples of Transient Literacies

Since I opened this chapter by contrasting the example of *Digital Nation* students' behavior in the open-style common settings of their university with their professors' office and lecture-classroom style environments, it may be helpful to further discuss how students' composing practices in shared social environments depend on and are enacted through transient literacies. The freedom of movement afforded by mobile technologies means that they are often used in environments that people inhabit for only a short time. Even for complex composing projects such as extended academic essays, composing processes are often "dispersed" through multiple places and times (Prior, 1998; Prior & Shipka, 2003). In these situations, networked mobile technologies become a hub of potential that is constantly carried to and relocated among new settings and materials. For example, students may use a laptop to compose a single project across locations such as a desk at home, an office space, a library carrel, a classroom, on the bus, using a laptop at the doctor's or dentist's office, and in a coffee shop, restaurant, or café. Simpler, less time-consuming composing events that often happen on cell phones (for example, posting on a social media feed, composing a text message, or responding to a tweet) likewise take place in unexpected locations. Whether acting as writers or audiences for these texts, students use networked mobile technologies to bring them in contact with literacy work in places that were not designed to support it. Both complex and simple (in terms of time required) composing practices have a spatial-temporal contingency, then, that require people to navigate complex environments on the fly. I'll start with two stories to introduce some concrete examples of what I mean.

Ed & Kathryn's Stories

With finals week looming, a J.D./Ph.D. student named Ed was working on one of the most important academic milestones he would accomplish during law school: a researched law review article that was a requirement for graduation. He was also sitting in a coffee shop. Ed occupied one seat in a line of back-to-back booths along the upper floor of the Gone Wired Café in Lansing, Michigan.[2] Rumored to have been purchased from the set of Pulp Fiction, each booth was large enough to seat four or more; however, Ed was alone with his laptop. His face was lit by his screen and a mural painting of a green monster kept guard from the wall above him. While the green monster itself might not be so important, the mural marked an important location: this particular booth was located within a power cord's distance to an electrical outlet. Enough people used Gone Wired for studying and working that the prime real estate he occupied around power outlets was often snapped up by café customers who arrived early, sat for hours, and left late. Finding the green monster meant working for several hours without interruption. It is also worth noting that downstairs beneath him, Ed's friend Kathryn sat at a similar booth facing Gone Wired's coffee bar—removed enough from Ed that she couldn't see where he sat. Like Ed, Kathryn was also completing an academic paper that was important to her that night: reading and reviewing primary and secondary scholarship she would later reference in a philosophy seminar paper. Like Ed, she also sat alone at a large, round booth that could accommodate four to six people comfortably, but she had made use of the materials around her in different ways. For example, she had stacked journal articles and book chapters she was reviewing into a fortress around her laptop, the stacks of paper warning people passing by that she was here for work and not for fun. Both Ed and Kathryn made distinct choices to create distance between themselves and other people, which enabled them to complete writing tasks.

Ed and Kathryn sat in places that created some social distance, and they agreed that there was something satisfying about the immediate social context created by sitting, reading, and writing in Gone Wired. The café enabled them to balance the demands of their respective graduate programs with the pulls of different professional and personal social interactions. They differentiated this environment's potential with that of other places they often wrote, such as their campus offices or carrels. Kathryn shared her office with

---

2   The Gone Wired Café has changed name, ownership, and purpose since I conducted the research study that inspired this book. I have retained the café's older name and identity to reflect the experiences of café patrons during that time. It is noteworthy that the café's name announced that digital, networked technologies were central to its identity.

other graduate teaching assistants in the Philosophy Department and Ed had a carrel in the law library. Both locales positioned them in social proximity to other graduate students, whereas the coffee shop provided social distance without isolation. Kathryn mentioned that her office was "shared with too many people [and was] too small to do good work there," adding that she "socialize[s] more in [her] office, or on the philosophy floor." Ed echoed her sentiment when describing the law library: "I find myself getting caught up in talking to people a lot more and I feel a little bit guilty about that." While working at home was a possibility, it had problems as well. Kathryn described how working at home was often a good idea "if there's a deadline." But even though Kathryn's house supported her work during some moments, she did not enjoy it. Working away from home helped her "feel less lonely." Ed, who lived with several roommates, said his house was always too distracting to get much done.

From observing and talking with research participants such as Ed and Kathryn, I began to understand how environments like Gone Wired offered access to materials that helped manage affective concerns and the difficulties of finding privacy in places closer to the university. To draw on Laura Micciche's (2014) words, they drew actively and deliberately on how "materials" present within different kinds of environments "are themselves endowed with energy and agency, contributing to the final product in nontrivial ways" (p. 497). While laptops, phones, roads, cars and bus routes made it possible to locate themselves in these physical environments, other technologies created connections and established boundaries that balanced their emotional needs with the demands of efficiency that graduate students experienced. Through an analysis of Kathryn and Ed's time-use that night, I learned that they interacted with each other while in the café, while keeping established but unarticulated boundaries. They used their cell phones to cultivate a connected distance, for instance. Every hour or so, Ed reached for his phone to send a text message to Kathryn, or Kathryn sent one to Ed. Through these messages, they made plans to meet outside for a smoke break, where they enjoyed a few minutes away from their respective tasks to chat. This was a regular routine, and Ed's roommates occasionally joined them as well. While Ed and Kathryn came to Gone Wired to escape distracting social environments, they also used the social web extensively from their laptops. The social web created an unpredictability to their movements, but both found connecting in this way to be tangibly and socially necessary. When I asked Ed about social media use, he said that he "generally [came] to do work" but often found himself "surfing the internet and talking to my friends online." Kathryn, too, said that even when under a strict deadline during the night I've been describing, she would take a few minutes to break and monitor her social networks on

Facebook. For both Ed and Kathryn, using social media sometimes involved talking to people that they knew well offline but also meant branching out toward connections and information with and from people and organizations they did not already know. Writing the longer researched pieces that mattered to their academic performance did not happen in isolation from the shorter social composing acts that kept them connected to their families and peers.

For Ed and Kathryn, mobile devices not only inscribed their words but also invited them to take up new practices to manipulate the social and material environments that would participate in their composing. As a result of the potential held in their laptops, they made purposeful choices to shape the conditions for writing, while also enabling other kinds of communication and social access that mattered to their livelihood. While their time in Gone Wired was important to them, it was also fleeting: they spent short intervals of time there before moving on to other places and organizing their composing in other ways elsewhere. Building on this more concrete example of transient literacies, let's now turn to another case, which illustrates some of the complex relationships among mobile devices, literacies, and dynamic social places.

Rebecca's Story

In 2012 when I began studying the second research site discussed in this book, the Technology Commons at the University of Central Florida, students and staff members were excited for the possibilities this new campus commons offered them. A campus Instructional Designer named Rebecca, for instance, talked to me about the opportunities that a place like this would offer her for moving around campus to address some unique demands of her position. On a campus with one of the largest undergraduate student enrollments in the country and nearly 2,000 teaching faculty, instructional designers played a mediating role between IT support staff and faculty members teaching online and mixed-mode courses. This work involved balancing multiple tasks: mentoring faculty members new to online teaching; responding to a steady influx of email questions; keeping up with the inevitable quirks of a learning management system scaled to accommodate 60,000 students; and reading and conducting research necessary for staying aware of trends in online and mixed-mode learning. Many instructional designers (including Rebecca) held advanced degrees and were also committed to conducting academic research, working individually or with campus teams.

The instructional designers' central workspace was a large open space with a conference table and several computer stations. Many instructional designers worked together in the open office at any given time. As Rebecca described it, the shared office was well suited to cultivating collective knowledge among the group, making it useful for problem solving or brainstorming new ideas. However, Rebecca recognized that she would need to move through campus to find alternative places for addressing some aspects of her job that could be difficult in an open office: for example, reading or writing extended prose among the ongoing talk could be difficult. The Technology Commons offered an alternative to the shared space of the office: it offered the opportunity to use a few moments to cultivate a focus that could be challenging in the presence of colleagues working out loud on projects that were too "close to home" not to pay attention. Furthermore, the Technology Commons represented a spatial "middle ground" that could be useful for meetings with faculty. Of course, the Technology Commons posed challenges as well. It was loud, students were everywhere, and finding a table required roaming around until something opened up. For Rebecca, as for many of the individuals I introduce over the next several chapters, it is important to understand that spatial movements through the university directly influenced composing practices and the usefulness of a given space was contingent on individual needs. The potential of social spaces to usefully support composing with mobile devices did not guarantee that those places would be inviting, accessible, or usable. The Technology Commons' feasibility as a workspace was intertwined not only with Rebecca's individual positionality and desires but also with how the place had been taken up and embedded within social and geographical networks of the campus, community, and city.

As with Ed and Kathryn, Rebecca's story similarly focuses on literacy practices enabled by mobile devices in a multi-use space to which the writer travels in or through for a short time. However, her example further emphasizes the contingency associated with transient literacies: the ways in which locating oneself in temporarily inhabited places designed for many uses brings individuals in contact with aspects of an environment that cannot easily be predicted or controlled.

Reflecting on Analyzing and Positioning

The two stories I have just told have transient literacies woven through them. People like Ed, Kathryn, and Rebecca take active, if not always conscious, roles in negotiating their surroundings when they compose with networked mobile technologies. Over time they build a sense of the capacity of materials and places and engage materials and infrastructures in ways that suit their needs. Sometimes they also experience misalignments among their goals and the potential of the materials that surround them. Ed, Kathryn, and Rebecca cultivated relationships of proximity and distance that oriented them in different ways to multiple shared social environments, and in so doing, they also participated in the creation of spaces and identities. As I will explain further in Chapter 2, composing with mobile, networked technologies in social spaces engages a "commons," or a shared space from which composers access social resources that have historically been understood as central to creating ideas (Lessig, 2001; McCullough, 2013), produces collective social interactions, and engages attention habits. This book focuses on how networked laptops in particular enable composers new locative potential, while also complicating the sociability of shared spaces. Within the transdisciplinary and public conversations about mobile device use, researched accounts of how people are interacting with networked mobile technologies can complicate generalizations and lore that totalize these experiences. Much of the current discourse operates through sweeping claims that rely on generational narratives or assume a totalizing deterioration of collective spaces. This book represents one possible step toward a more nuanced perspective on how mobile technology use intersects with writing through a focus on transient literacies in action, using a fieldwork approach that treats composing as a complex sociotechnical practice that engages both humans and nonhumans.

Focusing on Fieldwork

Composing in shared places with mobile computing devices is common, from studying in a Starbucks to telecommuting from a public park to using a shared university learning space for a team meeting. In spite of how familiar these practices are, rhetoric and composition researchers have produced relatively few systematic, detailed studies that focus both on the use of networked mobile devices and the extracurricular surroundings that influence these practices. There are notable exceptions. For example, in the years since Anne Ruggles Gere (1994) drew attention to the "kitchen tables" and "rented rooms" where community writers meet to exchange texts and ideas, Clay Spinuzzi (2012) analyzed the role the coworking spaces play for professional writers, and Huatong Sun (2012) traced how students write with mobile phones in dorm rooms and during travel. More recently, John Wargo (2015) researched how platforms like Snapchat become entangled with both place and affect in youth digital literacies, and Ty Hollet and Christian Ehret (2014) focused on the "real virtualities" invoked when youth use mobile devices in classroom contexts.

This research has been foundational; however, we still lack a qualitative study focused primarily on how college students create space for networked mobile devices outside dorms and classrooms. *Transient Literacies in Action* builds from a systematic, qualitative, IRB-approved study that observed how several individuals and groups across two research sites composed in and with mobile surroundings and learned more from how these composers discussed the practical knowledge that enabled mobile composing. In the vein of the research cited above, I have approached this task by researching the use of networked, mobile devices *in action*. The term "action" in literacy or writing research has typically signaled a focus on agentive potential. For example, Charles Bazerman's (2013a, b) recent two-volume rhetoric and theory of literate action theorizes how composers induce cooperation and achieve results. "Rhetoric is built for action," Bazerman suggests, and "it ha[s] to do with how to accomplish things" (2013a, p. 15).

This book interprets composing action as a collaboration among materials. That is, the arguments in this book rely on sustained observation of two shared social spaces over two periods of several weeks of normal everyday use, videotaped observations of networked mobile device use in practice in these places, and interviews with consenting research participants. These interviews enabled me to contextualize my observations, as well as share participants' voices. My grounding in qualitative fieldwork helps me understand how interactions with networked mobile devices unfold in the present moment. This focus on unfolding action has provided a way to describe the complexities of these practices, while attending to multiple materials that participate in that complexity.

Embodied Materialist Grounding

My fieldwork is informed by a materialist perspective that emphasizes mobile device use as embodied, emplaced situated action and that explores the bodily experience of that action in non-representative snapshots. As shorthand, I refer to this approach to fieldwork as an embodied materialist grounding. Rather than attempting to trace macro influences on micro practices, the embodied materialist research that grounds this project emphasizes the importance of relations and interactions as continually recreating composing agencies and experiences. In Chapter 3, I will discuss in more detail how the intersection of materiality and embodiment is unique within studies of digital rhetoric and literacy. To provide an initial foundation for that discussion, this introduction explains how I understand my fieldwork's concern with materiality and embodiment, before discussing an important methodological precursor to my approach in Lucy Suchman's situated human-machine interaction research.

My approach to fieldwork is *materialist* in that it assumes my phenomenon of interest (i.e., composing with networked mobile devices) to be a fundamentally collaborative practice involving humans and nonhumans together. My assumption is that mobile computing engages surroundings, which become generative participants in composing rather than backdrops for the real action. In so doing, it positions the agency of composing as a distributed enactment that is only possible at the intersection of bodies (human and nonhuman) and their surroundings. Importantly, when I suggest that materials are generative, I mean that they have capacity for shaping what rhetorical action is possible and how it takes place in a given situation. I do not mean that their capacity will lead to positive ends, or be helpful toward achieving human goals. Just as frequently, the collaborations lead to small and large failures, as several of my case examples will illustrate.

As I have argued, networked mobile devices complicate any sense of a pure, bounded domain for writing practices. Instead, these devices lend themselves to the continual production of densely layered spaces where information, values, and social actors conflict. As a result, I am further concerned with ensuring that my focus on the agentive nature of surroundings and materials does not oversimplify or "fix" the environments that I understand to shape networked mobile device use. Christopher Keller (2004) argued that a historical problem for ethnographic approaches in composition studies has involved the ways that research studies "imagine, minimalize, and construct our conceptions of spaces and places" (p. 206). Using the classroom as his primary example, Keller argued that research studies often position these places as "a simple microcosm of the larger social and cultural formations, as reflections or shadows of what's going on in the 'outside' world, therein erasing the classroom's status as a place where meanings, conflicts, and discourses are made" (2004, p. 209). The same can hold true for spaces beyond the classroom as well. Places are not generic, fixed containers that reflect overarching structures, and my fieldwork approach attempts to understand environments as continually shaped through interactions.

At the same time, my approach to fieldwork is *embodied* in that it locates an important form of composing knowledge in bodies and their spatial, relational, and time commitments to materials. I learn from humans' bodily intentions and perspectives when participating in enactments of agency with environments, materials, and infrastructures. In this sense, the bent of my approach is phenomenological in its concern for what Dorothea Olkowski (2006) described as "things as they appear to our experience, as well as to the meanings things have in our experience" (p. 3). In other words, my approach positions bodies as providing both a perspective and perceptual location for humans' experiences of practice, where bodily action is purposeful and yet not necessarily premeditated or controlled by conscious thought. Traditional phenomenological methods often generalize about human experience based on limited cases (often of white men); however, as I will further explain in Chapter 3, I approach the experience of lived bodies through what I have learned from accounts of the perspectives and practices of othered bodies and their embodied orientations (Ahmed, 2004; Anzaldúa, 2002; Young, 1980). Situating the experiences of net-worked mobile composers in this way is crucial for countering an assumed privileged, white, able-bodied subject as the general norm.

In the same way that my fieldwork pushes for a complex and agential reading of place, this approach also attempts to avoid an oversimplification of participants' experiences. Queer, gendered, and raced phenomenological research emphasizes that experiences cannot be reduced to normative bodily experiences. Further, I draw from Keller's further insights about the tradi-tional positioning of students within qualitative studies of composing prac-tice. In line with Keller's critique of traditional composing ethnographies, I do not position students' experiences as representative of their writing realities, nor as reflecting their experience as members of any particular bounded cul-ture or subjectivity. Instead, I am interested in creating new situated accounts from what Michel de Certeau (1984) referred to as the space "down below" the "threshold at which visibility begins" where "bodies follow the thicks and thins of an urban 'text' they write without being able to read it" (p. 93). At this point one can see not only consciously employed "strategies," but also the ephemeral "tactics" of practice that put environments, materials, and infra-structures to use toward the ends of desires not articulated in systems.

One important methodological forerunner for my approach is Lucy A. Suchman's (2007) *Human-Machine Reconfigurations: Plans and Situated Actions*, which introduced an interactional approach to understanding how people work with technologies. Based on an earlier study of how employ-ees used Xerox machines in a workplace setting, Suchman conceptualized human-computer interaction (HCI) by de-emphasizing human intention and refocusing attention on how interactions among people and technolo-gies continually co-construct the potential for future action. Responding to a field that had previously positioned human plans as deterministic, Suchman contributed a method for tracing how practices emerge and evolve in situ-ated moments. In this model, human plans, intentions, and perspectives are indeed one important kind of resource that shapes technology use, but they are always positioned as one resource among many.

Thus, where many cognitive approaches to studying technological interac-tion focused on human agents as guiding and shaping device use, Suchman's situated action research honed in on "how it is that actors use the resources that a particular occasion provides (including, but crucially not reducible to, formulations such as plans) to construct their action's developing purpose and intelligibility" (2007, p. 31). By treating action as an achievement depend-ing on materials and interactions that are never predetermined, Suchman urged HCI scholars to pay attention to how all participants in a given work event were made mutually intelligible to one another, finding ways to "cooperate" in order that work could be accomplished. As a result she built on the tradition of how ethnomethodology[3] and conversational analysis positions meaning as emergent structures built through, in Harold Garfinkel's terms, the "contingent ongoing accomplishments of organized artful practices of daily life" (1967, p. 11). By paying attention to situated actions rather than their stated plans, it became possible to see how many resources and representations contributed to action, while none fully determined it. The portraits of technological interactions that emerged from these approaches offered new ways of understanding the complexity of how people used and struggled with technological interfaces. This approach allows for deep description of interaction from a perspective that assumes distributed and enacted agency. However, it also allows for a focus on the micro-level embodied movements of lived human bodies in a composing scene. It brings materialist and embodied concerns into dialogue through new storied performances.

Using embodied materialist fieldwork to study networked mobile devices use offers the opportunity to see the relationships between people and the materials of their surroundings differently. As a researcher who tells the stories generated from this research approach, it is also important for me to account for how my own positionality, perspectives, and limitations shape the stories that can be told from fieldwork. To value the idea of agencies as co-produced and performed, it is important to position researchers not as privileged interpreters of action but rather as additional participants in what Karen Barad (2007) would call the entanglements that enact agencies. Thus, it is important for me to acknowledge how my own surroundings of "matter and embodiment come to matter in the process of research itself," becoming materials that participate in the accounts that form this book. The accounts that ground the knowledge in this book should be understood as "enactments rather than descriptions" (Jackson & Mazzei, 2012, p. 127).

---

3   Ethnomethodology is a helpful but complex approach to thinking about how social life is generated through everyday practices. Ethnomethodology was first championed by sociologist Harold Garfinkel (1967), who theorized that everyday actions provide a means for understanding how social worlds are produced and reproduced in the interactions of everyday life. Ethnomethodological approaches have been used in writing research that attempts to reconcile cultural/cognitive or structure/agency binaries (Brandt, 1992; Schneider, 2002), or that traces how semiotic practices such as talk, drawing, gesture, and/or inscription shape the processes of literate activity (Godbee, 2012; Prior, 2013; Olinger, 2014). While most ethnomethodological research studies analyze talk, these approaches have also been adapted to analyze interactions among people and elements of their surroundings. Although Suchman's situated action research has disadvantages for technology interface design research (Kaptelinin & Nardi, 2006; Nardi, 1996), applying ethnomethodologically inspired research has enabled closer tracing of human-machine interactions that are useful toward other goals.

Case Examples as Performances

When applied to the use of networked mobile devices in the Gone Wired Café and the Technology Commons, embodied materialist fieldwork shows how participants collaborated with phones, desks, emails, calendars, lights, and their own routines, mobilizing materials in ways unique to their situations and motivated by conflicting personal, academic, and professional habits and goals. While these cases emerge from my position as a scholar in rhetoric and composition and professional communication, the student mobile experiences discussed in this book relate to the broad interest of public and academic conversations about the impact of mobile devices, as well as to the questions raised by scholars across mobile literacy, learning, and information studies.

The experiences that I discuss come from people using laptops (and, secondarily, phones) in two shared social places that I introduced in prior examples. These two places are as much participants in the research as the humans who used networked mobile devices within them. The first location, the Gone Wired Café in Lansing, Michigan, was a coffeehouse heavily frequented by students, professionals, and people who lived in the local community. The second location, the Technology Commons at the University of Central Florida in Orlando, Florida, had been explicitly designed to support mobile study and work for students, staff, and faculty of the large metropolitan university where it was located. These places provided access to different kinds of assembled values and materials, while gathering different students, tasks, and activities. Although the two research sites were geographically far from one another and attracted different people, they shared similarities. Both were located on highly traveled pathways and were used for activities that varied from study to professional collaboration. Both invited interactions among teams with shared tasks, groups spending time together because of social relationships, and individuals connecting with others even when they appeared to be alone. As such, Gone Wired and the Technology Commons shared a relationship to social, technological, cultural, and organizational arrangements for learning, working, and socializing that have become commonplace in the United States and beyond. While I was familiar with both of these places from my time using laptops within them, I devoted six weeks in each location solely to observing everyday uses of mobile devices. The Appendix shares additional detail about this phase of observation.

As I have already suggested, my fieldwork further focused deeply on a limited number of cases of networked mobile device use. While my observations included many kinds of mobile devices in practice, I have focused my attention in this book primarily on the use of laptops in commons spaces.

Case research is often critiqued from positivist perspectives for its lack of generalizability; however, I do not intend the stories in this book to be generalizable. Instead, the case examples presented should be read as performances generated in a particular time and space. For example, although Ed and Kathryn experienced the coffee shop as a useful respite for cultivating the privacy they needed to write, it is not reasonable to suggest that this experience would be the norm among all graduate students, law students, or even students who share their race, class, gender, and/or age. Further, is also not reasonable to assume that Ed and Kathryn would feel the same way today, several years after their participation in this research project. The accounts in this book begin with small, fleeting moments in the lives of moving and changing people. The students in this book cannot be reduced to their practices, and each of them has already moved on to new devices, new practices, and new places.

Instead of generalizations, these case accounts serve the purpose of "respecification" (Hindmarsh & Heath, 2007). That is, they offer ways to concretely interact with phenomena that are often unproductively generalized. The goal of making oft-generalized actions specific is to provoke questions that challenge common stereotypes and that provoke new possibilities for moving forward. Commonplaces such as the distracted student, the isolated student, or the aloof student unaware of her shared social surroundings are often the norm in both public and insider lore regarding contemporary university students and their networked mobile device use. While there are inklings of truth in many stereotypes, respecification is necessary for better understanding how composing comes to be in the face of information saturation and constant movement. Paying attention to the action of transient literacies enables educators to rethink these commonplaces, which often position university students as universally connected, "always on," gadget-bound, and distracted. Such generalizations disregard issues of uneven access (Grabill, 1998; Moran, 1999) and ignore how relationships to space and technology are differentially experienced based on race, class, gender, ability, and a host of other influences.

It is furthermore important to position the performances of case examples in this text as informed by my own writing of them. Reclaiming attention to diverse embodiments and ephemeral practices while resisting positivist generalizations can prepare instructors and administrators for what Barad (2007) called a "diffractive reading," a way of interacting with data that reinserts those who encounter a story back into its frame. It is important for teachers and researchers to reflectively consider our own response to networked mobile devices and acknowledge how our assumptions play a role in the ongoing production of the social worlds in which students compose.

(Human) Participants

In order to understand these accounts, it is useful to know more about the participants in my research. As is the case with Ed and Kathryn, most writers I discuss as case examples in this book are students who used networked mobile devices in shared social places. As Table 1.1 shows, research participants in the Gone Wired Café and Technology Commons were diverse in terms of race, gender, and academic affiliations. In addition, they described themselves as traveling to Gone Wired or the Technology Commons for reasons ranging from homework to completing major writing projects to using social media to killing a few moments between classes. Given the openness of both locations and the tendency for mobile devices to blur personal, professional, and academic lives and contexts, it is hardly surprising that purposes for using these places spanned domains (i.e., personal, school, extracurricular), subject areas, and included both formal and informal writing.

The case examples that I have drawn out for discussion in this book are those where networked laptops are primary participants in composing. The people using these laptops reflect a diversity of embodiments and also have been grouped to reflect similarities in their composing purposes. The purposes for this writing align with broad-ranging academic, professional, and personal composing interests. For example, the cases covered in Chapters 1–6 highlight the following kinds of composing: writing alone to complete homework assignments, interacting with video media to complete homework assignments with others, interacting on the social web while "killing time" between classes, and research and writing for extended projects (i.e., a composition paper, a graduate-level research paper, a collaborative business plan). As such, the cases explore a range of academic, professional, and personal composing exigences faced by people who compose with networked mobile technologies.

Table 1.1. Research participants and demographics

Name	Location	Main Purpose	Subject Area	Gender[1]	Race[1]
Kim	GW	Homework	Rhetoric	F	White
Ed	GW	Major writing project	Law	M	White
Kathryn	GW	Major writing project	Philosophy	F	White
Dave	GW	Major writing project	Professional	M	White
Luna	TC	Homework	Calculus	F	Asian
Max	TC	Homework	Calculus	M	Asian and White

continued on next page

Table 1.1.—*continued*

Name	Location	Main Purpose	Subject Area	Gender[1]	Race[1]
Ann	TC	Socializing & homework	Criminal Justice	F	White
Heijin	TC	Homework	Tourism	F	Asian
Dean	TC	Homework	Graphic Design	M	Asian
Carly	TC	Homework	Graphic Design	F	White
Sofia	TC	Test prep	Organic Chemistry	F	Hispanic
Nadia	TC	Test prep	Organic Chemistry	F	Asian
Micah	TC	Killing time	Game Development	M	White
Charlotte	TC	Major writing project	Business Management	F	White
Owen	TC	Major writing project	Business Management	M	White
Gabriel	TC	Major writing project	Business Management	M	Hispanic
Sal	TC	Killing time	Web Surfing	M	Preferred not to disclose
Tiffany	TC	Major writing project	Business Fraternity	F	Black
Nora	TC	Major writing project	Business Fraternity	F	Black
Nicholas	TC	Major writing project	Business Fraternity	M	White
Ray	TC	Killing time	Gaming	M	Black
Theodore	TC	Homework	Accounting	M	White

1. Self-reported

Conclusion: Looking Forward with Transient Literacies in Action

In this introduction, I have defined the scope of this book by introducing the transdisciplinary problem of better understanding how composing is experienced when it is surrounded by the overlapping social environments and materialities that accompany networked mobile devices. I have introduced the idea of transient literacies to describe a practical knowledge of negotiating mobile composing environments, and I have positioned this project as one based in an embodied materialist approach to fieldwork. The following five chapters pick up on this foundation and further explore transient literacies by interacting with cases from research.

Chapter 2 begins the work of resituating mobile networked device use in space, time, and experience by exploring the intersection of shared social spaces and networked mobile device use. Shared social environments have long been important as inventive spaces for public or civic discourse when positioned as *public spaces*; however, networked mobile devices are used across places that are shared but not necessarily public in the sense that public sphere theorists have used that term. This chapter focuses on the Gone Wired Café and the Technology Commons as physical environments that become hubs for resources taken up in mobile device use. I argue that mobile device users frequently position these places as *commons* spaces rather than as public spaces. Framing shared social environments as a commons opens up the potential for exploring their role in providing resources that are adapted and shared to meet individual or collective needs. Focusing on shared places as arbiters of social resources brings new attention to the role that commons environments play in experiences of mobile, networked device use and also emphasizes the difficulties individuals experience when aligning individual needs to the capacities of shared environments.

Chapter 3 follows on this problem by offering an embodied materialist approach to understanding the intersections between individual experiences and mobile surroundings. This approach focuses on how surroundings are populated by materials that become co-participants in networked composing practices. The chapter offers a heuristic for understanding the mobile surround relative to composing as a cross-domain liminal space that combines materials from personal repertoires, productive settings, and eventual circulation networks. I further take up transient literacies as a form of knowledge performed in lived bodies' spatial, relational, and time commitments to these cross-domain materials. Finally, the chapter takes up Barad's (2007) idea of "intra-actions" to consider how the action of composing with networked mobile devices produces not only texts but also social contexts that matter to further composing potential. In particular, I focus on the feedback loops through which social relationships and attention are produced (and often troubled by) networked mobile device use.

Chapter 4 builds on this framework to explore the experience of *sociability* in the commons, asking how interpersonal interactions play a tangible role in composing with networked mobile technologies. This chapter looks beyond the commonplace of students "alone together" to discuss forms of social proximity and distance constructed in students' interactions with networked mobile devices (Turkle, 2012). I offer the concept of *ambient sociability* to describe the contexts in which available and/or potential social interactions abound, creating a situation in which social potential always occupies a background amongst other foregrounded potential. The chapter takes up how ambient sociability may shift the social focus in composing from "contact" to "potential," and introduces monitoring, contributing, and disengaging as a linked cycle of engagement that affects how people interact across platforms.

Next, the book turns to the relationship among *attention* and transient literacies in Chapter 5. If composing with mobile, networked technologies invokes shared resources and takes place in scenes in which some social resources are continually pushed to the background of focus, how does this affect attention practices? Would attention have different implications if we positioned it as dynamically co-constructed between humans and environments, instead of an internal process? Rather than focusing on mobile composers' distraction, the chapter traces how attention is composed in sequences of interactions and proximities. Positioning attention as a thing composed opens the door to new understandings of how people, environments, and technologies construct this assembled agency together. Rather than replacing old commonplaces about attention with new ones, the chapter avoids generalizations about students in favor of questioning and gesturing toward new implications.

Finally, the book's conclusion in Chapter 6 builds on this framework to reiterate the importance of looking outside screens to understand how networked mobile devices intersect with composing practices. Given the importance of these issues to academic literacies, as well as the changing nature of professional work and community engagement, this chapter reiterates the stakes of the argument and gestures toward a framework for the use of mobile, networked devices that centers the role of attention, sociability, and the commons as a means for managing proliferating information and interaction in academic coursework, distributed workplaces, and community sites. Across the case studies and questions raised through them, this book reveals hidden social, material, temporal, and spatial constraints that accompany the "freedoms" of using mobile technologies, but also articulates new ways that students are relating to and working with them.

Chapter 2: Sharing Resources in Places We Move Through

# #

> Where many old technologies inherently forced people together in factories, office buildings, schools, and libraries, new ones tempt them to stay apart, working for organizations without working in one, joining schools or libraries without going to one.
>
> –John Seely Brown & Paul Duguid, 2000, p. xix

Washington Examiner senior political analyst Michael Barone (2014) used "The Disconnected Generation" as the moniker of choice to describe U.S. adults born after 1980. To call millennials disconnected might seem strange, given the intense connectedness of many North American young people through social platforms and mobile technologies. However, Barone was summarizing the results of a Pew Research Report that focused on how the under-35 crowd is largely "unattached," tending away from organized religion, political groups, and even marriage. Barone associated this lack of connection with declining "social trust," citing well-known sociologist Robert Putnam's (2000) research depicting the shifting social fabric of the Western world. Building on this foundation, Barone argued that "the picture we get from the Pew numbers is of a largely disconnected generation, in touch with self-selected peers and distrustful of others" (para. 16).

The questions that Barone and others raised about community life and neighborhood connectedness resonate with those that Putnam posed nearly twenty years ago about the decline of local communities. Many scholars have long been worried about the degradation of places that nurture community life. When Putnam worried that Americans were "Bowling Alone," he lamented not only a loss of interaction among communities but also of places that support that interaction. Putnam did not believe that social places were completely disappearing. Instead, places where neighbors rubbed shoulders were changing. Public spaces, those shared noncommercial locations open to all members of a local community, were becoming replaced with places organized most explicitly to invite homogeneous consumer desire or to be moved through rather than dwelled in (e.g., see the concept of "omnitopia" [Wood, 2009]). In Putnam's terms, Americans were literally and figuratively reaching for fast food on the go over longer-term nourishment in places where they were likely to spend longer periods of time (2000). McDonald's replaced the neighborhood café, and the drive-thru window offered sustenance. As the epigraph from John Seely Brown and Paul Duguid (2000) suggested, technologies such as the car worked hand-in-hand with other cultural and economic dynamics to support people's tendencies to avoid community or organizational spaces, or opt for the privacy of their own homes over shared interactions.

While the "great, good places" of Ray Oldenburg's (1999) community life may be difficult to find today, readers and writers who use networked mobile technologies frequently turn to the social locations that he called third places—locations outside homes and offices—to access shared resources. To better understand some of the relationships among networked mobile device use and shared places, this chapter begins a conversation about how composing with laptops takes place in the *commons*. In discussions of economics and/or natural resources, the term commons typically describes a collection of shared community resources available for use that are not owned or controlled by a private entity. In common usage, many of us might be familiar with the "tragedy of the commons," a well-known economics concept used to describe how resources shared through open access by a community are likely to be depleted without long-term regard for maintenance and sustainability. However, the term also is used frequently in library and information sciences in concert with the idea of an "information commons," defined as an integrated place where people from all identities and backgrounds access resources such as learning guidance, technical support, hardware and software, physical space, and a cultural environments needed to achieve learning goals (Bailey & Tierney, 2002) or a "learning commons," which positions these integrated resources more explicitly toward learning as an outcome (Mirtz, 2009). In either sense, I will suggest that we think through how social potential and commons places intersect with mobile device literacies, given the widespread sense that community places and shared resources are disappearing due to privatization, globalization, and changes in technologies.

In this chapter, I examine the commons as a kind of place that shapes and is shaped by the embodied practice of composing with mobile networked devices. If we understand the places we move through as more than degradations of traditional community rootedness, what might we learn about the social environments that gather mobile people and technologies? What role do mobile interactions play in community places? What opportunities and challenges do they pose for composing that may differ from places that are perceived to be less flexible (i.e., classrooms, dorms)? Toward answering these questions, I examine how composers who use laptops in shared spaces often rely on shared resources that come from places maintained by and inhabited by others; however, the resources available in shared places we move through generally are not free for the taking. This creates a tension in which the commons is often perceived as flexible, customizable, or "blank" when it is highly situated and positioned. More closely examining how people use and discuss shared social places reveals challenges not only for local community organizing and civic efforts but also for academic and workplace collaborations.

Third Places and Their Roles in Invention and Community

Places meant to be moved through have long been important to how rhetorical scholars understand processes of generating new ideas and participating in community life. Historically, sites that gather mobile people and allow transient dwellers to enter them temporarily have been described as "third places" by sociological literature that discusses the importance of community locations that ground a domain of acquaintances (Oldenburg 1999). Most famously, third places such as the coffeehouses of eighteenth-century England were associated with rhetorical and humanistic theory because they were understood to support the critical, rational dialogue that grounds political social action. Jurgen Habermas (1989) in *The Structural Transformation of the Public Sphere*, for instance, identified the coffeehouse as a material foundation for newly developing late seventeenth- and eighteenth-century British publics, places where private individuals began coordinating in ways that radically shifted the possibilities for political agency. For literary critic Terry Eagleton (1984), the act of speaking in coffeehouses was considered unruly and threatened to break down power hierarchies, even if what was said was subject to norms of the occasion. As he put it, "the speech act itself, the enonciation as opposed to the enonce, figures in its very form an equality, autonomy and reciprocity at odds with its class-bound content" (1984, pp. 14–15). Coffee shops provided a space that facilitated a transition from an atomized society of private individuals to a "relatively cohesive body whose deliberations may assume the form of a powerful political force" (Eagleton, 1984, p. 9). Peter Stallybrass and Allon White (1986) also associated the rise of the coffeehouse with the development of print journalism, the birth of literary criticism, and the developing agency and self-fashioning of a late seventeenth- and eighteenth-century middle class.

Importantly, within public sphere theory, coffeehouses were positioned as foundations for two kinds of mediated social experiences. The first of these relates directly to literacy: coffeehouses were understood to be important because they facilitated the sharing of original print materials and a culture of reading. They were positioned as places for the exchange of texts that

31

introduced ideas to a newly formed reading public. Second, coffeehouses were positioned as important for facilitating oral discussion; they were places that enabled the rational/critical discussion central to dissecting those print materials when people met together publicly. Habermas thus described coffeehouses as "centers of criticism—literary at first, then also political" that were populated and enacted by a new "parity of the educated" (1989, p. 32). Importantly, Habermas portrayed the coffeehouse as beyond government control, a place where people could meet strategically and intentionally as a result of their own motivations and desires. Although feminists and historians have critiqued this reading on various grounds,[4] this collective memory of an accessible site for conversation and community organizing maintains a strong resonance, even while other theorists and historians have suggested that early British coffeehouses were sites for policing class-related manners and conducting business transactions, as well (Cowan, 2005).

Like social places of today that offer space for mobile travelers to gather, Habermas' ideal coffeehouse implied an openness and accessibility that meant it could be inhabited by different people over time. However, in Habermas' telling, the place was defined more by collective identity than by individual desire. The idealized coffeehouse of Habermas' theory was defined less by the individual than the collective: where conversations together were more important than individual transformations of place. In other words, within this theory individuals did not assign meaning to the coffeehouse so much as the coffeehouse assigned meaning to individuals by locating them inside a collective mobilized through persistent discursive exchange. Within public sphere theory, the coffeehouse has been positioned as a foundation where pamphlets such as the *Spectator* in eighteenth-century Britain created a persistent pattern of circulation, discussion, and response. Warner (2002) feared this sense of publicness would be lost as political dialogue adapted to the rhythms of online publication and circulation.

It is no wonder then that such places have long been understood as important to theories of civic action, as well as to the important role of literacy for supporting and sustaining relations among educated peers. For example, when Oldenburg described coffeehouses as one of the neighborhood "third places" of communities, he emphasized how they created accessible "neutral ground" where individual differences could be leveled in favor of identifications formed around shared issues of concern (1999). Literacy, as well, was

---

4   For an introduction to feminist critiques of public sphere theory, see Nancy Fraser and Seyla Benhabib's contributions to Craig Calhoun's *Habermas and the Public Sphere* (1992). Historians such as Brian Cowan have also argued, contrary to Habermas, that coffeehouses were more often spaces for social control and the manipulation of manners than for uncontrolled rational dialogue (2005).

understood to establish these identifications, as patrons read about and then shared news, opinions, and perspectives. As I have already suggested, these historically important communicative contexts have been understood to be under threat as a result to changes in the arrangement and ownership of space, as well as the changing expectations and values of the people who move through them. Relating these issues to civic and community rhetorics, Nancy Welch (2008) described the vast movement to privatize public space, through assigning it corporate control or altering human behaviors in ways that hide or isolate once-shared identifications.

In line with the shift away from shared places as community centers, the people I talked with during my study emphasized individual goals when using shared social places for composing, rather than understanding their time there to be related to overt participation in community or civic life. For example, the stories in Chapter 1 from Kathryn, Ed, and Rebecca illustrate a sense that laptop users often position shared social places as places to be used for an individual's unique desires. How then should we describe these places as related to the literacy practices associated with networked mobile device use, and how might these characteristics differ from traditional public spaces?

Places We Move Through

One answer to the previous question about the transformation of public space has been offered by theorists who focus on how shared places can no longer be understood as "localities" but instead illustrate (and serve the needs of) increasing globalization. Anthropologist Marc Augé (1995), for example, posited that if anthropology had historically depended on the idea that cultures or communities were bound in particular places, this notion was dissolving with the "excess of space" that accompanied global interactions, exchanges, and movements. When what had once been understood to be distant was suddenly perceived as local and when cultural contact with those far spread suddenly seemed inevitable, local places ceased to mean what they once had. In this "supermodern" world, time, space, and identity were increasingly homogeneous and defined by mass commercialization. Augé's theories intersected with problematics of space theorized by critical and feminist geographers (Massey, 1994; McDowell, 1999). In addition, Augé's theory echoed David Harvey's concept of time-space compression, in which the history of capitalism could be read through a lens in which time appeared to speed up as telecommunications and travel technologies shrank the distance between spaces. For Paul Virilio (1986), this compression was associated with acceleration that stripped away time for critical inquiry and contemplation (Kimme Hea, 2009).

Augé referred to the new category of locations unique to this situation as "non-places," focusing on their use and social impact:

> [T]he word "non-place" designates two complementary but distinct realities: spaces formed in relation to certain ends (transport, transit, commerce, leisure), and the relations that individuals have with these spaces. Although the two sets of relations overlap to a large extent, and in any case officially (individuals travel, make purchases, relax), they are still not confused with one another; for non-places mediate whole mass of relations, with the self and with others, which are only indirectly connected with their purposes. As anthropological places create the organically social, so non-places create solitary contractuality. (1995, p. 94)

Non-places for Augé, that is, could be identified not only by their intended purpose but also by the way of being in relation to others that they established. These places invited disconnection rather than assembling social collectives.

Augé's prologue to *Non-Places: Introduction to an Anthropology of Supermodernity* (1995) used the example of a traveler's experience to explore and develop the solitary experience of passing through places where individuals momentarily dwelled. Within this domain, institutional and organizational texts were used to maintain efficiency and regulate movement, rather than to enrich community understanding or provoke debate. In the airports and train stations that Augé described, it was less likely that people were reading newspapers that created a sense of collective relations to be discussed and debated among them. It was more likely that they were reading institutional texts that ensured that they effectively minded their individual pathways, moving in ways that facilitated their ability to reach another place (Augé, 1995). Thus people who found themselves together in airports, train stations, or malls often lacked a shared history or groundedness. They were thus likely to see themselves as on more individualized trajectories, each longing to be "a world in himself," where literacy was important for maintaining that perceived autonomy. Virilio (2012) further developed the temporal ramifications of shrinking geographical distances. He wrote, "what we are now seeing, after the topographic and geometric effraction of distances, is the anachronistic effraction of the time intervals required for effective knowledge and well as memory of the facts" (2012, p. 4). Our traditional means of perception and understanding are no longer equipped to deal with the speed at which both we and information can circulate.

As a result, the mall, the interstate system, and the airport terminal were more or less similar across geographical regions in highly developed Western places (Dickinson, 2002; Ellis, 2002; Wood 2009) and supported reading and writing texts that facilitated movement even as they gathered mobile people and devices. Today's coffeehouse is often understood to be functioning in a similarly individualized fashion. If Habermas' ideal coffeehouse epitomized a built environment that embodied the public sphere, the megachain Starbucks has often been invoked to illustrate the contemporary non-place. Although Starbucks cited the idea of third place in its description of its mission and purpose (2020, "Company Information"), in an interview with historian Bryant Simon, Oldenburg (2009) "scoffed" at the idea that Starbucks franchises could be described as third places in the sense he had intended the term. "It's an imitation," Oldenburg asserted. He continued by stating that Starbucks could not "achieve the kind of connections I had in mind" (2009, pp. 249–250).[5] Literary historian Markman Ellis (2002), known for his four-volume collection of historical materials referencing coffeehouses in the long eighteenth century, took a similar view of what social connection was possible in the contemporary coffeehouse, again using Starbucks as his exemplar. Ellis described "Starbucks sociability" as most related to a poster displaying the words "Taste, comfort, relax" that he observed on the wall of a Starbucks still under construction (2002). "In the sociability of Starbucks," Ellis wrote, "an atomized society finds a convenient representation of the city of individuals. This sociability is not collective and public but is rather about being alone together, about fragmenting public discourse into non-organized entities, about consuming rather than debating" (2002, n.p.). Although Sherry Turkle (2011) would later associate being "alone together" with the use of technologies, Ellis emphasized how this social state emerged from the social and economic arrangements of the place: changes that epitomized the difference between a coffeehouse that created a collective and one that stood to support individual trajectories.

Shared Social Places and/as the Commons

The kinds of places that Habermas described may be difficult to find in the twenty-first century, if they ever existed. The "great, good places" of neighborhood life that united communities have changed along with shifting technologies and economic arrangements. However, there is also reason to think that generalized critiques of shared social places likely overlook various neighborhood locations that seed arguments and serve as a grounding for both collective identities and neighborhoods. For example, Julie Lindquist's (2002)

---

5   While Oldenburg has denied that Starbucks can be a third place, Simon discusses how Starbucks owner Howard Schultz extensively used the theory of third place in creating the design and plans for this coffee chain.

A Place to Stand: Politics and Persuasion in a Working Class Bar discussed the role of a bar called The Smokehouse where discussion of politics, alcohol, and everyday life performed and constructed complex relations among those who spend time there. Many of us are lucky enough to have places like the Smokehouse in our neighborhoods, even if we do not understand them to hold positions as lofty or idealized as the historical coffeehouse.

Furthermore, recent research on the use and uptake of shared social places also suggests that worries about the isolating nature of shared space have been overstated. One strain of this scholarship is theoretical. The mobilities turn in social science scholarship has questioned the tendency to nostalgize localities and community rootedness. Tim Creswell (2006), for instance, described how a sedentarist metaphysics positions mobility as an inherent threat to the authenticity of local place—a dysfunction likely to result in the loss of tradition or community. A nomadic metaphysics, by contrast, celebrates fluidities and flows as potentially subversive responses to structuring forces, often romantically celebrating movement without attention to how mobilities are experienced differentially. The sedentarist metaphysics echoes through critiques from scholars such as Oldenburg and Ellis, who position movements away from localities as departures from rooted, rational foundations. Furthermore, recent studies suggest that people are less socially isolated in shared social places today than 30 years ago, and that women in particular are more likely than ever to be present and interacting in public spaces (Hampton et al., 2015).

Communication and information theorists studying the relationship between technology use and sociability also question whether threats to public space have been overstated. This research traces a long history of worries about collectivity that emerge during moments of technological change. These worries surface, for instance, in collective responses to technologies such as books, televisions, portable boom boxes, and Walkmans (Gergen, 2002; Hampton & Gupta, 2008; Meyrowitz, 1985). While cultural critiques associating global capitalism with the homogenization of public space remain compelling (Dickinson, 2002; Ellis, 2002; Wood, 2009), rhetoric and communication scholars have traced how individuals and groups collectively annotate and transform shared places through online social software applications (de Souza e Silva & Frith, 2012; Diehl et al., 2008; Frith, 2015; Gordon & de Souza e Silva, 2011; Rice, 2012; Varnelis & Friedburg, 2008), experiencing the world in hybrid spaces where contact is mediated both electronically and in person. Online applications support forms of connection that may not bound the same kinds of geographically rooted communities associated with public sphere theory but do create relationships and the potential for networked information exchange among neighbors and co-inhabitants. As the tools that enable collaborative learning and work in online places are often available online, the importance of offline places for gathering has not disappeared. However, these places take on different roles for workers, learners, neighbors, and community members seeking differently mediated social interactions as well as solitude and unofficial productivity monitoring.

The term "public space" no longer quite fits to describe many shared social locations where networked mobile technologies are used as a primary writing media, given the emphasis on individual needs and desires over and above collective interests. However, positioning these shared places as a commons emphasizes their roles as domains where people access shared materials that participate in their work, learning, and engagement with others. This function of social places as domains of shared materials might not be obvious at first. In Starbucks, we may not borrow newspapers or magazines or other historically significant shared literacy materials. However, we are likely to borrow the free Wi-Fi connection, the surface of a tabletop, and the values and attitudes that enable literacy work to take place. In the most overt cases, places such as the Gone Wired Café or the Technology Commons become temporary destinations for work particularly because they contribute relevant materials to literacy practices. For example, Johndan Johnson-Eilola's (2005) *Datacloud* describes how both students and symbolic-analytic workers construct personalized workspaces combining physical spatial infrastructures (e.g., surfaces such as whiteboards, desks, chairs, etc.) that they access with online interfaces to create layered, multiply mediated settings where they sample, juxtapose, and transform information. Such constructions frequently make use of resources available in coffeehouses, coworking facilities, or libraries. These resources range from technologies and archived texts that enable device functionality to arrangements of built environments, values, and people that enable interpersonal social support.

Composers who write with networked mobile technologies also frequently and simultaneously make use of shared online domains that enable access to materials that participate in literacy. Social media sites, bulletin boards, Wikipedia: these sites have in common that people navigate to and from them temporarily in order to access shared information that participates in their composing. Readers and writers often position the places they move through in this way: as collections of materials rather than as homes for communities. In so doing, users compose documents but they also simultaneously participate in and co-construct multiple social environment through their user-generated participation. This includes complicated and potentially troubling participations: for example, the passive data collected, used, and manipulated whenever composers interact in social media or log in to a Starbucks Wi-Fi connection.

To bring this conversation to a more concrete place, the chapter now turns to the two sites in which I researched transient literacies to reflect on how we might read both as a commons for networked mobile composing. Both sites were more complex than either Habermas' traditional collective sociability associated with the coffeehouse or Ellis' atomized "Starbucks sociability." Across their functions as community centers and workspaces for academics and professionals, both places emphasized flexibility through multiple zones and changed as people accessed and maneuvered toward materials that supported a range of literacy needs.

The Great Good Non-Place

Located on a central avenue in a city that had once been in the center of the US automobile industry, Gone Wired was part of a broader rebuilding and rebranding that could be seen throughout the East Side of Lansing, Michigan. That central avenue was Michigan Avenue, which divided the city and moved travelers in a direct route from the state government district in Downtown Lansing to the large research university in neighboring East Lansing. Along this route, a large teaching hospital was positioned between these centers of academia and state government. This highly traveled thoroughfare collected and supported the movement of individuals affiliated with the area's academic, health-care, and government sectors—people likely to be transient in their relationships to the city and state. The research participants lived in this neighborhood (the East Side), which put the café in close proximity to their homes.

Gone Wired, however, had positioned itself to *feel local*, defining itself against the corporate coffee scene that Ellis described or that rhetorician Greg Dickinson (2002) evoked in his material rhetorical analysis of a Colorado Starbucks. Echoing Augé, Dickinson noted how Starbuck's generic corporate text, combined with the sights, sounds, and materials that come with experiencing coffee beans transformed into sippable lattes and mochas, enforced an aesthetic that made globalization local and comfortable, while covering over material contexts and practices that supported the brand. Gone Wired had, by contrast, encouraged its materiality to be developed as an ongoing, community-produced endeavor. Instead of seeing generic advertisements for products in the café, patrons who entered Gone Wired through its glass entry doors encountered announcements for community reading groups or local music acts. The bulletin board along the back entryway and the floor-to-ceiling columns near the cash register were tacked and stapled with notices for community meetup groups, musicians, and artists—many of whom hobnobbed there during free time. The newspaper available near the bar was the "City Pulse,"

Lansing's "alternative weekly newspaper." Gone Wired served coffee roasted by a local roaster and distributor, whose plant had been releasing the smell of roasted coffee beans into Lansing's downtown district since the 1930s. Gone Wired never hid its history as a place built over the remnants of another former small business on the Ave. The foosball table and glass cabinet counter visible on the first floor reminded patrons of the building's previous life as an outdoor sporting goods shop. Patrons commonly propped bicycles against the unused counter and storage area in the front entryway. It was far from a controlled aesthetic.

Figure 2.1. The front entrance of the Gone Wired Café.

Figure 2.2. The Gone Wired Café as viewed from the upper level.

Although Gone Wired resisted a corporate coffee ambiance, perusing its use on any given day revealed literacy practices that differed from either the historical sketches of face-to-face conversations among citizens in Habermas' coffeehouse or the scenes of isolation in Augé's conception of non-place. Gone Wired negotiated a middle space as a community site that invited locals to read the local news and drop by to talk local politics. However, it also served as a composing workspace for those who wanted to pass through without much interaction. This was true not only for graduate and professional students who attended local colleges and universities, law schools, and medical schools, but also for state government employees, attorneys, and local businesspeople. As in many other gathering places (including Starbucks!), it was not uncommon to see community groups drafting out plans to organize a volunteer drive or locals dropping in to say hello to the barista and scope out the local paper. This activity happened simultaneously as others entered the café explicitly to get personal or professional work done, laptop after laptop often lining the upstairs space. The fact that Gone Wired was so local in the ways I have previously described makes it even more interesting that many research participants referred to it as "blank" or "clean space," a tabula rasa on which to write their own needs and desires. The place in many ways worked as hard as it could to counter this notion of its own positioning. Permanent fixtures—such as the burgundy, cream, and green-tiled fountain holding an aging, metal sculpture in its reservoir—reminded patrons to view it as a unique, local place. And yet individual desires were key to many of its dwellers, who focused on what it offered as an escape from more socially saturated places in their lives.

A Resource "Epicenter"

The Technology Commons differed in substantial ways from the Gone Wired Café, but even its name emphasized how it positioned itself as a commons providing resources and bringing people together. As much as the Technology Commons hoped to be a gathering place that synthesized a community, it also emphasized the importance of its community's diversity, which was evident in the design features that attempted to support students' individual information management practices. The website described it this way:

> UCF's old computer center has been transformed into a welcoming, convenient place for all students. The Technology Commons is an epicenter for students to gather, communicate, interact, study and receive technical support. A state-of-the-art facility open to all of UCF, providing the resources for students and staff alike to find, assemble, and synthesize the information needed to tackle numerous diverse tasks. The individual areas of the computer center buildings amalgamate to form a diverse, thriving, technical community at the heart of UCF.

The description implied that the Technology Commons could fulfill two needs at the same time: to exist as an "epicenter" where the community could meet and to provide the resources students needed to "find, assemble, and synthesize the information needed to tackle numerous diverse tasks." Importantly, the Technology Commons would attempt to achieve its mission by "providing the resources" that would be put to use by students and staff and would do so by creating "individual areas" that could be taken up for different uses.

To provide more context, the Technology Commons opened its doors in January 2012 and was located on the most frequently traveled pedestrian pathway at the University of Central Florida (UCF), a large, metropolitan research university of over 60,000 students. University campuses, whether by design or as a result of use, can be seen through student eyes as collections of linked places inhabited temporarily before moving elsewhere. At UCF, this dynamic of interconnected dwelling places was shaped by its large student population. Campus social places were saturated with people during the busiest hours of the day and were never completely deserted. In buildings where classes were conducted, students transformed hallways into study zones, sitting on the floor in front of open textbooks. Against this backdrop, UCF had recently invested in renovating or constructing several new, flexible campus locations for temporary study, gathering, and information access. For example, when I arrived at UCF in the fall of 2011, the entry floor of its John C. Hitt Library had recently been renovated from a traditional "stacks" setup and print repository into a knowledge commons built on a "Commons 2.0" model of library space design (Bilandzic & Foth, 2014). The new knowledge commons featured a coffee shop, mixed-use seating, and portable white boards that could serve both as inscription surfaces and barriers to interaction (Allen 2011). UCF also operated several computer labs dotted across its 1,415–acre main campus, including in highly frequented locations such as the Student Union, as well as places local to particular majors such as in the Business Administration building. The campus also featured two flexible study sites called "All Knight Study," which were available to students at all hours, after many computer labs ended normal operating times.

Prior to remodeling, the Technology Commons had played a role in this broader campus spatial organization by providing students with access to technologies and resources without a dual focus on gathering. Called "Computer Center 1 and 2," the building had been a large traditional computer lab, lining rows of black computers against gray carpets and white walls. The new Technology Commons by contrast emphasized diversity and flexibility by combining a series of contrasting arrangements that suggested diverse forms of social interaction. These zones corresponded with different technologies, lighting, and materials and stretched across the two buildings joined by an outdoor walkway and patio. Both instantiations of the place had gathered mobile students traveling across campus and provided them with resources, but design choices in the new built environment had a different rhetorical impact on the movement and positioning of mobile bodies. The remodeling emphasized students' ability to choose—and, to some degree, manipulate—their immediate material surrounds, rather than occupying a predetermined set of relations among bodies, furniture, and devices structured through bolted-down materials and technologies. Students were confronted by choices about what resources to use amid the following multiple zones that the space assembled.

The BYOT Lab, Coffee Shop, and Technology Product Center

Figure 2.2 shows the Bring Your Own Technology (BYOT) lab, which included a small coffee shop, a technology product center (a technology store), and modular-style café furniture. One side of the BYOT lab included cushioned chairs with printed upholstery, often arranged to face a large flat-screen display at the far end of the room. Students used the BYOT lab for everything from coursework to playing video games on the PlayStation to eating lunch. The right side included café-style tables for two that could be pushed together to accommodate larger groups. Students often brought in or purchased food and used this area simultaneously for eating, socializing, and studying.

Figure 2.3. The Technology Commons BYOT laboratory.

The Collaboration Lab, Tech Repair Desk, and Transitional Space

Students accessed the Collaboration Lab by passing from the BYOT lab through a hallway with a tech-repair desk, storage for charging mobile devices, recycling centers, and vending machines containing small study items (headphones, blue books for test taking, etc.). As Figure 2.4 shows, the Collaboration Lab featured pod-style desktop computers arranged with rolling desk chairs. Groups often huddled together around one desktop computer for collaborative projects, and individual students moved chairs to empty desks to work alone while sitting near friends or strangers using desktop computers. In addition, the Collaboration Lab housed glass-walled private rooms designed for group work and specialized technology needs (e.g., an audio- and video-recording studio).

Figure 2.4. Technology Commons collaboration laboratory.

The PC Lab, Cubby, and Meeting Spaces

Both the BYOT lab and Collaboration Lab opened onto an outdoor patio space, which was usable almost year-round in Orlando's climate. Across the patio was the second building in the Technology Commons, which housed a large conference-room space and a standard computer lab with traditional rows of desktop computers. While arranged more traditionally, this laboratory was busy with students, many of whom used headphones to create privacy. The transitional hallway that led from the front door included a small "cubby" area with sofa-style seating, a large central table, and a flat-screen panel from which students could project from laptops.

Given this design for flexibility, it is hardly surprising that students' uses for the Technology Commons spanned domains (i.e., personal, school, extra-curricular), technologies, subject areas, and reasons for interpersonal gathering. In the interviews I conducted, students frequently discussed their use of the Technology Commons by positioning it as one of several competing campus social spaces, which they used strategically for different reasons. In other words, the Technology Commons' position in spatial and social campus networks was associated with particular uses and challenges. The ongoing use of the Technology Commons for convenience and social interaction, in turn, shaped the activities, attention, and social arrangements cultivated there. Specifically, the Technology Commons was often positioned as a place to complete study tasks that could be accomplished while purposefully splitting attention or "hanging out" with others. This was in part because the Technology Commons was bustling with activity. It was loud, bright, and dynamic. For example, business major Max described how the Technology Commons was a perfect location for conducting "low-level research" for finance classes while socializing. By "low-level research" in this case, he described running an investment simulator and monitoring the ongoing performance of his simulated choices over the course of a few hours. Students like Max often worked on tasks that did not require full attention in the Technology Commons, which enabled them to be with friends at the same time. However, individuals and groups often found themselves in the Tech Commons for more sustained composing work as well.

The Cost of Composing with the Mobile Commons

The Technology Commons and Gone Wired were different kinds of places. They were built as a result of different funding models, and they evidenced different trends in space design and retrofitting. However, the environments were similar with respect to how they foregrounded individual freedom and choice in how their built environments would be navigated and used. Both places had been designed for flexibility and configurability and offered patrons a range of possible materials to support tasks they encountered. What was less clear was whether users of these places possessed capacity, access, or time needed to effectively mobilize the available resources. Furthermore, both locations required that users possess technologies and other social support that would transform empty surfaces into fully functioning learning or literacy ecologies. While the Technology Commons provided some remaining desktop computers, the majority of its zones offered tables on which to place laptops. While the Gone Wired Café did not purport to offer learning or information management support, the commons still emphasized flexibility across its multiple zones: a "living room style" seating area, booths, and tables.

In places that serve as a commons but not always as "public space," the flexibility to organize one's own learning practices comes with costs, in at least two senses. Although these places offer flexible resources designed to appeal to many needs and desires, it is generally necessary to invest in food or drink in order to occupy space in a coffeehouse, and it is difficult to miss the consumer goods that line the Technology Commons walls (see Ryan Moeller [2004] regarding the consumer impulses of wireless technologies). This is not to mention how costs for constructing and maintaining University places funnel back to taxpayers and/or students. In other ways the cost of using these commons spaces was more hidden: the usefulness of shared places for composing depended upon factors that varied for individuals: their social embeddedness, their habits of time use and attention, and their material and social access to technologies and discourses. This cost for entry meant that some potential users were more likely to have the opportunity to participate in the commons than others. Recognizing the "cost" associated with taking up shared materials is crucial for understanding the challenges of composing in flexible commons spaces. How are students and professionals negotiating these costs and where do they run into roadblocks and challenges in assembling the resources needed for composing?

In order to reflect on the complexities of positioning shared social spaces as locations for networked mobile composing, the chapter discusses two cases of extended writing projects, one of a professional writer in the Gone Wired Café and the other from a group of student writers in the Technology Commons. These cases focus on the costs of taking up shared resources, positioning these relative to participants' perceptions of the spaces in which they collaborated.

Dave's Story

Let's begin with Dave, who is a research participant I've discussed at length.[6] Dave was a professional rather than a student; however, his story is relevant to the challenges and costs of transient literacies. A technology consultant who writes, teaches, and lends advice to a number of different academic, community, and nonprofit organizations, Dave used the Gone Wired Café for many aspects of his job, including his personal/professional blog. Dave was also a new father with a partner who worked outside the home. Not surprisingly, the birth of his daughter had significantly altered many parts of his life, including assigning him the new identity of stay-at-home dad. As a self-employed contractor and full-time father, he lacked an official organizational workspace, and working at home was filled with crawling and crying challenges: "My house is busy with the baby. So really the only time I really can sit is if I negotiate some time with my wife . . . or when they go to bed." The Gone Wired Café had been a central work location for Dave long before this most recent

---

6   I have written about Dave's case previously focused on the role of social media in building capacity for his professional writing identity and career (i.e., Pigg 2014a). Here I write about Dave again, but emphasize different details from my interviews with him in order to develop a different theme from our conversation: the difficulties that transient literacies present for navigating the commons as hybrid space, given individual desires for its use.

shift in his personal and professional identity. When I asked Dave about why he first started coming to Gone Wired, he mentioned his laptop, the Wi-Fi connection, and his work, which had taken a winding path across several local organizations in the past several years.

Dave positioned the café as a place for private time. Although he was preparing to "meet with one other group" later that day to discuss an ongoing project, he emphasized Gone Wired was a place for time and space alone. When he discussed the need for a private workplace, he stressed that finding personal time as an independent contractor in which to focus on work was an issue with which he was currently struggling. As he put it, "I just have no space and time for myself, and I really . . . when I'm here, I just really want to be left alone, you know? And not chitchat, you know? I don't have any time for myself unless I make it." He used the café on Fridays "mostly to write or to catch up on things" alone with his laptop, external hard drive, and mobile phone. He contrasted how the café offered different affective associations than that of his home. While his home was familiar, he felt confined there, adding that he was "kind of stuck in the house a little bit more. And more comfortable there too, but it still takes me longer to write if I'm there. If I have to write a blog there, it will take me a lot more time."

Finding alone time was tricky in Gone Wired, however, because Dave was well established in professional networks of the city as well as in the social networks of the coffeehouse. While Kim and Ed, for example, were able to find privacy upstairs in Gone Wired away from the in-and-out traffic of local patrons, Dave found the upstairs space uncomfortable because of the temperature. Sitting downstairs, Dave found it almost impossible not to run into people he knew from prior work and community organizing efforts. This posed problems for Gone Wired's capacity to support the privacy Dave craved when he worked outside the home. He was increasingly ambivalent about spending time there. As he put it, "Because I'm not here a lot, if people see me, they tend to just come over and think they can talk to me. So I'm getting where I want to go hide when I'm here." Hiding for Dave meant working in a small meeting room that was typically not visible to patrons entering through the café's front door. He described how the pressure to complete tasks during the hours he had available was leading him to feel agitated, both with others and himself. As he described, "I think I am putting more pressure on myself to get more done, and I think it's made [my outlook on working here] a little more negative." He described how when heading home on Fridays after a day in Gone Wired, he nearly always felt that he did not accomplish enough and transferred that attitude to the rest of his life. Relying totally on mobile workspace to support his career, he could never easily leave his frustration at the office.

Charlotte, Owen, and Gabriel's Stories

The second case example is a writing group involving three students named Charlotte, Owen, and Gabriel. These three senior management majors had been assigned to work together on a large-scale writing assignment, a business plan, that required extensive research and invention over a semester. While members of the group were relatively close in age, the one woman and three men had different racial and socioeconomic status and experiences, as well as different prior and current life experiences. The business plan writers were collaborating as a direct result of an assignment that required them to become a team, rather than because of their own motivation to do so. Their course met face-to-face one night a week, and each meeting represented a process deadline toward completing the business plan. Working to meet this weekly deadline, the group had the opportunity to set the terms of their collaboration and their composing process.

When Charlotte, Owen, and Gabriel's group started working together on their business plan, at least some of them had a rather idyllic conception of how the collaboration should unfold. Owen, for instance, described the plan that he and fellow group member Charlotte had imagined for the collaboration at the beginning of the semester. As he put it, he and Charlotte had "heard glorious stories of groups where everyone comes in on Saturday, you're in the library in one of the cubby areas . . . with five computers for about eight hours and all just knock out the work, the assignment right there. Everyone's right there. Just reach around and touch someone." Thinking back on this original vision as he approached the end of the semester, Owen reflected, "We'd envisioned that for this group. That hasn't worked out."

During the hour-long work session I observed during the last week of January, three group members were huddled around a high-top table with one laptop in the BYOT lounge of the Technology Commons working on the market analysis section of their business plan. Their goal for the day was to combine four individual contributions that had been composed prior to their meeting into one coherent draft of the market analysis. If possible, they also hoped to align their finished product with two example texts they had received from the instructor: one printed in the book and another successful version the instructor had provided from a previous course session. This meeting in the Technology Commons was the closest they would come all semester to the rosy vision of collaboration Owen and Charlotte had imagined. Even on this most successful day, however, not all group members could carve out five or six hours from their schedules to be in the same place at the same time to complete the plan. Owen and Gabriel were available earliest at around eleven in the morning and met in the Business Administration building computer lab—

where both of them typically completed coursework. They worked together on the early portions of the market analysis until Gabriel needed to leave to attend a class. When Charlotte arrived on campus a few hours later, she texted Owen and suggested he meet her at the Technology Commons because of the power outlets, coffee, and large tables. Owen agreed, though he and Gabriel both stressed later that the Technology Commons is not a place they would typically work—both had visited only once or twice before. Their fourth collaborator did not respond to text and email messages inviting him to join the group's work session, though he had contributed writing toward the project. The group eventually did finish a draft of their market analysis section before the course deadline and submitted it for their instructor's review.

The Costs of Freedom and Challenges of Flexibility

Using laptops is often associated with flexibility, in ways that are illustrated by both the cases that I just described. When Dave left the confines of his home and had childcare for his daughter, he felt a freedom to conduct his work in ways less constrained by the needs of others. He could compose where and when he wanted. The business plan group experienced a similar freedom and flexibility in their writing assignment: though they needed to complete a particular task, they enjoyed the freedom of organizing its completion based on their personal desires. Though Dave and the business plan writers both enjoyed freedom, they needed resources to transform their flexibility into a tangible composing process.

Let me begin to illustrate by discussing Dave in more detail. For Dave, the flexibility offered by freelance work enabled him to be a primary child-care provider in his household but simultaneously replaced the stability offered by affiliation with a singular firm with the necessity of organizing contract positions across organizations in a way that allowed for the development of emergent opportunities over time (Pigg, 2014a). Dave is not unique in this way. According to some, "flexibility is the modus operandi" of global capitalism (Garsten, 2008, p. 14), which means that individuals must be prepared to adapt and shift their career goals continually in response to potential opportunities. This adaptiveness involved ongoing watchfulness and the cultivation of "negotiation" and "agility" in creating, maintaining, and reorganizing alliances (Spinuzzi, 2007). As I have argued before (Pigg 2014a), flexibility in a career like Dave's requires him to cultivate a relationship to a range to online social media sites that were not provided to him by an employer but instead were his responsibility to assemble. However, the same was true for his physical workspace, creating the need to continually construct hybrid space that effectively layered the affordances of online and physical materials.

For Dave as for many others, this flexibility and construction of space revolved around his use of a laptop computer for everyday work. Dave's laptop was a portal to the online resources he used to insure the possibility for future action (i.e., more jobs in the future), but also required a built environment that served to anchor a *production setting* for his work. The places that served a function as his resource commons were unlikely to be tailored to the particular needs that he brought to them, however. Twitter was not a perfect medium for establishing his professional identity, and Gone Wired was not a perfect production setting for his work. Dave was frustrated with the café's flexibility. The fact that Gone Wired served not only as a workplace but also as a community hangout meant that he was often faced with people who did not share his need for privacy. Through no fault of theirs, Dave experienced their presence as a distraction because it did not align with his personal goals for the production setting.

Recall that Susan Leigh Star and Karen Ruhleder emphasized that a central problem of infrastructure uptake is that collections of resources designed to be taken up by many different people will always struggle with the space between what is generally available and what is specifically needed. In their terms, "it is impossible to have 'universal niches'; one person's standard is in fact another's chaos" (1996, p. 112). In Dave's case, Gone Wired's status as a production setting for professional work had begun to feel like "chaos," even though the café functioned well for people like Ed and Kathryn, whom I discussed earlier. The flexibility offered by the built environment of the café came with a cost: it would be used in multiple and diverse ways and might only effectively serve one's goals for a time. Dave's time for Gone Wired seemed to be running out. This issue affects students as well as professionals. In the same way that professionals define and orchestrate workplaces and workflow routines, students with laptop computers gain responsibility for cultivating their end of the bargain to organize their "workflows." These choices require students to work with and assemble resources associated with values and materials embedded in their immediate physical locations, the disciplinary cultures of their coursework, and their personal routines and habits.

In a similar way, the key benefit of the Technology Commons for Charlotte, Owen, and Gabriel was its flexibility: it accommodated their seating, power, and noise needs, which enabled them to discuss their project out loud without interrupting others. Its café tables were well suited to group discussion, rather than dispersing them across a row of computers side-by-side. However, the presence of useful materials did not stop the group from struggling to effectively combine them with personal repertoires. When I first approached the group, there were stacks of paper, flailing arms, cans of energy drinks, and stress-relief toys sitting on the café table where the group huddled. Charlotte began in front of the Dell laptop, which was connected to the Wi-Fi network and plugged into a power outlet behind them. She read aloud contributions that the group members had composed prior to their meeting, taking feedback from Owen and Gabriel and making changes to the official text as they debated vision, ideas, and phrasing details. Things had become tense as it was around three in the afternoon and the deadline for their section was at the beginning of their course at six. During this process, Owen and Gabriel cracked jokes, discussed mixed martial arts, and ultimately annoyed Charlotte to the point that she turned her laptop toward Owen and asked him to take over the central composing role.

It was not a design flaw in Technology Commons that made the group struggle: they had scheduled their work near the deadline and created a stressful situation for completing their assignment on that night. However, what I want to emphasize is that the group was generally unprepared to collaborate well with the materials in the space, even if they were somewhat cognizant of the need to plan and carefully orchestrate a collaboration among humans. I have already emphasized that most of the group preferred working face-to-face with one another in a way that simultaneously involved composing separately in a division of labor model and having immediate access to one another's feedback and interaction. However, they did not ultimately use this process, in part because the Technology Commons did not help them achieve this kind of social arrangement. Looking back on their composing session in the Technology Commons that day, Gabriel laughed, "We haven't really met [in person] since because we weren't really productive. I'm sure you could tell by the tape—we weren't really productive." Charlotte, herself, explained: "We agreed not to meet [face-to-face] anymore just because we don't get anything done. Not that we don't get along well, we do, as people but as a . . . like a work . . . a working group? No. We can't." In place of a face-to-face meeting, Charlotte took responsibility for centralizing interpersonal coordination via a different kind of commons: a Facebook group, which provided options for both synchronous and asynchronous communication and which all group members seemed to find more convenient. With Facebook creating an archive and online gathering place for conversations and materials, group members planned ad hoc face-to-face meetings when necessary by contacting each other through the page. Importantly, as the group delegated project coordination to Facebook, they divided the labor of the project differently. Instead of working to generate text together, they allowed one team member to work more or less independently on each week's contribution and rotated this responsibility among the group. Not surprisingly, all group members did not contribute evenly. Mediated through Facebook, they enacted a full division-of-labor model and collaborated in ways that prioritized their individual convenience. Though the Technology Commons offered flexible space for organizing the deliberative approach to collaboration that most of them preferred, their ability to mobilize the materials came at a cost: of knowledge, time, and access that they were not able or willing, in this case, to pay.

The Conflicts of Individual Desires and Routines

There's a related challenge at the heart of both Dave and the business plan writers' stories: the individual needs and motives writers bring into commons spaces often create problems when they attempt to align them with the material possibilities afforded by socially rich gathering spaces. I have already suggested, for instance, that the highly individual needs Dave brought with him to Gone Wired were at odds with how the café functioned as a community hub. When the social atmosphere of the place required him to make small talk with his neighbors rather than focusing on writing or editing, he experienced intense frustration. The business writers' experience produced an interesting parallel: Dave increasingly found himself interested in seeking out online commons for shared resources rather than working where others could access him face-to-face. If Dave frequently spent time "hiding" in the café, he worked to make himself as visible as possible across online spaces and valued contributing to the online commons above conversations in the built, physical one. To give an example, Dave recently had been invited to deliver a short TED-style talk at a popular local conference. Interestingly, Dave was excited about this opportunity because it would develop his online visibility to his dispersed network, rather than because it would better establish an identity in the local community. He said, half jokingly, "I'm doing it more so I can get it on video," which he knew would be circulated on YouTube and could be linked to his blogs and social media accounts.

His needs for professional identity construction were so specialized, so individualized, that reaching out to garner contacts for future work was more likely successful in the crowd-assembling online commons of YouTube than the community-assembling local commons of the neighborhood meeting space. His central focus, then, was on what the physical commons offered him in terms of resources to be used in connecting through online media to communities dispersed geographically. He was not even particularly interested in the online commons associated with his local region because it did not effectively support his career goals. For instance, Dave described how Twitter was not useful for cultivating local connections because Twitter users often posted personal details ("I don't care that you had a date tonight. Okay? That's for Facebook. Do it on Facebook"). Dave perceived the personal, local, friendship-based identity and relationship building that happened on social media outlets to be connected with a local young professional ethos that was less interesting to him than geographically distributed affinity networks connected to his personal and professional needs and development. The online commons offered something that the local commons could not.

In Charlotte, Owen, and Gabriel's case, the challenges of individual needs, materials, and assumptions worked hand-in-hand with the costs of freedom in that each group member brought conflicting perceptions and materials to the physical commons. Each member not only had disparate writing styles and uneven access to technologies but also different philosophies about how, when, and where collaborations should be accomplished. As with any collaboration, the group found itself in a situation where these individual trajectories needed to be bridged through negotiations to set an agenda and work plan for the group. However, the group seemed to believe that the flexibility of the commons itself would be overcome their differences: that the very act of being face-to-face together in a location that offered technical materials that could aid in completing the task would outweigh the disparate goals that the group had for the business plan. Before returning to this central problem, let me further outline how individual experiences and goals created problems for the business plan group in mobilizing resources available in the Technology Commons.

Uneven Access to Mobile Devices

First, uneven access to mobile was a central issue that created challenges for the group, and that its members experienced in an immediate way during the composing moments I observed and in a more pervasive sense beyond that group writing project. For example, when the group worked together in the BYOT zone, they used one laptop computer, which was one group member's personal device. As a result of using one member's personal device to complete the task, not all group members had equal access to see the screen, or control what happened on it. This created a difficult power dynamic, enabling one group member (Charlotte at the beginning of the session) to feel as if she were taking on a larger share of the workload—and other members of the group to feel as if their input could not be heard or to become distracted and fill time with other interactions. Beyond this composing moment, the uneven adoption of mobile devices (including both phones and laptops) among the group created confusion and tension while coordinating group planning. Charlotte, a self-described "constant texter," was the only student in the group who frequently checked her phone. The constant presence of a smartphone was not shared among the group, and neither was access to a personal laptop that was easy to transport. While Charlotte chalked this up to generational differences (she was between 5 and 12 years younger than her teammates), she was also aware of how socioeconomic privilege influenced device use and ownership. Speaking about her group, she mentioned, "What I've noticed with them is none of them really have a good laptop." She continued, "I'm lucky enough for my parents to pay for my school [and] my dad provided me with a good laptop." Gabriel noted that his laptop had been an issue for his mobility. While he did have a laptop, he described it as "a little heavier," which made it inconvenient for carrying from his job to his internship to his three classes. In addition, he had recently "cracked the screen," and as a result he explained that "now I've been using the computer labs a lot more."

Owen, the third group member, emphasized this uneven access when describing how working together with personal devices only worked well when every group member had access to one, and when the group could draw on a social composing program (e.g., Google Docs) displayed on a common screen for making individual efforts visible to all. Owen believed that, to effectively write the business plan, group members should work both collaboratively and individually at the same time. This would allow all group members in Owen's words to be "researching separate things" at the same time while contributing to a master document. Notably, this was not a situation easily enacted in the section of the Technology Commons that they had chosen for their work, where no large, master screen was available. It was, however, precisely what the Technology Commons was designed to enable with its flat panel displays and café style tables—except that the students either had not chosen this setup or had not arrived in time to secure this section of the commons or one of the private collaboration rooms.

Different Expectations about what Productive Writing looks like with Mobile Devices

In addition to the differences that uneven material access created for mobilizing the commons, Owen, Charlotte, and Gabriel struggled to effectively carry out team writing because their expectations about time and productivity were in conflict. These conflicts involved different expectations among group members about what mediations constitute productive time use, as well as conflicts when their own expectations about productivity conflicted with the realities of working with co-present people. While Owen and Charlotte both were committed deeply to arrangements that included all members together in a face-to-face gathering space, other group members either had a difficult time making this arrangement work or understood time spent working face-to-face on a classroom assignment to be a waste of time. For example, Owen recounted how the tension that had begun mounting during the work session

I observed became explosive during the following week's face-to-face writing meeting: "We were sitting across from each other at computer screens, so we were looking over computer screens at each other, and [another group member[7]] was really resistant and kind of really rude." He explained, "He was pretty against the [idea of] everyone getting together and do the same project all at once. He thought it was a big waste of time." While Gabriel was more "low key" (in Charlotte's words) than the student who actively resisted co-present group meetings, he too had issues with spending so much time together in one place. Reflecting back on the hours spent in the Technology Commons, he laughed and said, "Oh, that was horrible." For him, the issue was explicitly related to all that he was trying to fit into the current semester, which was making it nearly impossible for him to engage in a five-to six-hour meeting with his group members. He explained that during the "first month of school, I was a little more free, but then I accepted an internship." This internship was layered on top of a job, at which he worked fifteen to twenty hours per week, and two additional senior-level courses. As all his peers acknowledged, Gabriel did his best to align with the group consensus about when and how to divide the labor of the group and when to meet in person. And yet he was not continually available for touching base. From an outside perspective, it is not surprising that other group members at times felt that his work was rushed, given his schedule and the resulting reality that he generally completed assignments during short breaks between scheduled work or classes.

Expectations about how face-to-face time should be spent were also not shared among group members, and this created further challenges. For example, Charlotte's preferred approach to revision was to follow the models given by the instructor sentence by sentence and line by line, bringing the structure and form of their draft material into alignment with the market analyses their instructor had provided. Since they were working on her laptop, she spent most of the session typing while comparing their initial drafts with the two available models. Owen, for one, found this approach of beginning with models to be limiting because it overdetermined what was possible for them to say. From his point of view, sticking so closely to models was not in the generative spirit of what the assignment called for: they were supposed to be inventing a business and learning to be creative entrepreneurial thinkers, after all, not filling in a template. While Owen often brought up philosophical issues related to their business plan during the work session I observed, Charlotte reflected later that she often interpreted his interjections as slowing down the process: smart ideas, but not appropriate for discussion in the few hours before the

---

7   This group member was not present during the face-to-face meeting that I observed and was not a participant in the research.

deadline. The pace of working face to face was also slowed down by inevitable social detours, mostly involving small talk not directly related to the task. The group members clearly liked each other socially and enjoyed spending time together, and some members were more comfortable than others with including social niceties during their meeting. Social interactions unrelated to the content created ways for the group to resolve some of the increasing stress, but while the group giggled and bantered easily, their time spent joking also removed them from the immediate task, which bothered Charlotte in particular and Gabriel to some degree (not to mention the member who did not attend the meeting and later asserted that face-to-face meetings were time wasters). Both the social conversations and Owen's creative impulses were interpreted by some group members as inappropriate uses of time, given the duration they had left themselves for composing the draft before the deadline. Although she remained good natured during the work session, Charlotte later described feeling an urge to constantly manage the direction of the conversation to keep it on task.

When I asked Charlotte how she would describe her role in the collaboration, she said that she felt like the team manager. Referring to another team member, she remarked, "I was trying to focus him, but at the same time I know that I don't have any real control over him, you know what I mean?" She elaborated that she felt like she was the team member who "want[ed] to get it done," while he was the team member who thinks, "I have all these great ideas" and wants to talk about them. Notably, Charlotte also perceived the role of overseeing the group's written online coordination to be a gendered task, and she remarked that women were often assumed to be responsible for this work within team projects in her major.

Conclusion: Collaborating with the Places We Move Through

As I stated earlier, the challenges that Dave and the business writing group faced were not caused by the designs of the Technology Commons or the Gone Wired Café. Certainly, the business writing group lacked a focused approach for organizing collaboration (e.g., Rebecca Burnett, L. Andrew Cooper, and Candice Welhausen's [2013] seven-term heuristic). And Dave was facing challenges in locating a workspace and interacting with locals that stemmed from unique personal needs that would never be wholly in line with what a neighborhood hangout could offer him. What I want to emphasize, however, is the lack of preparation or perceived options writers seemed to have for how to effectively collaborate in the hybrid space of the commons, particularly when their individual habits for orienting to space and materials had to become temporarily aligned with conflicting habits from other people. While shared social places provided resources that aided teamwork and interaction, neither technology nor social places alone led to stronger or better teams or more fruitful collaborative endeavors. People need strategies for how to work with and among both people and materials in the contemporary commons.

Information commons research bears out the point, for example, that the presence of a built environment designed for collaboration is not in itself enough to initiate interpersonal encounters within those places, particularly among strangers or around particular learning tasks. Users of social commons spaces or labs have positioned those places as "cool, hip space[s] with computers" in ways that downplay the potential they offer for collaboration and collective gathering (Mirtz, 2010, p. 248). Or, as Mark Bilandzic and Marcus Foth (2014) suggested, a physical environment designed for collaboration may not explicitly communicate its purpose to users, who often perceive the built environment in light of their own desires rather than for the potential it offers. That's worth saying again: users of shared social places often perceive a place in terms of their own desires rather than in terms of the potential that it offers. As hybrid space layered becomes a new norm for public places (Gordon & de Souza e Silva, 2011), librarians and learning center directors are beginning to invest in a range of ambient social media, signage, and connections among online and offline resources to help create lower barriers to collaboration among peers and increase the chances that students will connect with resources and library staff.

This is important as research has shown that people spend time in shared spaces for reasons that range from focused collaboration to serendipitous encounters to the experience of working alone among others (Crook & Mitchell, 2012). Bilandzic and Foth describe five archetypes of users of flexible social space: (1) coworkers who want to be away from distraction; (2) the "what can I do here" person, who happens upon a space but does not intuitively understand its purpose; (3) the "doesn't care" user who comes for particular technological resources but is not particularly interested in meeting others; (4) the "learning freak," who is interested in interacting because she wants to learn; and (5) the "I wanna share" user who has expertise in very particular domains and would like to meet with others to discuss these particular interests only (2014). These diversities of interest and spatial uptake layer with the differences that emerge from experiences and perceptions about space that come from users' race, class, sexuality, gender, and ability.

Looking forward, the biggest challenge for the interactivity of social gathering places is not the lack of contact experienced within them. With a move from public space to commons space as a controlling metaphor for how socially rich gathering places support composing practice, working through how shared places intersect with individual goals requires new ways of thinking, acting, coordinating, and assembling for which many participants in this study were unprepared. If the commons is to remain fruitful, individuals will need to see shared social places not only in terms of their own interests but in dialogue with a stewardship that places their own needs and interests in dialogue with others', aware of differential access to materials as well as diverse viewpoints about time and productively. The following chapter builds on this theme of individuation in order to offer a framework for more closely analyzing how users of networked mobile technologies take up resources of the commons in everyday practice.

Chapter 3: Orienting to the Mobile Surround

> [A] nonrepresentational approach describes literacy activity as not projected toward some textual end point, but as living its life in the ongoing present, forming relations and connections across signs, objects, and bodies in often unexpected ways.
>
> –Kevin Leander and Gail Boldt, 2013, p. 28

Imagine what you perceive as surroundings when you compose with a networked mobile technology like a laptop computer. You might sense a screen on your device. You might be vaguely aware of the backdrop of a wall or other horizon. If you are sitting, a table or other surface might collect objects that participate in your composing process: a cup of coffee, a stack of papers, books, food. Likely, you also sense things that have nothing to do with your writing. For example, when revising this chapter at a local Starbucks in Durham, a fellow patron brought in a two-foot-tall 1970s tape deck to restore at the table beside me. I couldn't help but turn toward what he was doing. He was using a strong cleaning fluid that smelled like alcohol and, as he told me later, was removing layers of musty cigarette smoke to try to make the technology functional again. People use shared places for pretty much every activity that matters to their lives, and this means that unpredictable and unrelated materials can shape the choices we make when composing with networked mobile devices. In this case, while I enjoyed talking to my fellow patron about his hobby, I had a hard time focusing on my writing once the tape deck restoration was underway. I wanted to ask more questions. I also had a difficult time ignoring the smell.

Materials like these, even when unusual, are somewhat easy to identify as participants in a composing session. But, what about all of the materials that are less easy to see. If you take into account the invisible infrastructures that impact composing, you would have to think about all that lies below the tip of the iceberg: the cultural, social, economic, and technological networks that extend across time and space to influence your movements. You'd also have to think about your own prior experiences as a writer and technology user and how these experiences travel with you into the places where you use your laptop. The surroundings that shape networked mobile composing extend broadly and deeply across the page, the building, the city, the social sphere, and the networked space of the internet.

Chapter 1 introduced transient literacies as negotiations with places, materials, people, and values that take place during networked mobile composing practices, and Chapter 2 examined how shared social places function as particular kinds of environments with respect to transient literacies by supporting perceived "flexibility" but actually influencing composing process through their situatedness. In Chapter 2, I argued that individuals and teams often choose common places for mobile writing based on personal desires, histories, and expectations but struggle to effectively align their needs with what the place affords. This chapter uses an embodied materialist approach to dig further into how individuals interact with surroundings when they compose in the transient commons places that collect people and their mobile technologies. In this analysis, I emphasize the role of human perception, given the strong role that experiences of place play in choices around locating mobile composing. My argument thus begins by drawing on Sara Ahmed's (2006) concept of *orientations* and Lucy Suchman's (2007) ethnomethodological approach to human-machine interactions. Taken together, I suggest that a focus on orientations and interactions provides a way to understand composing as an ongoing collaboration between writers and surroundings, while valuing how movements across places instill a familiarity with materials that influences future actions and perceptions of writing. I further offer a four-part heuristic framework—*materials, proximities, interactions,* and *sequences*— that researchers and instructors can use to refocus attention on how transient literacies are enacted in real time. Taken together, these four concepts offer language for positioning networked, mobile device use as a complex sociotechnical entanglement pushed forward by many materials (Barad, 2007).

After introducing this framework, I return to the question that I posed in the opening paragraph: How do we describe the surroundings that matter to networked mobile composing? Although there are multiple ways to parse this space, the chapter offers two frameworks unique to composing with networked mobile devices. First, I discuss three *dimensions of materiality* engaged during mobile composing. Rather than bifurcating physical and virtual space, I argue for thinking through the materiality of mobile composing by examining three dimensions that cut across physical and information spaces, as well as both apparent materials and invisible infrastructures. Second, I discuss three *dimensions of interaction* at which mobile composing practices result in the generation of complex agentive entanglements. My focus on dimensions of interaction takes seriously recent critiques of literacy research that locates the ends of literacy practices only in textual products. Drawing on Barad's (2007) concept of intra-action, I identify interactional spheres that influence and are influenced by networked mobile composing. The commons, sociability, and attention are three important interactional agencies co-constructed during networked mobile composing. By offering these frameworks, this chapter takes a step back from the challenges identified in Chapter 2 to lay the groundwork for closer attention to how and why individuals turn toward particular arrangements of information and materials when they compose with laptops.

Orientations as Links Between People and Surroundings

To inform an embodied materialist approach to researching composing, I draw from scholarship across disciplinary boundaries that was produced in response to problems and questions that are not my own. As Wiebe Bijker and John Law (1992) argued, "a model or theory, whatever its form, is a kind of statement of priorities: in effect it rests on a bet that for certain purposes some phenomena are more important than others" (p. 7). In this project, I have foregrounded theories that help me better understand how bodies move in relation with materials that they encounter as they cross spaces and times. Thus, I have turned to theories that emphasize human bodies as interactive confluences of histories, locations, technologies, cultural identities, and memories. Queer and feminist scholars of color have provided particularly compelling accounts of meaning-making from and with the body as a complex intersection of discourses and materials (Spillers, 2003; Williams, 1992). Theories in the flesh are a useful starting point for understanding bodies as active, living, and interactional processes at the cross-sections of people and their surroundings.

Theories in the Flesh

The Chicana feminist concept of a theory in the flesh links body, history, and cultural location to processes of making meaning. In the introduction to *This Bridge Called My Back*, Cherríe Moraga (1981) described the concept of a theory in the flesh as "one where the physical realities of our lives—our skin color, the land or concrete we grew up on, our sexual longings—all fuse to create a politic born out of necessity" (p. 23). What I want to emphasize here is that flesh is positioned as an interaction of various "physical realities" that coinfluence a drive to produce meaning. Importantly, theories in the flesh position these physical objects of life (e.g., skin color, land) as rhetorical or discursive, at the same time that typically rhetorical or discursive elements of life (e.g., social locations, desires) become physical, tangible, and material. Thus, by allowing for flexibility in what we understand as an influential or agential object, theorists in the flesh are able to understand bodies as produced in the intersection of multiple influences, as well as to trace this confluence as central to the impulse to act, speak, believe, and make meaning.

Theories in the flesh influenced later post-positivist realist theories of identity (Alcoff, 2006; Moya, 2002), which emerged in respond to a backlash against "identity politics" in the academy and activist circles. Post-positivist realist theory positioned social and cultural relationships that had previously been understood as barriers to individual rationality instead as agentive objects informing the experience and existence of bodies, as well as the potential for critical reflection and creative making. As Paula Moya (2002) explained it, "different social categories of a woman's existence are relevant for the experiences she will have and that those experiences will inform her understanding of the world" (p. 50). Social categories and identifications were positioned not only as active but also tangible, concrete, and identifiable. Importantly, while social relationships, individual geographies, and past experiences become "objects" or physical realities in these embodied theories, those objects are not assumed to be static. Rather, as Moya emphasizes in her reading of Moraga's work, experiences change over time but interpretations of our own experiences also change, affecting how prior experiences and relationships influence actions. Moya illustrates this idea through a close reading of the change over time in Moraga's understanding of her own positionality as a light-skinned person of Mexican descent. This act of interpreting and re-interpreting the relationships between self and the objects of life is key to a theory in the flesh that is distinct from other feminist standpoint theories (Harding, 1991). Moya draws a distinction, in particular, between theories that "seem to imply a self-evident relationship among social location, knowledge, and identity" and a theory of the flesh which "explicitly posits that relationship as theoretically mediated through the interpretation of experience" (2002, p. 50). Working from this idea, the interpretation of one's own embodied experience becomes an object—an active and agentive object—that can be understood to influence future choices and actions.

Literacy and composing scholars have largely overlooked the usefulness of theories in the flesh and post-positivist realists theories for understanding composing practices. Chela Sandoval has argued that the academy has often positioned U.S. Third World Feminist theories as relevant only to issues related to the raced experiences of people of color rather than as generative frameworks that can help explore more general experiences. These theories are relevant to composing in their unique physicalization of lived experiences and their positioning of bodies as confluences that are continually becoming and also continually interpreted. At the same time, it is important to keep in mind that Moraga and Moya are both discussing lived experiences of trauma that emerged from living a raced life in a racist society. These theories thus emphasize that interpretation and generation of meaning is not always a learned art, but can arise from trauma. By focusing on "a politic born out of necessity," Moraga emphasizes that composing sometimes is less a conscious strategic course of planned action but instead an inevitable, tacit response to conditions that meet and cross in individual bodies: a form of "making do."

Michel De Certeau (1984) in *The Practice of Everyday Life* described how mundane interaction with environments and structures of others' creation—cooking, walking, renting—position people as producers of new embodied scripts. In De Certeau's terms, production can happen inevitably, as an oppositional response to contexts and structures that attempt to structure behavior. Interestingly, De Certeau articulated these meaning-generative practices and tactics in behaviors practiced across a culture such as reading or walking. Chicana feminism's theory in the flesh resists a totalizing descriptive meta-discourse. It exists as more overtly "multiple" in terms of voice and story than the descriptive mode in which De Certeau operates. A theory in the flesh is multiple and situated because it lives in bodies and, by extension, in accounts of experience. The advantage of seeing theory as living in bodies and accounts of bodies is that the objects that are associated through accounting for experience are specific, not generalized. As collections, U.S. Third World Feminist works such as *This Bridge Called My Back* and *Making Face, Making Soul* amass stories that explode easy categorization or identification, and Moraga explains that "the theme echoing throughout most of these stories is our refusal of the easy explanation to the conditions we live in," but rather to explore the contradictions of experience and to respond to the exigencies created by their tensions and confluences (1981, p. 23)

This multiplicity and focus on situatedness helps theory in the flesh to remain relevant for a project like the one described in this book, despite how the spaces and times differ radically from those that were emphasized in Moraga's or Moya's work. These texts offer a theoretical grounding for a phenomenological approach that emphasizes the role of both environment and interpretation of prior experience on individual choices and actions. Philosopher Robert Sokolowski (2000) describes phenomenology as "the study of human experience and of the ways things present themselves to us in and through such experience" (p. 2). By using the term *phenomenology,* I am aligning theories in the flesh with research approaches that emphasize "the activity of giving an account, giving a logos, of various phenomena, of the various way in which things can appear" (Sokolowski, 2000, p. 13). Phenomenological thought explores how the experience of the world, coupled with intense reflection and accounting for how that experience appears to us, can be a viable methodology for knowledge-making. The central methodology of phenomenology has typically been understood as Edumund Husserl's (1970) "transcendental reduction," a move to radically reflect on how objects in the world are understood and experienced. In traditional approaches, this reduction initiates radical reflection that involves understanding a separation between the "natural attitude" of experiencing everyday life and the "phenomenological attitude," which attempts to read that experience as a detached observer through a process of "bracketing" or setting aside objects in the world in order to reflect on how they appear and are experienced. For Husserl, this act is transcendental because it works through "the motif of inquiring back into the ultimate source of all the formations of knowledge, the motif of the knower's reflecting upon himself and his knowing life" (1970, p. 97).

Turning to Orientations

A problem for traditional phenomenological methods, however, is that experiences of individuals are often universalized in order to generalize about human nature, movement, and perception in ways that lose the situated perspectives that emerge from the accounts of Moraga, Anzaldua, and other collaborators in the queer and Chicana Feminist collections that I have described. Sara Ahmed (2006) confronts this problem in *Queer Phenomenology*, which offers an alternative phenomenological approach that resists the impulse to normalize experience. Ahmed used the term *orientations* to describe tendencies built over time and through experience, through which bodies relate to space, time, people, and materials. Orientations are important because they create ways of "registering the proximity of objects and others," and "shape not only how we inhabit space, but how we apprehend this world of shared inhabitance, as well as 'who' or 'what' we direct energy and attention toward" (Ahmed, 2006, p. 3). Orientations, Ahmed suggested, create potential by influencing how bodies extend into the world, as well as when people are liable to feel "at home" or what objects are likely to be within their reach (2006, p. 10). Importantly, in Ahmed's estimation, orientations are never neutral but instead constructed through encounters with cultures, institutions, and designs that shape embodied tendencies over time.

Although orientations shape practices, we often experience them as invisible or transparent. In composing, we often realize that we have developed an orientation when we try to change our habit in some way. Have you ever noticed, for example, how difficult it can be to type on a keyboard that is not the one that you use routinely? The slight difference in spacing between the keys or alternative labelings can be enough to throw off your entire process. In her extended example of orientations, Ahmed focuses on sexual orientation, noting how often normative heterosexual and patriarchal orientations are assumed and encoded onto bodies. These normative ways of moving appear natural until we begin to deconstruct how cultures naturalize particular ways of being, which could be otherwise. Importantly, then, Ahmed suggests that "the body gets directed in some ways more than others," which means that bodies become habituated over time into normative associations and movements (2006, p. 15). In terms of sexual orientation, bodies are frequently socially directed in heterosexual directions: for instance, men are most frequently socialized to understand women rather than other men as sexual objects. To take on a non-normative orientation—to live queerly—means doing active work to build new proximities: to put one's body into proximity with other materials that shift, over time, how we move and what appears to be near us. Ahmed's conception of queering orientations builds on individual mindfulness or recognizing one's tendencies but extends beyond recognition into an attempt to actively resist socially naturalized orientations. Orientations to technologies, place, or materials are never "natural" or "pure" in spite of the extent to which they become transparent or seem inevitable. Constructions of tendency always shape how we move through the world, even as we continually reconstitute them through new interactions. And those tendencies are socially informed, rather than merely individual preferences.

Ahmed's concept of orientations, positioned in relationship to the theories in the flesh, offers a useful way to interrogate how people interact with surroundings when they compose. Because I am particularly interested in human-environment, human-machine, and human-information orientations that shape the circumstances of composing when people interact with their surroundings, I focus particularly on bodies in relation to and with technologies and other nonhuman materials. As I introduced in Chapter 1, Suchman emphasized how technology use can be understood as an ongoing production that takes place when humans and machines interact in specific circumstances. Placing Suchman's interactional theory in dialogue with the phenomenological theories I have just reviewed, I introduce four terms that can shape accounts of how mobile composers collaborate with their surroundings. As Figure 3.1 illustrates, my framework for understanding transient literacies in action focuses on materials, proximities, interactions, and sequences. In order to further elaborate this framework, let me first introduce a story of composing that can serve as an example for what each term can reveal about how bodies and surroundings meet in networked mobile composing.

Kim's Story and a Framework for Transient Literacies

A masters' student named Kim[8] sat on a burgundy vinyl-covered bench seat with her laptop resting on the table in front of her. I observed about an hour

8   This chapter draws from a case participant, Kim, who is also discussed in Pigg, 2014b. My argument in that chapter uses Kim's case to argue for the embodied and emplaced character of mobile writing. This chapter makes use of Kim's case to illuminate a method and set of vocabulary for establishing how transient literacies are enacted in practice.

of her study session, which involved attention directed toward the screen, privacy protected with noise-cancelling headphones, and stamina maintained with a muffin and coffee that she had just purchased downstairs at the barista station. Kim was completing an assignment for a theory course for her degree: a reading response that asked her to synthesize and reply to ideas articulated in four assigned scholarly readings. To complete this task, Kim was reading PDF documents on her laptop, taking notes on them, and using these notes to draft a reading response that she would later submit to her instructor and classmates. While drafting the response, she also moved fluidly among less time-consuming literacy events such as reading emails or checking for updates to her social media accounts. She was occupied by the "page" on which she typed (a word processing document positioned at the right side of her screen to make room on the left side for the PDF course readings she perused simultaneously), as well as the positioning of her body in the room. She sat in a particular place within in a particular building located in a particular spot within Lansing. Her "page," her laptop, and her body were also shaped by cultures and histories that were not immediately visible to an observer. All kinds of actors were involved in Kim's composing process, becoming relevant to how and why she wrote in the ways that she did.

As for what made Kim's environment unique, the materials interacting with and around her (including intangible actors such as values and histories) were shaped by needs, desires, and inevitabilities that enabled her literacy practices to be physically mobile: taking place across a number of locations in temporary bursts of time. When I interviewed Kim, she explained that she would never have started using the Gone Wired Café as a workspace if not for her decision to purchase a laptop computer. As she explained, "Before I had the laptop, I had a desktop, so if I was writing, I had to be at home, I had to be at my desk. And I had to be, you know, in that space, which was a lot different. Using a laptop, I can take it anywhere" (Pigg, 2014b, p. 259). While the idea that purchasing a laptop would require an individual to decide where to write might seem like an obvious point, Kim described that her newfound mobility also had immediate effects on how and when composing took place and what kinds of materials were involved. For example, she generally only used digital reading materials because, without weight and mass, they were easier to haul around on the move. Furthermore, she only took digital notes and annotations for similar reasons: she was likely to have faster access to online annotations via her laptop. Since she did not read print copies, the digital notes she took shaped her eventual draft. Building upon materials such as her laptop, the PDF readings, and these notes, she developed and practiced habits that massaged elements of the mobile environment into a coalition. The materials interacted as participants in her process and sometimes her written product, as well.

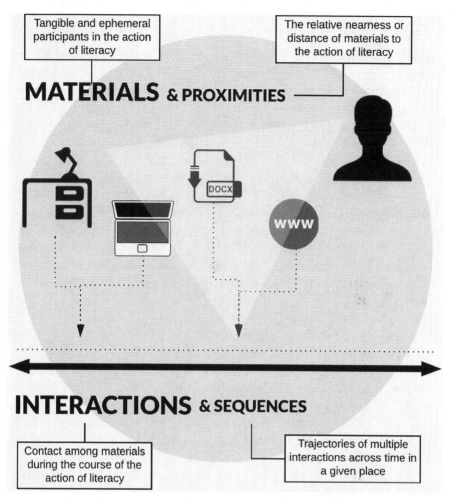

Figure 3.1. Tracing transient literacies in action.

Materials: The Resources of Environments

This book refers to participants in mobile composing simply as materials. Materials are agential, vital, active participants in composing: participants or collaborators in the sense described across a range of recent socially informed materialist theories of composing (Micciche, 2014; Shipka, 2011; Wysocki, 2004). The term allows researchers and educators to position these influences on composing as participants, rather than inert objects in service of a human subject who puts them to use. To draw on Suchman's language, one advantage of situated action studies is that they enable researchers to "identif[y] the resources by which the inevitable uncertainty is managed" in a given case (2007, p. 86). I have chosen the term "materials" here as opposed to "resources" in order to reflect the sense in which these actors exert their own influence on unfolding scenes, rather than being taken up inertly in service of human interests. As the previous chapter established, using mobile networked devices for composing is always associated with attempts to manage uncertainty and impose temporary stability to flux. Composing processes in mobile frameworks involve decisions that could be carried out in a number of different ways. For example, when a classroom assignment is relayed to a student, there is typically no predetermined method nor preordained set of materials to follow to complete the task (even if the course has an expected genre format). The materials that (or who) become invoked as participants meaningfully shape composing's texture and outcomes. For example, a student like Kim might have chosen to script her reading response in her car during a commute using a voice recognition software that would transcribe her talk into text, or she might have chosen to sit with a composition notebook at her desk at home and write the reading response in one sitting after having read the articles from printouts collected in the university library.

But Kim's particular choice on that Tuesday in Gone Wired was different, and her choice to use a laptop in Gone Wired invoked materials that needed to be brought into temporary alignment in order for her writing process to be effectively accomplished in ways that met her goals. To return to Kim's example in more detail, it is relatively simple to categorize some of the materials she perceived as relevant to her composing task. For example, she discussed the importance of the built environment that surrounded her, such as the booth where she sat, technologies and interfaces ranging from her laptop computer to her headphones to the software platforms that provided the "page" on which she worked. However, she also referenced ephemeral "structuring resources" (Lave, 1988) that shaped the act but were less tangible in the scene, such as curricula, organizational schemes, categorical ontologies (Bowker & Star, 2000), languages and symbol systems, "ordering devices" such as plans, scripts, or routines (Suchman, 2007); and gestures (Prior, 2010) just to name a few. While no tally of materials that participate in literacy practice can be fully complete, Figure 3.2 visualizes and categorizes materials that Kim discussed when reflecting on her networked mobile composing practices when I observed her. As the visualization suggests, Kim invoked materials that included feelings, personal routines, and aspects of the room alongside those that take on more physical and observable mass: her PDF documents, laptop, and phone, for instance.

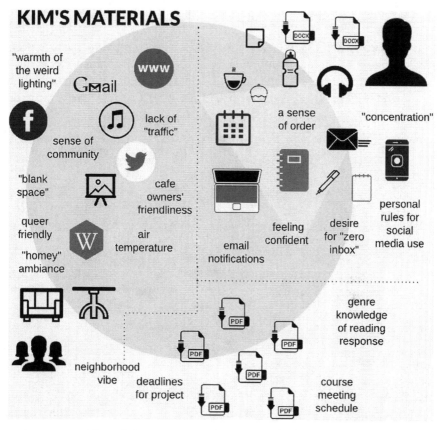

KIM'S MATERIALS

"warmth of the weird lighting"

Gmail

www

f

sense of community

lack of "traffic"

"blank space"

queer friendly

air temperature

cafe owners' friendliness

"homey" ambiance

email notifications

feeling confident

desire for "zero inbox"

a sense of order

"concentration"

personal rules for social media use

neighborhood vibe

deadlines for project

genre knowledge of reading response

course meeting schedule

Figure 3.2. Selected materials that participated in Kim's reading response.

For Kim, then, accomplishing the reading response in the Gone Wired Café not only depended on access to readings, a software platform that enabled her to read the articles, and word processing software where she could see the letters that she struck one-by-one on her laptop keyboard. She also depended upon values like the perceived expectations of her graduate course, which shaped when and how she approached the reading response. For example, Kim's reading response was a weekly activity with a deadline before class began once each week: a temporality set in motion by course constraints. As in most cases of academic writing that are not timed tests, her instructor had assigned a product ("the response") that had taken on particular genre expectations as the course progressed as a result of feedback from her peer classmates and her instructor. Just as important were materialities that emerged from her identity and social positioning as a LGBTQ student. These more ephemeral issues became active participants shaping how she went about accomplishing the task assigned to her.

Proximities: The Relative Position of Materials

Infrastructures supporting practice are dynamic: they are relative to a user's needs and circumstances as experienced at a given time. To put this another way, materials with the potential to become participants in networked mobile composing practice hold relative positions in place and time that bring them closer to or farther from potential action. I use the term *proximities* to describe the nearness or distance of materials as they are positioned relative to a mobile composer moving across her trajectories of everyday practice. In my prior work describing Kim's case, I highlighted that proximities to relevant materials must be established in order for writing practice to take place even when mobile devices appear to enable use anytime and anywhere (Pigg, 2014b, p. 261). Here, I want to extend this idea by focusing on how social factors influence human perceptions of what is near or far from us. As Ahmed suggests, discursive and material relationships of nearness and distance affect whether or not particular materials become collaborators in our compositions. These proximities are not natural, but are continually culturally and socially produced. Suchman describes how "questions of location and extent" matter more to situated action research than assumptions about how "macro" structures such as cultural-historical systems or ideologies affect practice (2007). As with the role of plans or purposes, this does not mean that cultural artifacts or "social facts" are not meaningful to action. Instead, it means that materials are not assumed *a priori* to be active within a given scene as a result of a structuring macro-level institution (i.e., a culture, an economic model, a technological structure). Situated action research begins with a local scene and observed moment with an eye to identifying what materials are active and how they have been positioned, rather than assuming agencies that are predetermined by a given cultural or social frame.

To give a basic example of proximities that resonated across cases in my research, students described the Technology Commons and the Gone Wired Café as locations useful to them in relationship to each location's nearness to or distance from how they walked across campus or traveled across the space of the city, respectively. To echo Ahmed's point again, these proximities depended upon social positioning; people using a wheelchair to navigate a campus or a screen-reader to navigate device screens would no doubt experience the Technology Commons or the Gone Wired Café in a different proximity to their movements across campus space. Students tended to position these locations as useful merely because they were available and/or convenient, and we can deduce that they met personal requirements for comfort, safety, or emotional needs. Students frequently mentioned materials such as power outlets, coffee, comfortable chairs, Wi-Fi networks, computers, and software applications as materials that drew them into the center. Business fraternity pledges Tiffany, Nicholas, and Nora, for instance, chose the Technology Commons for completing a digital video production project because it offered iMovie software. While their individual work toward the project had taken place using networked mobile devices (i.e., they recorded individual video clips using their cell phones), they needed this software in order to bring their individual online work into dialogue. Conversely, students I interviewed who rarely worked at the Technology Commons explained its challenges in terms of proximity as well, including how it positioned them either too near or too far from materials (e.g., often too near to other people, or too far from their homes or classrooms).

Table 3.1 illustrates a few proximities that shaped the use of the Technology Commons as a workspace. Many students described using the Technology Commons because it was centrally located near classes or parking spaces. Located in a central position near the student union and university library, the Technology Commons was near buildings where classes were conducted, the restaurants and food courts housed in the student union, and parking garages where many students began and ended their days on campus. Many students chose to write in the Technology Commons because it was convenient to locations they had come from or would need to reach. For example, sophomore engineering major Dean noted that he made locational choices "just depending on where I am." Other students described walking to the Technology Commons after a class that had just ended in a nearby building. For example, Luna says that where she studies on campus "depends on the time of day" because her courses lead her to particular areas of campus. Luna described using the Technology Commons on a particular schedule: on "Monday, Wednesday, Friday" and "usually after my lab class" where she completed homework with a friend. The amount of time spent in the space was also shaped by proximity to deadlines created by course schedules. For example, Luna described how on those particular days she had two hours between her courses and thus spent around two hours in the Technology Commons. Students frequently measured time spent in the Technology Commons in this way—as filling in openings or "dead time" (Perry et al., 2001) created by course and meeting schedules.

Proximities like these recall Nedra Reynolds' (2004) focus on how spatial practices such as dwelling and navigating link people's habitation and navigation to how they make meaning about it. However, race, class, gender, socioeconomic status, and ability affect proximities and personal perceptions of which spaces are near and which are far. As Ahmed emphasized and scholars such as Terese G. Monberg (2009) have explored in writing studies, movements accessible to composers depend upon the unique confluence of physical realities that are manifested in their bodies. Materials appear as accessible or not to composers as the result of the meaning that they take on in relation to particular embodiments, and systematic oppression denies access to materials. Furthermore, the kinds of movements that are culturally valued and accessible often vary based on race and gender. Gesturing to Luce Irigaray's reading of the how acts of building rest on "the materiality and nurturance of women," Iris Marion Young recovers a lost sense of dwelling as preservation, an activity she associates with building a home through the collection and arrangement of particular objects. The politics of this work happen when cultivation extends beyond making the home a "commodified construction of personal achievement and lifestyle" or is enforced upon women as an oppressive, normative labor as in De Beauvoir's descriptions (Young, 1980, p. 132). It becomes a politics when it involves "maintenance" through the arrangement and preservation and use of things that give meaning to life and that connect past to present and future (Young, 1980).

For mobile composing, not every student owns a laptop computer, and not every student finds shared social spaces comfortable or usable. Understanding proximities as having a discursive dimension is important for less tangible forms of access as well. As Kathleen Blake Yancey and Teddi Fishman (2009) argued, mobile composing requires proximity to ephemeral materials such as social knowledge. As situated action researcher Michael Lynch (1993) described, collections of materials, or "equipmental complexes," become arrangements that "provide distinctive phenomenal fields in which organizations of 'work' are established and exhibited" (p. 123). In the case of transient literacies, how one is oriented to space, time, and knowledge plays a distinct role in shaping the material arrangements that will ultimately participate in composing practices.

Table 3.1. Proximities that led users to the Technology Commons

Kinds of Proximities	Sample Interview Excerpts
Travel Patterns	"I usually just park here at garage A or I and I just make my way through the campus [and choose the first available place]" (Heijin)
	"[I choose to study at] whatever I'm closest to." (Dean)
Social Relations	"Sometimes I'll just study with people who are in different classes just for the company" (Luna)
	"We were planning to go to the library, but we were already there, so we were like let's just go and find a place to sit. And we had to really study for that quiz. So, we were like well, you know, let's just find a place to sit. And we found that place that was empty so we just sat there." (Sophia)
	"Tech commons is like a lot more livelier, I guess, so, not too quiet . . . I like to go to tech commons when I'm kind of like, kind of tired." (Max)
Daily Schedules	"[I go to the Tech Commons] usually after my lab class" (Luna)

To continue with the example from the Gone Wired Café, positioning proximities as meaningful, relative positionings is useful for understanding why Kim accesses different materials in the café from Ed, Kathryn, or Dave, whom I have discussed over the past two chapters. To draw again on Kim's example, we might start by discussing how her positioning in time and space makes the Gone Wired Café a possible workspace. In her interview, Kim detailed how she lives in the neighborhood called the "Eastside" where the café was located and passed by it to get to campus. The café literally existed on her trajectory across the time and place of the city, as she uniquely knew and experienced it. Kim also found herself aligned with the cultural vibe of the coffee shop, which emphasized inclusivity for non-gender-conforming bodies. Once she entered the shop, Kim's location upstairs in Gone Wired with headphones sitting alone at a booth positioned her so that her laptop computer was in her direct line of vision. Comparatively, she was positioned at a relative distance to the incessant social traffic to the barista stand, and was unlikely to hear the chatter around her thanks to the headphones. As I have discussed in detail (Pigg, 2014b), Kim's proximities to online incoming social information were active as well. Instead of putting up barriers to interaction as she did with headphones or bodily positioning, Kim invited information from outside her immediate goal-orientation to enter her composing scene. Kim had signed up for notifications, desktop alerts that let her know immediately when an email or Twitter message was posted to one of her accounts. Thus, the word processor screen where she was drafting was interrupted repeatedly by incoming information that clued her into how her social networks had been updated. Although my example focuses most clearly on tangible materials that can be directly observed in her surroundings, metaphorical proximities were also in play. Across both observable and more hidden aspects of location, proximities describe why and how certain materials are invoked during the action of transient literacies while others are present but remain inactive or disengaged. When materials are near, it is more likely that they will participate in interactions, an idea I discuss in the following section.

Interactions: When Materials Meet

While materials are important to action, proximities create the likelihood that materials will be transformed, engaged, or mobilized—in short, that they will exercise rhetorical capacity. Situated action researchers often used the term interaction to refer to what happens when people related with materials in such a way that shaped their future capacity for action. In Suchman's terms, "interaction is a name for the ongoing, contingent coproduction of a shared sociomaterial world" (2007, p. 23). Within situated action frameworks, interactions among materials both depend upon and generate temporary negotiated alliances that accomplish action. Suchman emphasized that her use of the term interaction for situated action theories built on the idea of interaction in the physical sciences to mean "reciprocal action or influence" but also in the social sciences to mean "communication between persons" (2007, p. 34). In this way, interactions among people and technologies implies working toward a "mutual intelligibility or shared understanding" while also influencing and being influenced by the other (Suchman, 2007, p. 34). To put it another way, interactions generate agencies. In this way, Suchman's older conception of interaction resonates with the more radical co-involvement suggested by Barad's conception of intra-action, which I will discuss in more detail. For her part, Suchman adapted her approach to interaction from the sociological research traditions of conversation analysis, but emphasized interaction among humans and nonhumans as co-producing agencies as various elements of local circumstances factored into action in unexpected ways. Because "circumstances of actions are never fully anticipated and are continuously changing," Suchman argued, plans act in concert with what we encounter in particular places and times (2007, p.26). From the perspective of situated action research, action could always have been otherwise, as ongoing adaptations, transformations, and negotiations shape the texture of everyday practice (Suchman, 2007).

Similar frameworks have been useful for translingual literacy studies, focusing on the mobility and mutability of language. For example, Suresh Canagarajah's (2013) approach to translingual practice focuses on how languaging practices depend upon a complex interplay among resources and their mobilization. In his terms, "The process of communication also reflexively alters context, changing the terms of engagement and meaning. The meanings and forms that are thus created are situational, arising from the modes of alignment between participants, objects, and resources in the local ecology (2013). Illustrating this orientation, Canagarajah's study zooms in to focus on how what he describes in this quotation as "modes of alignment" are achieved in diverse language use scenarios. For example, Canagarajah traces how a group of migrant students use strategies and resources from their surroundings to come to an understanding of others' codes, which often differ from their own and thus cannot be predetermined (2013).

To turn back to Kim's reading response, interactions with participating materials in literacy happened constantly—so quickly that it is difficult to keep track of them. Through video recording, I was able to trace many of these interactions, making it possible to discuss forgotten, ephemeral, or fast-paced movements as they unfolded in contingent circumstances. As Pam Takayoshi (2016) described, the micro-level practices of digitally mediated composing are difficult to account for retrospectively. In Kim's case, as she worked through various stages of composing the reading response (and attending to other smaller literacy tasks), a range of interactions became pieced together as the response slowly developed. Tracing these interactions at a granular level enabled me to pay attention to experiences with technologies and surroundings that were tacit and would be difficult to recall in a retrospective account. For example, during this session, Kim's interactions with social software were so fast paced and threaded through interactions with her word processing software that it would have been easy for her to forget how much of her composing time they comprised. As I described in the previous section, she often checked Twitter or Gmail as a result of receiving an on-screen text alert. As a result, these interactions with social media became braided through her interactions with the word processor page. I want to note here that, much like Suchman, my framework emphasizes interactions between humans and machines and explores composing through the lens of embodied encounters with materials. I have purposefully centered human bodies in this framework in order to better understand the bodily perspective from which an individual's composing practice takes place. However, it would be possible, and indeed is necessary, to think about how materials interact with other materials in a composing scene separate from the involvement of human bodies. This is a limitation to which my current framework cannot speak, and one that I trust other scholars working from materialist frameworks are also exploring through frameworks such as Thomas Rickert's (2013) ambient rhetoric.

Sequences: How Materials Interact Across Time

Situated action studies typically represent interactions that unfold during an observation of a bounded moment in time, and these interactions are described as a series of events (Lynch, 1999). Tracing interactions, then, not only illustrates how materials participate in action but also how they are arranged into meaningful sequences. Paying attention to sequences of interactions can illustrate how trajectories of action take temporal shape as a result of the unique circumstances of being in a given place in time responding to what has happened before. In Kim's case, for example, we could begin to look at whether and how the interaction of the on-screen text alert was or was not likely to influence her to stop composing in her word processing document and to check her email or social media. From there, we could trace whether and how this movement created challenges or new opportunities for the reading response she was drafting at the time. When read as linked together in sequences across time and materials, tracing interactions provides a way to ask new questions about how materials play an agentive role in composing.

This way of thinking about composing is unusual, but similar techniques have been used to understand embodied action in different domains. As ethnomethodological scholar John Hindmarsh (2009) pointed out, nineteenth-century physiologist Etienne-Jules Marey used chronologically sequenced photographs of human and animal movements to understand how activities like walking, running, jumping, or pole vaulting took place in real time. By capturing a series of snapshots that visualized and sequenced the relative positioning of bodies over a time scale, Marey parsed out how small movements compiled to form a way of operating that would nearly invisible while people were in active motion. Most of us do not stop to think about the positions that our bodies inhabit between where we begin and where we end an action, and attending to practices as sequences with duration enable a view on practice that is difficult to have while in process. Of course, literacy-in-action is not precisely the same kind of action as walking or pole vaulting, in spite of the similarities that Michel De Certeau has described. Furthermore, sociologists such as Paul Atkinson (1988) have argued that privileging sequences has led ethnomethodologically informed research to problematically assume all action is ordered rather than chaotic.

Figure 3.3. Example of Marey's embodied sequences.

Composing research tracing sequences of practices have typically focused on cognitive processes of expert writers with the goal of describing normative sequences of thinking (Flower & Hayes, 1981); however, the use of sequences that I am calling for is different. Rather than generalizing example sequences into normative models to describe what we should do when we write, I am calling for sequences as a tool for understanding the complex interactions that take place during situated moments of practice. More than anything, I understand tracing sequences as a useful tool in the repertoire of researchers and instructors who want to have conversations with people about the precise impact of materials such as technologies and elements of environments on their composing. In specific contexts (informed by histories, cultural members, and other knowledge held in active bodies), tracing sequences of interaction offers a means for understanding how environments and embodiments intersect, and as a result, how composing conditions and processes blur. Sequences of interaction can illustrate when and how materials are mobilized and how they temporarily stabilize embodied, emplaced literacy processes: giving texture to composing process that we usually overlook or marginalize.

Dimensions of Materiality: The Spheres that Affect Composing

In the prior paragraphs, I have introduced an embodied materialist framework that can offer ways to shape accounts of composing practice, focused in particular on human-material interactions. Now I want to return to the question of how accounts produced through this framework can inform how we understand the surroundings that shape composing with mobile networked devices. When people like Kim read and write with laptops in places like the Gone Wired Café, materials emerge from different discursive positions relative to participants' values, capacities, and social positionings. One way to describe the surroundings of networked mobile composing is to focus on how these materials relate to the goals of composing that writers bring to their use of laptops and other mobile technologies. Understanding how different dimensions of materiality intersect when we write with networked mobile devices in shared social settings can help writers, educators, and researchers anticipate potentially divergent participants that composers must attempt to reconcile through the embodied action of composing.

To explain further, I have already discussed how prior research explores how participants in a composing process emerge from environments that surround individuals, as well as more hidden dimensions of infrastructure. Take, for example, Danielle DeVoss, Ellen Cushman, and Jeff Grabill's (2005) discussion of how the materiality of infrastructures affected a multimodal composing course. While creating short multimedia videos in Cushman's class, students' and instructors' plans were constrained by the classroom around them, the expectation of IT professionals at their university, and students' own choices and preferences. When mobile technologies are used for a composing task, they invite further complexities. Composing's materials are assembled from across divergent environments or domains, and the immediate surroundings in which mobile devices are used often do not harmoniously gather materials that are conducive to completing writing tasks. Jason Swarts (2007a) highlighted this issue while researching the integration of

PDA devices in veterinary students' learning practices. When using a mobile device while making rounds, students did not operate in the immediate vicinity of all information that they needed to usefully interpret available texts that guided their practice. Because information was not assembled in a way that formed intuitive context, Swarts suggested that these students operated more in "non-places" (Augé, 1995) than in coherent places. Based on his analysis, Swarts argued that "mobile technologies short-circuit locative assumptions and transfer more of the burden of interpretation back to readers and other resources in their environment" (2007a, p. 280). Transient writers are often responsible for making their environments, so to speak, because the places in which they compose are not already prepared for them.

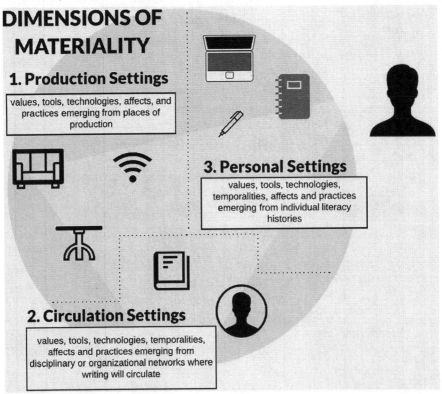

DIMENSIONS OF MATERIALITY

1. Production Settings
values, tools, technologies, affects, and practices emerging from places of production

3. Personal Settings
values, tools, technologies, temporalities, affects and practices emerging from individual literacy histories

2. Circulation Settings
values, tools, technologies, temporalities, affects and practices emerging from disciplinary or organizational networks where writing will circulate

Figure 3.4. Three dimensions of materiality.

To return again to Kim, the physical surroundings in Gone Wired were not designed explicitly to support composing an academic paper. In order for Gone Wired to become an effective workplace for this task, Kim needed to bridge several gaps. In this case, she used materials such as her laptop (and the range of materials to which it enables access), her own knowledge, and other personal technologies as participants that mediated this issue. Closely analyzing Kim's and others' composing processes in places like the Gone Wired Café, relevant materials emerged from at least three dimensions of their surroundings that intersect physical and information space, which are visualized in Figure 3.4:

1. the *production setting* or the immediate surroundings,
2. the *circulation setting* or the context related to a composing purpose and audience, and
3. the *personal setting* or *repertoire*, or the individual composer's technologies, habits, practices, and social positions.

When students compose with mobile devices, they take up materials from across these dimensions, which are already complex in themselves. Notably, these dimensions suggest that we need to be thinking in more complex terms than just the bridging of "physical" and "virtual" spaces during the action of mobile composing. Each dimension involves materialities and virtualities that emerge from across the multiple dimensions of hybrid space.

Production Settings

The first dimension of materiality important to composing with mobile networked devices is the production setting or immediate surroundings that emplace composing, inviting interactions with the tangible locale. Production settings always involve complex histories, cultures, and social meanings that are taken up as tangible materials shaping process. For example, as I have already described, Kim's booth created an inscription surface on which to place her laptop, as well as a barrier creating space between her body and others located around her. Although these tangible materials participated in how she was positioned, the values of privacy assumed in the café also allowed her to focus her attention almost completely on her screen without offending others around her. As I discussed in Chapter 2, this space was also accessible to her because of the history and redevelopment of historical buildings in the district where the café was located. Food, drink, and power outlets became different forms of sustenance, and their availability was uniquely tied to place. There were norms and economic expectations associated with the place that mattered as well (i.e., if you occupy a table, you should buy something).

Circulation Settings

Second, composing with networked mobile devices always engages a dimension of materiality related to an audience or domain where an eventual composition will circulate. The dimension of materiality described by the circulation setting refers to the discourse communities or networks that exert powerful influences on composing through issues such as genre conventions, appropriate style, and delivery media. When transient literacies are practiced, circulation settings are often distinct from production settings, so materials from across them need to be reconciled. For Kim's reading response, materials from her theory course actively participated in how her processes took shape as a sequence of interactions. For example, the curricular expectations and timescales in place as norms of the class environment were central to Kim's process. She was writing on that day because the deadline for the course followed soon after: all students in class were required to submit a written response to readings two days before class so that other course members could read them to prepare for discussion. She was able to write in the café to meet this deadline because she had portable PDF journal articles and book chapters assigned as part of the course. The expectations and curricular organization of the class, then, became important materials shaping her choices and processes.

Personal Settings

Finally, a third dimension of materiality invoked in transient literacies are personal settings, or the repertoires associated with literacy habits and practices. Individuals bring technologies, organizing schemas, dispositions, and other relevant materials with them into their mobile workspaces, and these materials interact with those that emerge from both production and circulation settings. Although "personal," these repertoires include knowledges and gestures shaped by prior experiences, connections to cultures, social norms and constructions, land, economic positionings, built environments, and technological systems (Haas & Witte, 2001; Sauer, 2003; Spinuzzi, 2003). Individuals' idiosyncratic technologies, habits, and ways of organizing can run counter to or align easily with materials emerging from production and circulation settings. Imagine, for example, how time use habits associated with constantly checking one's social media accounts intersect with the expectations of time use associated with the deadlines of a course schedule. Imagine then reconciling both of these structuring materials with the rhythms of time-use encouraged by a coffeehouse setting, where the norm is to sit in a particular location with a cup of coffee for a finite amount of time. The forms of practical knowledge that I have called transient literacies involve assembling together materials from across these dimensions.

For an example of a particularly relevant material from her personal repertoire, Kim's process took place in the café, drawing on her course materials, and what she referred to as "her workflow" (Pigg, 2014b). This workflow used a number of personal materials—including devices like phones, laptops, and social media sites—to bridge gaps among production and circulation dimensions. Kim generally began writing by invoking a cognitive and embodied blueprint for how she imagined she would spend her time; in Suchman's terms, this plan became a relevant resource contributing to how her composing session would take place. What Kim called her "workflow" began with checking her social media feeds and interpersonal communication channels before settling into more focused tasks. At a more granular level, Kim's workflow for the reading response was ordered purposefully: "so the readings, and then the notes, and then the reading response." Specifically, she opened each PDF document one by one in the left-hand side of her screen. While reading the article, she took notes by transcribing or cutting and pasting text directly from the PDF into a new Microsoft Word document entitled "Notes" and marked the page number from where she took each direct quotation. After composing one notes document that contained the material she found most important from all four readings, Kim moved the notes document to the left-hand side of her screen and opened a new Word document on the right. Into this document, which would later become her response, she cut and pasted information from the notes document that she wanted to address (quotation marks around all cited material) and began to "compose around" this information. While Kim's response text began by looking like patches of others' quotations, she eventually cut bulky quotations, added elaborations and commentary, and synthesized across multiple readings until there were no traces that indicated she had used this technique.

Dimensions of Interaction: Agencies and Productions Beyond the Text

While it is useful to think about mobile networked surroundings by focusing on the kinds of materials that participate in goal-oriented production of texts or other artifacts, recent mobile literacies scholarship argues that texts and goals do not alone determine the shape of mobile literacy activity. Leander and Boldt (2012) emphasize this point in their critique of design pedagogies. They argue for a conception of literacy that does not imagine it as "projected toward some textual end point, but as living its life in the ongoing present, forming relations and connections across, signs, objects, and bodies in often unexpected ways" (p. 26). This way of thinking about literacy is consistent with the research approach that I have described thus far, and it opens the door for researchers and instructors to think about the different kinds of productions beyond text that are generated during mobile composing. I have come to think of mobile composing practices as generating not only texts but also **dimensions of interaction**.

I use the term *dimensions of interaction* to name a way to take seriously how networked mobile composing practices entangle materials in ways that reinvent individuals' own habits and identities as well as shape the social contexts in which action takes place. While Suchman's concept of interaction remains helpful to thinking through this issue, Barad's use of the terms intra-action and engagement can extend Suchman's focus on mutual influence in order to better understand the new inventions generated when materials meet in everyday practices. Barad offers a complex way of thinking about matter as both always materially and discursively meaningful, as people who use networked mobile devices "intra-act with the matter of their worlds in ways in which they are transformed by matter and vice versa" (Jackson & Mazzei, 2012, p. 125). Composing continually co-constructs both subjectivity and context, supporting a reinventing of oneself and the world. By focusing on dimensions of interaction, I intend to name a few slices of context that we can understand to be reproduced through networked mobile device use and that provide examples of how interactions participate in the "ongoing, contingent coproduction of a shared sociomaterial world" (Suchman, 2007, p. 23). Based on fieldwork, this book focuses on two contexts for/productions of networked mobile composing that are central to the experience of shared social space in commons places: *interpersonal sociability* and *attention*. As I will describe in the following sections, the influence of and production of each dimension entangles materials from across production, circulation, and personal settings.

Sociability

Sociability, a term I'm using to refer to interpersonal social atmosphere, is a dimension of interaction both invoked and composed with and in the presence of networked mobile technologies. Composing always involves interpersonal interactions, although this might not be obvious when looking at a lone individual sitting in a public place with a laptop. The social potential of mobile environments is mediated across platforms (i.e., face-to-face, online, phone lines) as well as across synchronous and asynchronous timescales. As a result, as Chapter 2 suggests, the sociability that matters to composing might differ from the ideal forms of social contact expected and cultivated in public places. For example, when composing with mobile devices, people often interact with others through multiple textual forms including text messages, blog and social media replies, and instant message communication. The people with whom they interact can be associated with the production, circulation, and personal material dimensions of their composing, even when those interactions have nothing to do with the production of a given text. As a result, composing often blurs the boundaries of social domains and calls on people to reconcile social connections from their immediate surroundings, personal life, and work or school life. Sometimes these interactions are invited and centrally important to accomplishing a given literacy task: for example, receiving a peer review or consulting a text message that responds to an idea. Other times, as the cases I have discussed imply, social interactions that become part of composing processes are not easily integrated or aligned with our composing purposes or tasks.

Kim, for example, interacts with a range of other people who I describe more clearly in Chapter 4 as audiences, collaborators, and eventual influencers. Some of these people are directly related to the course context; however, Kim also threads interactions with different social media outlets through her workflow and accesses social contacts that are unrelated to her immediate task. The text alerts that I previously mentioned, which keep her updated about her social media feeds, are necessary from her perspective for staying informed about issues and people that matter to her. Of course, these social interactions are not always easily reconciled with interactions that are more directly task-related, including the online internet research that Kim accesses through Wikipedia. Reflecting on the role that the internet played in her work session, Kim said it's "multifaceted. It's a distraction, it's a resource." For example, she commended Wikipedia for providing important collective information but understood that introducing it into her work session also brought the lure of other places: "I can go look it up and find out more about this writer or this movement or whatever it is that I think I need to know about. But at the same time, when I open up Firefox, all those other tabs are there too. So it's not just a resource, it's a resource that I then use to distract myself." Although Kim largely relegated the in-person social potential of Gone Wired to the background (i.e., she did not interact with others face-to-face), she struggled at times to bring together interactions from personal and circulation settings.

Sociability has already become the subject of debates about the effects of mobile device use on contemporary student reading, writing, and learning. As I discussed in the prior chapter focused on the changing nature of shared social places, students who use phones and laptops in public frequently are assumed to be socially isolated. It is important that students develop means for accessing people who can provide feedback; texts that reveal shared information; and even search engines, online encyclopedias, blog pages, and other wired locations that hold collective knowledge. However, the steps that lead toward interactions with these kinds of materials, including those completely unrelated to a given task (e.g., a Facebook messenger conversation) and those partially or fully related (e.g., co-present friends), often bring proximity to social potential that may not align well with the task at hand. As a result, cultivating the sociability around composing is central to successful academic, workplace, and community writing. By more closely analyzing how sociability is constructed in mobile composing situations, educators have the opportunity to better understand how students negotiate the often-dissonant social contexts that intersect as they cultivate proximity on the one hand to "enablers" of their literacies and on the other to the range of social potential surrounding them. This sociability also has implications for the role and function of shared social places, which I have already positioned as a commons where people access shared resources.

Attention

Finally, when students compose with mobile devices, their process depends upon and generates *attention*, or a changing state in which some materials appear salient to a writer and others fade into the background. An individual's attentive horizon orients her to materials perceptible and accessible for literacy practice at any given time, and attention describes how a writer assigns prominence to those materials in ways that bring them into composing's action. As I describe in Chapter 5, this way of thinking about attention assumes it as an ongoing production or invention: something composed. Positioning attention in this way opens it up to analysis, enabling us to understand it as a performance created in collaboration with places, technologies, and personal memory systems and habits. In this way, attention is always a production of mobile composing, and it is entangled with the burgeoning online information and densely connected interpersonal networks mobile composers bring from their personal repertoires.

When literacy activities are supported by mobile devices, materials that emerge from production, circulation, and personal settings often are not easily reconciled in writers' attention. For instance, Kim described how working at home was difficult because materials present in her home space weighed so heavily on her focus that it was difficult to ignore them. In her words, "There are certain things that I can't do at home because I get distracted. So the TV's at home, my dog's at home, all these things sort of either need my attention or demand, in some way, my attention. Here I can put my headphones on and be in this world." At the same time, Gone Wired accommodated her body and mobile technologies (i.e., providing Wi-Fi and power outlets that would allow her to use her laptop) in ways that aligned with her preferences for how to do things. Her routines, available technologies, and course assignments aligned with what was available to her in the Gone Wired Café in ways that created workable assemblies. And yet as I have already suggested, using her laptop in Gone Wired also introduced new materials that pulled at her attention and created the need for other kinds of negotiations in her composing process. For example, she often ignored people who sat around her in the café, even though she appreciated their presence and was attuned to many of their movements and actions. Attention is not always so neatly maintained, as Kim suggests when discussing her struggles with attention in production settings that offer different kinds of resources. Attention is often described as a central problem of contemporary university students, and so this dimension has already become an important point of tension and contention taken up and debated by instructors, employers, and public intellectuals.

Conclusion: New Focal Points

People who set up shop with laptops, smartphones, earbuds, and the social configurations that abound in coffeehouses, cafés and other similar locations give many reasons for being there (Sayers, 2009). Some need a place to sit between scheduled meetings, some need space to support collaborations on a "neutral ground," some desire access to technological infrastructure that they do not have in their homes, and some want to get away from people, pets, or objects who are difficult to ignore when in their presence. In a sense, mobile surroundings are stable: their locations can be located on a map. However, they are also shaped by situations of the moment: deadlines that are approaching, the groups and individuals who happen to be around, the level of charge available on a laptop. The time/space of composing in these places, then, is always an experience of transience, an impermanent event shaped by conflicting forces. Furthermore, the "integrative" quality of mobile technologies and online social platforms (Levinson, 2006) that are common to contemporary writers blur boundaries across domain categories that researchers typically use to differentiate lifespheres for communication practice (e.g., personal, professional, academic, civic). This chapter has positioned networked mobile composing as a performance that engages the potential force of materials, while forging relations that produce new social spaces.

Attention and sociability represent new focal points for what matters to composing and provide frames for further exploring how mobile networked composing is experienced. These dimensions depend upon one another, as well. As Kim's example in this chapter illustrates, cultivating attention depends on managing sociability using shared materials available in the commons. The social atmosphere of a place likewise depends upon how shared materials are taken up and how attention is distributed. Both of these dimensions of interaction furthermore shape the shared social locations that I have identified as a commons for mobile composing: how attention is paid and the developing norms of sociability within places can affect how composers access shared knowledge. Although these dimensions are intertwined, the following two chapters take them up separately to continue tracing how intersecting dimensions of materiality create challenges and complexities for networked mobile composers, while responding to ongoing debates about how students use mobile devices in daily life.

Chapter 4: Composing Social Potential: Ambient Sociability and Mediated Contact

> What is the place of those who are physically present and have their attention on the absent? At a café a block from my home, almost everyone is on a computer or smartphone as they drink their coffee. These people are not my friends, yet somehow I miss their presence.
>
> –Sherry Turkle, 2011, p. 156

For the past several years, social psychologist and new-media theorist Sherry Turkle (2011) has noted a link among computing and social isolation that has grown into a common refrain. In the epigraph above, Turkle reflects on this connection in the context of a neighborhood café much like Gone Wired and the Technology Commons. Scanning the room she shares with other people and their technologies, Turkle interprets café-goers' use of laptops and smartphones as a lack of "presence." She imagines, in turn, that individuals like those she describes are spending time "alone together," a phrase now frequently circulated in the scholarship of humanist critics of public space as well as technical and professional communication researchers (Büscher 2014; Ellis, 2002; Spinuzzi, 2012 & 2015). Elsewhere in her popular text, Turkle uses a different metaphor to describe the social tendencies that surround networked mobile device use. She describes digital natives as "tethered": bound to connections they access through mobile technologies and their networked, digital reserves. Although critical of the generation's device fetishes, Turkle explains that the situation is complicated. Being tethered means keeping close ties like the one that enables her to converse in real-time with her college-aged daughter studying continents away; however, it also conjures images of restraint and lack of control. For Turkle, tethered people are "marked absent" from physical social surrounds when committed to mobile screens (2011, p. 155). To be absent in this way, for Turkle, is a tragedy for communities as well as for individual emotional wellbeing, which relies upon authentic relations with people around us.

Turkle's remarks highlight the complicated ways that mixed-use, shared social spaces initiate contact among people who might not otherwise meet, while also reinforcing relationships that are close relationally but far-flung spatially: best friends, family members, significant others. These social overlaps must be negotiated through ongoing orientations toward and away from people and other objects. To use language that I have introduced throughout the book so far, Turkle laments how orientations toward digital reserves can represent orientations away from people sharing a place such as a café. She perceives the tendency to orient toward digital reserves in public places as abnormal, a deviation from healthy social behavior. In this way, Turkle suggests an unspoken norm: that people located in proximity to one another should first and foremost be oriented toward one another, and only after that spatial immediacy is achieved, establish geographically dispersed or remote connections.

I have focused on Turkle's example to open this chapter because her work has become well known in both public and academic circles, but the sentiment that she expresses is common. The perception that mobile device users should connect first with physically co-present people and secondarily with distant relations is a perceived norm worth further discussion as it intersects with how we interact in social environments that shape our mobile composing. While writing scholars have long argued that composing practices are affected by interpersonal contact, this chapter argues that networked devices necessitate a closer look at how we collaborate with social actors to compose the social environments that surround us, as well as how writers navigate the social potential that intersects when they use mobile technologies. This chapter is an extension and complication of my earlier discussion of commons spaces in Chapter 2. Positioning the social contexts of networked mobile device use only in terms of negative divergences can lead educators and researchers to misunderstand or stereotype mobile composers. As a result, the generation who has grown up with mobile, networked technologies is often generalized not only as the most distracted generation but also the loneliest one, charged with "attempt[ing] to substitute *real* relationships with *online* relationships" (Beaton, 2017, para. 13, emphasis mine).

To better understand how interpersonal contact intersects with the mobile surroundings of transient literacies, this chapter takes a closer look at moments of literacy practice that could easily be labeled as nonpresence or social isolation. By taking a granular lens to interpersonal interactions in these scenes, it is possible to see how individuals enact social proximities and social distancing that challenge traditional norms of public interaction as well as traditional understandings about how the forms of social interaction most valuable to writers should be mediated. At times, these new social arrangements develop as a result of a search for privacy. As I have introduced through the examples of Ed and Kathryn in Chapter 1 and Dave in Chapter 2, finding a place to write is a challenge for many of us even if we have dedicated office spaces. We seek places like cafés and coffeehouses to serve as what Kate Zabrowski and Nathaniel Rivers called "an oasis for weary travelers" (2015). These places offer moments away from the everyday social interactions that we want to have but that make it difficult to focus on text: conversations with our families, our colleagues, our friends, our pets. When sitting down in a coffee shop for composing, some of us do not intend to interact very much with those around us: we've come here to get things done while we can! However, even when writers are not actively seeking to distance themselves from those around them, people who write with networked mobile technologies are likely to end up facing surroundings that are saturated with people but that also invite impromptu interactions through incoming emails, text messages, and social media posts. The experience of dwelling among people while "marked absent" from them is central to composing in shared social places.

In order to draw out questions and challenges related to the intersections of transient literacies and sociability, the chapter first discusses the practical interactions through which social influences on composing were accessed and performed in my study. Next, the chapter turns to stories from research in the Technology Commons. By reading these stories through the concepts of materials and interactions introduced in Chapter 3, I describe how interactions of varying intensities across different social platforms are braided into the use of networked mobile devices in action, in turn producing unusual social dynamics within commons spaces. As a result, I argue that negotiating the interplay among salient social actors and those that fade to the background is central to information management practices of transient literacies and that this practice is meaningful for establishing connections among people who share commons spaces. Living among information not only means deciding how to attend to the generative and disruptive potential of physical social presence, but also requires negotiating the spontaneous and ephemeral social potential that lives in digital reserves, or what I call ambient sociability. Ambient sociability is characterized by dispersed potential social connection across physical and virtual platforms. Understanding this social atmosphere and its relationship to how we compose today complicates a simple reading of the mobile surround as positioning people as "alone," "together," or "alone together." The social interactions that support literacies proceed along multiple proximities and pathways, observable in how networked mobile composing's action often takes place across face-to-face, direct communication, and social media platforms.

Composing, Isolation, and Interactions

The idea that social influences matter to literacy practices is a belief that has so infused writing research that it usually no longer needs to be overtly articulated: it is often an unstated warrant behind more controversial claims. Because this is a longstanding issue, it is worth returning to a context for this development in rhetoric and composition studies that predates the current challenges of networked mobile technologies. We might recall, for example, Linda Brodkey's (1984) famous deconstruction of the modernist writing scene: the vision of a writer alone in a garret, closed off from the social world and jailed to the confines of language alone. Brodkey argued that the stereotypical vision of the writer working alone resulted from associating composition and authorship with literary production rather than the realities that accompany more diverse purposes for writing practice. For Brodkey, this modernist scene "places social life on the other side of writing, that which occurs before or after writing," rather than a more generative vision that imagine writers as "social activists" who are part and parcel of the worlds that surround them (1984, p. 397). Marilyn Cooper (1986) offered a similar often-cited deconstruction of the isolated "solitary author," who "works alone, within the privacy of his own mind" before he turns over his text to "the world of which he is not a part" (p. 365). In Cooper's model of writing as informed by and embedded in overlapping, dynamic social systems, it is "contact" that drives forward our writing: "ideas result from *contact*, whether face-to-face or mediated through texts" (1986, p. 369, emphasis mine). Cooper's statement emphasized that the social contact that matters to written invention can be mediated and practically achieved in different ways: through reading texts that provide access to contact, as well as through face-to-face talk.

The Practicalities of Social Interaction

Alongside Brodkey and Cooper, Kenneth Bruffee's (1984) well-known "Collaborative Learning and the 'Conversation of Mankind'" also associated the social turn in writing pedagogies not only with theoretical shifts but also with the changing social needs and demands of university students. In the late 1970s, Bruffee suggested, college students were struggling and refusing needed support because the "kind of help provided seemed merely an extension of the work, the expectations, and above all the social structure of traditional classroom learning" (1984, p. 637). As Bruffee explained, university instructors and administrators responded to this situation by introducing new learning techniques that worked outside of the typical social setup of lecture classrooms. In Bruffee's history, peer learning, group work, and other forms of collaborative interaction first emerged as practical responses to students' needs and demands for new forms of sociability, and they were only later connected to and justified by theoretical developments emphasizing knowledge as a social construct.

Building on developing social constructionist theories of knowledge, then, Bruffee drew from his practical experience of successful social interactions in writing classrooms to argue that a particular form of social contact should be used to support composing practices. He argued that students learning to write should read texts that provide access to disciplinary knowledge, and then educators should be "engaging students in conversation among themselves at as many points in both the writing and the reading process as possible" (1984, p. 642). Importantly, Bruffee positioned the social contact that mattered to composing as enacted through dual processes with different mediations for expert and peer interactions. In order to access experts, students would read texts, and in order to access peers, students would have conversations about those expert ideas. Bruffee was clear that the kinds of peer interaction supporting effective composing processes in classrooms were connected to the experience of talk about ideas, rather than collaboration on other aspects of composing processes: "What students do when working collaboratively on their writing is not write or edit or, least of all, read proof," and "What they do is converse. They talk about the subject and about the assignment" (1984, p. 645). For Bruffee, then, the conversation among peers that best supported literacy development in classrooms was direct conversation, conducted orally, among educated peer communities that invoked the "normal discourse" of that community. It was not, for instance, two students working in separate locations on a shared Google Doc, or carrying on an IM conversation in writing. By positioning collaborative learning as a way to overcome social isolation and access shared discourse of educated peers, Bruffee emphasized *talk* as a particularly important form of social contact that matters to composing.

However, other forms of practical social interaction were beginning to emerge as relevant to social theories of composing. For example, Karen B. LeFevre's (1987) *Invention as a Social Act* published a few years later named a range of interpersonal interactions that fueled invention, where that term refers to the creation of new texts and ideas. As pictured in Table 4.1, LeFevre articulated several perspectives on sociability that shape assumptions and attitude toward written invention. Platonic approaches, for example, often assumed the ideal of solitary authors much like those that Cooper and Brodkey critiqued. These theories, according to LeFevre, emphasized the usefulness of social isolation, emphasizing that an individual should turn inward to discover ideas. LeFevre's "internal dialogue" model fell in line with Bruffee's conception of writing as internalized social thought re-externalized through writing. However, LeFevre's "collaborative" and "collective" perspectives encompassed forms of social interaction that might extend beyond direct conversations such as those Bruffee emphasized. For example,

LeFevre's collaborative model was built on an assumption that social inter-actions are meaningful across relatively long spans of time in which texts are created and exchanged. Sometimes interlocutors who participate together in collaborative models are co-authors who talk or exchange while creating text together. However, LeFevre also emphasized that the social influences that shape invention may, from a collaborative perspective, be involved implicitly rather than explicitly. She captured this idea by referring to relevant social influences as "enablers, resonators, friends, sponsors, liaisons, or brokers" and by focusing in particular on "those who attempt to assist invention by bridging the distance between inventor and audience" (1987, p. 78). In addi-tion, LeFevre emphasized the importance of direct interactions from readers and listeners who complete a chain of meaning that does not exist solely with the writer, including user feedback (1987). Finally, LeFevre's collective model of invention focused on the impact of social interactions that hap-pen through tacit structuring forces in culture. Contact with these forces not only comes through face-to-face talk or text, but also through implicitly observing the norms of others' behaviors and action. For example, in this vein, LeFevre emphasized the impact of language as a social force, the role of local communities and disciplines as constraints, and institutions and ideol-ogies as indirect but steady pressures.

Table 4.1. Karen LeFevre's schema for types of social influence on invention

Platonic	Internal Dialogue
Individual is an agent of invention	
Invent by recollecting or finding and expressing content or cognitive structures that are innate. Asocial mode of invention; internal locus of evaluation of what is invented.	Invent through internal dialogue or dialectic with construct of internalized other. Inter-nal locus of evaluation, but influenced by social codes and values.
Collaborative	**Collective**
Two or more people interact to invent.	Invention influenced by social collectives
Invent by interacting with people who allow developing ideas to resonate and who indirectly support inventors. Listeners and readers receive and thus complete the act of invention. Locus of evaluation may be one person influenced by judgments of others, or a pair or group of people who invent together.	Invention is hindered or encouraged by the force of supra-individual collectives. Locus of evaluation is a social unit beyond the individual (e.g., an organization, bureau-cracy, or socioculture).

I have provided a deep dive into the intersections of social contact and invention to suggest that many writing specialists have developed and internalized beliefs about what kind of social interaction writers should engage. Over 30 years ago, LeFevre's schema opened the door to acknowledging that different kinds of social interactions shape composing. Writers make contact with meaningful social actors through practices that include but extend beyond direct talk about topics of interest or reading accepted discourse of a discipline or profession. LeFevre emphasized co-writing, peer review, written audience response, as well as reading and listening to language. LeFevre largely left the audience to consider how interactions are established with "enablers" of literacy, those "friends, sponsors, liaisons, or brokers" that can be more informally connected than through academic or classroom networks. But what, if anything, happens to this contact when it is mediated by mobile devices or dispersed across geographies? Do these new developments that remediate social interaction matter to literacy practices and development? And, if so, how?

Remediating Social Interaction

How has the sociability of composing been affected by technological change since Brodkey, Bruffee, Cooper, and LeFevre theorized the importance of social contact? For example, would Bruffee amend his focus on "talk" that provides access to educated peer discourse to include the "conversation" of a chat room linking people at a great distance from one another? What about the complexities of social interactions such as those that Turkle describes as marking individuals absent from their immediate surrounds? Scholarship theorizing the impact of the internet and new technologies on social literacy has had to grapple with similar questions, although often in tacit ways. For example, the New London Group's (2000) framework for multiliteracies shifted common assumptions about what kinds of interactions matter to literacy performances in a world shaped by the "textual multiplicity" emerging from increasing linguistic diversity and competing communication platforms. For workplace life, the New London Group emphasized how an emphasis on teamwork and collaboration has given rise to the importance of "informal, oral, and interpersonal discourse" as well as "hybrid and interpersonally sensitive informal written forms, such as electronic mail" (2000, p. 12). In public and community life, they emphasized the complexity of social interactions in contexts where standards are no longer centralized and where understanding difference is more relevant than identification as a skill "to negotiate regional, ethnic, or class-based dialects" (2000, p. 14). Finally, they argued that personal lives would change as identities are more complex and performed through informal texts and everyday technologies. In place of the importance of "singular national cultures," it was increasingly the case that communication across "less regulated, multi-channel media systems . . . undermind[ed] the concept of collective audience and common culture, instead promoting the opposite: an increasing range of accessible subcultures" (2000, p. 16). In the world that the New London Group described, multiple channels for social contact were the norm, and the meaningful communicative interaction that enabled people to work, organize, and perform their identities took place across them.

The related New Literacies paradigm championed by Colin Lankshear and Michel Knobel (2011) took a step further in positioning the social contact afforded by the internet as central to literacy learning, by emphasizing how digital environments enabled self-motivated learning nurtured by persistent connection to people and information online (see also Gee & Hayes, 2010; Ito, 2009; Lankshear & Knobel, 2011). While the term social learning has a longer history with Albert Bandura's (1977) work in cognitive and behavioral psychology, Lankshear and Knobel advanced a conception of social learning dependent upon the internet and with foundations in contemporary workplace management theory. Drawing on John Seely Brown and his colleagues' (2011) "Situated Cognition and the Nature of Learning," Lankshear and Knobel called for teaching strategies that "embed learning in activity and make deliberate use of the social and physical context" (2011, p. 215). Lankshear and Knobel called these contexts "platforms": web architectures that they described as "arrangements" providing access to "people, websites, written texts, and any and every kind of helpful support—as and when they need it" (2011, p. 232). In this framework, initiating "contact" was largely understood to be the responsibility of the learner, who calls on individual ingenuity to effectively mobilize available resources. In line with their roots in management theory and workplace learning, Lankshear and Knobel argued that social learning builds on individuals' inclinations toward "innovation and productiveness," characteristics they believed individuals practiced most genuinely through their online interactions with affinity groups in digital networks (2011).

When relevant social contact is mediated by the internet and changing global interconnection, collaborative or collective literacy practices are emphasized. However, the historical categories used to describe the forms of social contact that matter to composing are limited in their ability to account for what Howard Rheingold (2012) called the changing "shape of the social" associated with having immediate access to distant people who may be closely or weakly affiliated. Sociologists such as Barry Wellman (2001) have long argued that many individuals in highly developed countries are moving from a close-knit community-based organization of social connection to one that is more loosely organized. Institutions that historically have grouped people into dense, highly interconnected social units based around identity categories like church, organizations, or neighborhoods still exist; however, their influence may not produce the same bounded sense of social groupness that it once did. In its place, Wellman recently joined Pew Internet Research Center director Lee Rainie in *Networked: The New Social Operating System* to discuss how an emerging paradigm of "networked individualism" shapes the forms and functions of social contact that shape workplace, community, and personal life. In their words,

> It is not the World According to Me—it is not a world of increasingly isolated individualists. Rather, it is the World According to the Connected Me, where people armed with potent technology tools can extend their networks far beyond what was possible in the past and where they face new constraints and challenges that are outgrowths of networked life. (2012, p. 19)

Where a scholar like Sherry Turkle saw social isolation, Rainie and Wellman saw a radically changed model of sociability: one that is networked rather than bounded. Recent social media scholarship also has used the term "networked publics" to describe a similar focus on how emerging social mobilizations form when networked individuals come together across geographies to address issues of concern (boyd, 2010; Ito, 2008; Varnelis, 2008). Digital rhetoric scholarship also took up this social context through a range of scholarship that outlines the changing nature of collaboration and crowd-based user-generated participation (DeVoss, 2018). This scholarship explored examples ranging from social bookmarking (Brooke & Rickert, 2012), to YouTube Composing (Arroyo, 2013), to textual curation in Wikipedia and other online systems (Kennedy, 2016).

The move toward networked individualism, networked publics, and networked collaboration has important implications for how networked mobile composing takes place. This understanding of social connection de-emphasizes bounded communities as the central organizing social units shaping contemporary life and brings more attention to fragmented, fast-paced interactions that build up over time and across collocated communities in digital platforms. For online affinity groups such as those described above, this model of social contact means that contributions from across millions of people and far flung geographies can be easily assembled. However, for individual learners, the experience of networked individualism means facing increased pressure to use networked technologies to initiate contact with these potentially far-flung contacts that might become their "enablers" of literacy, LeFevre's "friends, sponsors, liaisons, or brokers" (1987, pp. 75–76). Individuals bear an active burden for assembling social contexts and initiating social inter-actions that support literacy goals across personal, workplace, and academic life, rather than relying on assembled and bounded communities with clear hierarchies and discourse norms. Digital and mobile technologies, along with the social platforms accessed through them, offer a means of reach through which social contact can be sought out, established, and maintained. How-ever, that coordination is hard work and time consuming. As a result, the ties that hold the networked social together are the same ones that scholars such as Turkle identify as responsible for social disconnection and isolation among digital natives. This paradox is a central tension of the practical knowledge of transient literacies.

On the one hand, if the "isolation" observed by Turkle and others indi-cates that contemporary students experience difficulty connecting with others, educators have reason to worry about students' ability to access needed social resources. However, on the other hand, there is reason to believe that students in highly technologized societies are initiating—and bearing greater responsibility for—the interpersonal contact that provides them access to literacy resources. As digital devices and online resources become participants in connection, the mediated social interactions that support learning may contrast with those that supported traditional interactions in classrooms. Important learning contact may come through blogs written in cafés, emails composed on smartphones, or text messages to collaborators. To better understand contemporary literacy and learning, educators need to refocus on the role that interpersonal sociability plays in composing through the lens of multiple modalities and mediations of interaction, drawing not only on the importance of face-to-face talk but also on interactions associated with networked social arrangements.

Usefully, writing centers long have functioned with complex ideas about the kinds of social interaction that are meaningful to composing. In writing studios and writing centers, environments are often carefully cultivated to sup-port social interactions among peers and mentors. For example, studio ped-agogies have been described as "interactional inquiries" because of how they distribute learning across formal and informal social interactions in ways that many contemporary students find meaningful (Grego & Thompson, 2008). Multiliteracy centers that actively incorporate digital technologies often use similar methods, while also mediating support through online feedback and emphasizing the importance of digital genres as important sites of learning (Sheridan & Inman, 2010). Educators need new vocabulary to name and describe the range of mediated social interactions that matter to composing outside campus environments that actively cultivate literacy coaching, social support, and guidance. Furthermore, we need to understand how students negotiate the complicated terrain of balancing attention to both screen-based and physical social interaction.

Sociability and Transient Literacies in Two Case Examples

To take a step in this direction, let's now look more closely at how two students collaborate with people and technologies to compose sociability while spending time in the Technology Commons. As opposed to the prior cases discussed in Chapters 1, 2 and 3, both stories here involve students "killing time," rather than purposefully working on coursework. However, both cases involve a range of self-sponsored literacy practices.

Micah's Story

The first student I'll discuss, mechanical engineering major Micah, entered the Technology Commons between two classes. This was his habit. As he put it, he would come here to grab a cup of coffee and use the power outlets to charge his technologies. While doing so, he would sometimes "study or do coursework, but more often . . . [he is] just killing time between classes." When "killing time," Micah still actively read and wrote on his laptop. On the day that I observed them, Micah and a friend were "geeking out," to use Mizuko Ito and her colleagues' (2010) term for social learning that makes use of online participatory culture. In this case, Micah and his friend across town (i.e., sitting in front of his own computer screen) were working together on an ongoing game development project. The project interested them because they enjoyed playing around and learning how to use new software development technologies. Micah described their purpose for the project as motivated by learning and participating in something together rather than by desire to produce an actual game for themselves or others. When I observed Micah, he was using his laptop to navigate a range of social-media and direct online communication sites: partially to discuss, plan, and work on this gaming project and also just to speak with his friends. Micah's literacy activity, then, aligned well with the self-directed, online collaborative social learning and literacy practices described by Knobel and Lankshear. However, as I will discuss in more detail, Micah was not completely shut off from the face-to-face social scene around him. He engaged with other students who were co-present in the Technology Commons.

Sal's Story

The second case discussed in the chapter comes from Sal, who sat alone in the Technology Commons with his laptop facing toward a group of students he did not know. He, like Micah, was taking a break between classes. In his case, killing time involved looking at his laptop and using it to shuttle through a site that aggregated new online memes. He was checking out the latest content posted on the site and laughing along with what he found funny or surprising. He also used the opportunity to send a direct message through the online social marketplace, Etsy, to a product seller regarding a sticker he'd been considering purchasing for his laptop. Unlike Micah who was working on a particular project, Sal did not have any central objective for what he intended to accomplish during his time in the Technology Commons. He was not working toward course deadlines or projects. Sal's interactions happened in clusters associated with the smaller literacy tasks that he was performing, including reading online circulated meme content, perusing Reddit, and corresponding with a "social seller" on Etsy. Sal did not directly establish contact with those students around him, though he sat facing into their group conversation. Still it is possible to understand the students around him as direct participants in the mobile surround—and in Sal's use of networked mobile devices to make sense of the world around him.

Interactive Platforms and Sociability

I chose Micah and Sal as cases for discussing sociability because they might easily be described as socially isolated in the Technology Commons. Unlike many students who used that location to collaborate with others, Micah and Sal were both oriented primarily toward their laptop screens and did not appear to be interacting with students around them. However, taking a more granular look at the sequences of their interactions illustrates how they move across layers of social channels, while engaged in networked mobile computing in public places. To illustrate what I mean, I will discuss Micah and Sal's interactions by first introducing three kinds of social platforms that they and other students in the Technology Commons and Gone Wired negotiated simultaneously while using mobile technologies. These platforms do not represent all channels through which students access social resources (i.e., books, articles, or other assigned resources are not emphasized here). However, they name key social spheres that complicate traditional assumptions about how meaningful social contact takes place during composing.

Social Media and Platforms for User-Generated Content

Many participants in this research wrote with social media platforms frequently during their time using mobile technologies. Participants described social media platforms as central to their use of shared places and interweaved them with attention to materials associated with longer, goal-based literacy projects such as the kinds of projects discussed in the first three chapters of this book. This finding is not surprising, given what we already know about the high percentages of social media use among those with access to mobile, networked devices. The more interesting questions for transient literacies revolve around why and how these platforms were used and what they represented for individuals. For participants in this study, social media platforms were only partially important for contacting already known peers, family members, or acquaintances to which they were "tethered." Many participants actively used social media to engage those beyond the boundaries of their known social connections.

Micah and Sal's examples of social media use during time spent in the Technology Commons illustrate this diversity. Micah primarily used social media platforms, first, to keep up with people he knew through offline affiliations: university friends, family, and high school friends. Second, he used them to access information related to specific personal interests such as fitness or game development. Micah browsed Facebook to check who was currently active online so that he could potentially chat directly with them. Alternatively, he browsed social sites for inspiration or humor. Sal, by contrast, exclusively sought encounters in virtual places where he did not already know those present. He did not have a Facebook page or Twitter account. Sal reported that he distrusted the ethic of "friendship" on sites such as Facebook that led to social surveillance at both micro and macro scales. In his own words, he reported learning that when he used Facebook, "I was the product and refused to allow myself to be marketed and bombarded by advertisements tailored 'just for me.'" Instead, he used social media platforms such as Reddit that assembled crowds who did not need to know one another to interact.[9]

As he put it, "I feel Reddit is the lesser of the [social media] evils, as it doesn't come with the promise of 'companionship' and 'friendship' that social media tries to offer. I can simply retrieve information from a variety of subjects via the subreddits, and be on my merry way." Sal further positioned his impulse toward Reddit as driven by (1) a desire for information, and (2) the unknown: "Since it's a site that is used by people around the world, it provides new perspectives and news that I may never have heard about. For example, when Edward Snowden first blew the whistle, /r/News and /r/Politics exploded with information about him, and within days, news was constantly being circulated about the questionable means of information gathering being done by the NSA." I will discuss the blurred lines among negotiating people

---

9   Reddit is a social news and entertainment site that is organized like a bulletin board system. Its threads are called "subreddits" and users post to and lurk in subreddits, most of which include links out to other sites. Often these links are links to photos or visual memes. Many of them are supposed to be funny, cute, or raunchy, while others are informational and link to breaking pop or political culture news.

and information in social media platforms. For now, though, it is important to understand that these channels support a diverse range of social "contact" that should not be generalized.

Direct Electronic Communication Platforms

In addition to interacting through social media, participants also made social contact through online platforms that supported direct and often immediate communication. For example, students in the study used sporadic text messages with friends, family members, peer classmates, and significant others to make immediate and later plans. Richard Ling and Bridgette Yttri (2002) described how these shifts affect the use of mobile devices for microcoordination, or the orchestration and planning of meetings and other face-to-face interactions. This microcoordination leads to a state they describe as "hypercoordination," where peer groups rely on short, mobile, networked interactions and the expectation for reciprocity for affective purposes to retain a sense of connection to peer and family groups. Additionally, email also should not be overlooked as a central online electronic communication platform—especially for students enrolled in universities. Finally, many participants on laptop computers used IM communication technologies, frequently choosing instant messaging (IM) packages connected to their social media or email accounts (i.e., Facebook Messenger and the Gmail chat). IM enables participants to directly engage with people that they determine to be present and active. They often checked in with these people after perusing their feeds or inboxes in order to determine whether there were updates to check.

Unlike with social media platforms, it is not surprising that participants used direct communication channels primarily to interact with people they knew (with the exception of email, which functioned for interactions with both known acquaintances and to receive information with unknown others, corporations, organizations, and institutions). In Micah's case, for example, the Gmail chat function enabled him to carry on an extended conversation with the friend collaborating with him on the game development project. The two friends used IM to exchange links to shared materials: the tutorials, explanations, and discussions of game development that they found on various social media and content aggregating sites. After watching or reading this information, they also used direct communication channels to discuss it and make plans. Sal also used direct communication to connect with his significant other, as well as to contact an Etsy seller with a question. Though most direct-channel use connected participants to known others, Sal again stressed using direct online communication platforms to interact with people he did not know while using his laptop. Following the same general philosophy that oriented him toward Reddit rather than Facebook, Sal was excited about sites like Omegle, which in the same fashion as Chatroulette, created a forum for accessing strangers. Sal explains, "Omegle is . . . its basis is you talking to strangers, it's, I don't know if I'd say it's a platonic sort of relationship. It's a casual acquaintance, but not really, it's sort of like being stuck in a room with someone random for 30 seconds and saying hi." Direct communication platforms, however, were typically associated with social contact that took place in quick episodic bursts.

Face-to-Face Platforms

Finally, contrary to popular assumptions, participants spending time in social places with their mobile devices did interact face-to-face with others present. As with social media platforms, interactions with people in the same geographical location took place with both previously known and unknown peers. Interactions with known friends and acquaintances often followed one of two models that align with cases already described in this book. For example, students often met purposefully with someone they knew who was a close friend, significant other, or acquaintance to spend time. Sometimes these meetings were specifically related to course content, as was the case with many study participants such as those working together on a digital video project for a campus fraternity or students studying together for organic chemistry. Sometimes, instead, students met with others to spend romantic or platonic friendship time while also studying on the side. Finally, even students such as Sal and Micah who entered the Technology Commons alone interacted with co-present others; however, their interactions with surrounding people were subtle and nuanced, complicating the idea of being "alone together."

Participants who spent time alone in both the Technology Commons and the Gone Wired Café were highly aware of other people present in the room. Ed and Kim, to whom I referred in Chapters 1 and 3 respectively, both referred to this interaction with their co-present social surroundings as "people watching," and described it as a benefit of writing extended projects in a café rather than at home, which felt more isolating. However, these interactions did not take place in ways that might easily be identified as traditional conversations, certainly not in the sense in which Bruffee used the term. Instead, interactions were indirect, often more akin to curious but casual surveillance than direct interaction. Their social contact was not organized by shared affiliation within a community; instead, these were interactions of shared presence that only occasionally led to more in-depth conversations.

Micah and Sal, once again, provide examples of what this face-to-face interaction among co-present students entailed, as both interacted with others sitting near them in the café space. Micah appeared to be ignoring students around him who were organized into a group and carrying out an extended conversation—until he began to talk with them. The students had been discussing problems with their computer science coursework. While Micah was studying to become a mechanical engineer, he had extensive computer programming experience as a result of his game development hobby and additional coursework in that area. After listening to students complain for several minutes about struggling in computer science classes, Micah interjected with advice from his own experience.

As the student responded, Micah tabbed back to Facebook and hovered his cursor over pictures of his friends listed on the right-hand column of the screen—looking more closely at those who were available for chat. Micah clicked another browser tab where Reddit was already open before he looked up and spoke more deliberately once again: "Well, you know maybe you're not . . . " He chose his words carefully. "I'm in those classes . . . and a lot of the projects we are given just aren't really covered in the book. You have to figure it out." When the student explained that he was having a difficult time relating his coursework to what he imagined himself doing later, he revealed that he wanted to be a video-game developer. He said, "I feel like game programming doesn't involve half the things I'm being taught in these classes. I haven't been taught a dedicated game programming class." Micah looked up at the student at this point in the conversation and continued: "Part of me thinks this is ridiculous, but then again in the workforce, when you get out and get a job, they are going to give you an assignment and you have to figure out how to do it." Micah was looking down at Reddit as he spoke. "And this is kinda . . . you know . . . teaching you how to figure things out." Figure 4.1 illustrates how these moments of his discussion with other students were layered with his ongoing use of both IM and social media platforms.

For Sal, interaction with co-present others was more passive and indirect, but still observable. As the group around him simultaneously explored Reddit and discussed a number of recent news items they encountered there, Sal listened intently. As their conversation turned abruptly from a recent college basketball star's season-ending injury to animal decomposition to sushi, Sal responded with non-verbal cues—sometimes by wincing or visibly reacting, other times by looking up information on his laptop that corresponded with their conversation. As the group took conversational topics and cues from Reddit, he listened and visibly reacted. He read Wikipedia entries that aligned with their debates, his laptop screen evidence to his spectator involvement and the integration of their debates into his own thinking. This interaction with the group's conversation was persistent through Sal's session. When Sal and I later discussed his time in the Technology Commons, he opened our

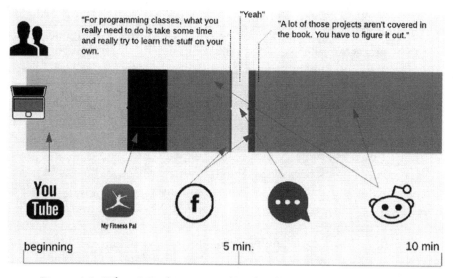

Figure 4.1. When Micah interacted with other students face-to-face.

conversation by saying that he'd been listening to the conversations of students around him.

Sociability with/in the Mobile Surround

To return to questions about the mobile surround, what are we to make of the interpersonal interactions that are central to everyday transient literacies but fall outside the norms of direct communication, such as what Turkle might expect, or collaboration, such as what Bruffee might expect? These interactions are not easily separable or discrete in terms of when and how they take place; they are messy and overlap in the space/time of sequences of interaction. Like other students I have profiled, Sal and Micah were comfortable interweaving a range of social interactions that expanded the scene of their learning (i.e., Micah's hunt for online gaming resources) or that made it possible to inch toward multiple personal and/or professional purposes in short spans of duration (i.e., both students' combining of multiple leisure activities while "killing time"). With so many social materials across platforms in close proximity, not all could be at the forefront of their perception at once. As a result, an important part of Sal and Micah's basic negotiations when using mobile devices involved practices to prioritize when to foreground each of the multiple, overlapping social platforms that existed around them simultaneously. Sal, Micah, and other students created dense social arrangements that brought unrelated contacts into proximity. Figure 4.1, which illustrated how Micah interacted with IM, social media, and face-to-face peers in the span of just a few minutes, provides a good example of this thickness. While working on his game development project, Micah used the IM function associated with Gmail to talk about the task with his friend; he accessed two development platforms to view and manipulate code; and he watched a YouTube video featuring a professional game developer discussing a new game released at a recent conference.

Micah used the game development engine, Unity. While manipulating objects in the visual view and opening internal files related to the project, Micah interspersed his activity with discussions with his friend and game development partner in Google Chat. Although Micah was already alternating between the metadiscussion of the project with his friend and the actual manipulation of it within the development platform, he needed still more software to make the changes that he had in mind. Thus, he opened a program called StarUML, a modeling tool that works in unified modeling language. The program creates diagrams that can also generate code to import when building different kinds of computer programs. While StarUML began to open, he quickly tabbed over to Google Chat and typed in the message box. Micah also needed to manipulate code directly, so he opened a text editing program and began typing code, using the drop-down menus that appeared on screen to add tags directly to the document. During the next several minutes, he tabbed between Unity, StarUML, and his text editor.

Sal, too, floated from Tumblr, to Reddit, to his phone, all the while listening to the students around him. The kind of social contact that influences students' composing processes outside the classroom very often involves movements across different social platforms nearly simultaneously. I refer to this dynamic by the term ambient sociability.

Ambient Sociability

I use the term ambient sociability to describe a context in which potential and actual interpersonal interaction exceed the level to which an individual can attend at a given time. Literacy researchers and video game designers have used the term ambient sociability to describe social presence and awareness cultivated through the use of massive online social systems (Gillen & Merchant, 2013; McGonigal, 2011; and "ambient affiliation" in Zappavigna, 2011). When social media researchers use the term ambient sociability, they describe the experience created within virtual game play or the use of a massive online system like Twitter. I build on this research, but position the term ambient sociability to refer to relations unfolding across offline and online places. Within rhetoric studies, Thomas Rickert has described ambient rhetoric as encompassing the agential conditions of rhetoric often too ephemeral to rise to human salience (2013). Rickert explores ambience as a theoretical problem for rhetoric studies, theorizing how rhetoric's emplacement creates new possibilities for invention through its own activity.

Through my concept of ambient sociability, I bring attention to the ambience in commons spaces when networked mobile devices are used. Under these conditions, some form of potential social exchange must always be rendered to the background when another form or platform becomes the focus of attention. Ambient sociability is key to the negotiations of transient literacies, as well as to the ways that the passive social interactions that happen in the background of mobile surroundings become relevant to learning and development. Ambient sociability provides a new frame from which to read to interpret the social interactions that take place when we write with mobile devices, often even when students appear to be "isolated."

Sal and Micah's stories illustrate ambient sociability. Their interactive sequences suggest that they constantly negotiate interactions across multiple social platforms to which they have access. That includes people who enter the Technology Commons by walking through the door, but also those that enter through phones, laptops, social networks, and mobile messages. Neither Sal nor Micah entered the Technology Commons to find solitude or privacy because they needed to complete a writing project. Instead, they were happy to engage others during their "down time," but saw the primary locations for this interaction as online social media and direct communication channels. While both students directed attention primarily toward screens, they also frequently were aware of social potential outside their laptops and smartphones. Though they did not always attend to people within the space in ways that would be immediately recognizable as conversation, they were in tune with and often responsive to them. Observing their time spent in the café revealed a movement across layered and often competing social interfaces. Their movement across these platforms while using their mobile devices produced a rhythmic set of social interactions. Across the Gone Wired Café and the Technology Commons, participants used a rhythm of monitoring, contributing, and disengaging with people and other social resources surrounding them, creating a cycle that is visualized in Figure 4.2 and discussed in the following section.

Monitoring, Contributing, and Disengaging

The literacy demands associated with networked individualism and participating in networked publics shifts the requirements of how individuals orient to other people. In order to participate in quickly shifting networks (as

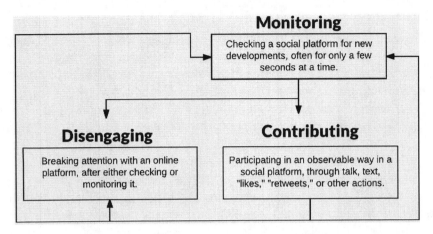

Figure 4.2. A Cycle of attention to social platforms.

opposed to more durable communities), it is necessary to be able to move quickly, to adapt, and to find ways to interact at once with crowds, parochial or close-knit groups, and known close connections. As a result, people who participate in online networks tend to shift among and engage different platforms constantly. During this process, interacting with a given social platform often moves through phases of monitoring, contributing, and disengaging. By monitoring, I refer to an interaction that enables an individual to keep informed about the status of a social platform that is frequently updated with new information. Monitoring a social platform might involve frequent checks of an open browser tab in order to check for new information or notifications in a social media feed. However, it might also involve continually "tuning in" to the conversations of people located around someone sitting in a shared social site. By contributing, I refer to interactions that perform a contribution to unfolding conversation in a social platform. Again, contributing might involve writing a social media comment or "liking" or "retweeting" a social media post. However, it might also mean answering a text message or joining in a social face-to-face conversation. Finally, by disengaging, I refer to interactions that signal moving one's attention from a particular social platform in order to turn toward another kind of social material. Disengaging might be accompanied by a practice that signals actively moving away from a platform. For example, an individual might close an active browser tab. Or, disengaging might simply mean moving attention away from one given platform and toward another one. For example, for Micah, disengaging from the face-to-face conversation around him was as simple as looking down to his laptop with a nonverbal gesture. In turn, this allowed him to resume working on his game development project.

The linked practices of monitoring, contributing, and disengaging may be most familiar as a way to think about how the practices of social media use typically take place. For example, social media use generally involves some combination of keeping up with changes in a social website's activity due to the influx of user contributions, providing content to a site or adding value to the contributions of others through an identifiable action (e.g., commenting, liking, retweeting), and then walking away. These forms of engagement are not unlike interacting with print-mediated texts through activities such as "consuming" and "producing." In social media exchanges, monitoring and disengaging are central to effectively contributing. For example, anyone who has ever been part of an email list community can identify users who contribute without monitoring—often lumbering into the middle of an ongoing conversation without attending to how it had preceded before they arrived. Or users who fail to disengage, becoming obsessed with the incoming information flow such that they are unable to walk away from it.

These rhythms typically associated with digital participation, however, are not limited to how social interactions take place on social media platforms. The same kinds of monitoring, contributing, and disengaging take place across face-to-face and direct communication platforms as well. Just as if they were "tuning in" to Twitter briefly to get a sense of what others were saying, Sal and Micah both moved in and out of monitoring face-to-face conversations around them. As I suggested above, they also drew on materials offered by mobile technologies to disengage from interactions with strangers. Positioning those around them as potential points of information, Sal and Micah treated the social platform created by the face-to-face context surrounding them much like their social media platforms: as a feed that could be sampled and from which it was practical, and even necessary, to occasionally disengage. Sal's, Micah's, and others' passive interactions, when practices together in a social place like the Technology Commons, invited a kind of co-spectatorship. While their attention to people on social media and in present space was less purposeful than what might typically be called eavesdropping, Sal and Micah each monitored conversations around them.

As a framework for understanding the rhythm of social interaction associated with networked mobile composing, monitoring, contributing, and disengaging suggests an ongoing commitment to participation that unfolds over the course of time and involves incremental, dispersed attention distributed to particular platforms for social contact in small bursts. This looks different from the ideal of ongoing focused, direct conversation that is often assumed to ground interactions among strangers in shared social places.

Instead, monitoring, contributing, and disengaging creates an iterative, reciprocal process of continued checking and occasional responding. When monitoring and contributing to social networks is conducted through mobile devices, the social contact that shapes literacy practices works itself temporally and spatially through the kitchen table, the bus, and the lecture hall in ways that are both incremental and continual. Importantly, this structure of interaction does not negate the importance of (or, I would suggest, the ability to participate in) the kinds of conversations that Bruffee and others associate with community sociability. However, the cycles of networked, mobile participation can begin to resemble an embodied mode of being. Importantly, monitoring in social media (and perhaps across social platforms) is a habit that is difficult to break, leading users through a "drift logic" in which they begin to move without consciously intending to follow traces of online activity (Nunes, 2006). Because habits of movement are so important to this rhythm, proximities help explain why people develop orientations toward particular kinds of social interactions.

Negotiating Social Proximities with/ in Ambient Sociability

What does all of this mean for the interpersonal relations associated with and composed through transient literacies? Ambient sociability shifts the central keyword associated with the social influence on composing from "contact" to "potential." Where Cooper, LeFevre, Bruffee and theorists of the early social turn in composition studies focused centrally on direct social contact as a means for accessing resources and discourses, contexts of ambient sociability highlight the experience of cultivating and maintaining social potential: creating the possibility for social contact by constructing and then navigating the surroundings through which connections to others can be made. This work not only requires the direct contact of conversation or reading, but also indirect actions that include checking for updates in discourse and turning away from some platforms in order to tune into others. As we can see from the examples of Micah and Sal (but also from Kim, Kathryn, and Ed in previous chapters), students organizing and practicing composing negotiate an interplay between the social potential that is foregrounded and focal—the center of immediate attention—and social potential that is offloaded to the background, ready to be engaged more directly later. Proximities create familiarity or nearness that position particular kinds of materials as naturally in line with our immediate surroundings. As a result, composers often orient in familiar directions repeatedly as a result of their position relative to our habits of movement. This same dynamic is in play with people surrounding us: writers develop ways of moving and negotiating place with technology that orient them toward some and away from other forms of social potential.

To continue moving forward, I want to outline two implications of social potential for how we understand networked mobile device use. First, indirect social interactions increasingly should be understood as important to composing processes. Second, the social potential that enables mobile literacy practice increasingly exists in tension with social exclusion and isolation.

The Importance of Indirect Social Interaction

Whether "killing time" or working on focused projects, passive or indirect social interactions are important factors in composing with mobile devices. Across social platforms in my study, participants spent more time monitoring than directly interacting with others, looking to social platforms as clouds of information that hold promise but incrementally demand attention. This describes both anonymous posters on Reddit that offer information on a topic of passing interest, as well as collections of bodies encountered because of the proximity in a room. While focused, persistent conversation among connected people remains an important form of interaction to developing ideas and texts, educators and researchers would be remiss to overlook the influence of more ephemeral and temporarily important social encounters that matter: some of these encounters involve listening and lurking rather than directly speaking.

Indirect interactions challenge many assumptions about the kinds of social encounters that are positive, useful, and necessary for successful composing. This is particularly true in dialogue with the model of conversation that Bruffee suggested be integrated into classrooms as the central pedagogical tool preparing students to externalize social discourse. The social resources described briefly by LeFevre as "resonances" and "enablers" are emerging as important to students in the practice of their everyday lives. Although metaphors such as Turkle's concept of "tethering" assume the net generation avoids unknown peer communities because of a preference toward more intimate social relations, both Sal and Micah's practices and perceptions hint at new motivations for why individuals seek social potential in common spaces—online and offline—that assemble unknown people, rather than in smaller affiliation communities.

Sal, for instance, articulated an ethic in which individuals understand their most meaningful or authentic interactions to happen outside of known peer networks because those relationships are so heavily subject to surveillance and the influence of networked systems. His purposeful strategies for social learning in crowds attempted to escape, if only in small ways, the algorithmic "filter bubbles" of homogeneity that come with life in a hypermediated and connected society (Pariser, 2011). By seeking out places that acted more as an information commons than building (and enforcing) strong awareness of known peers, Sal most highly valued interactions that pushed against the tendency toward forced consensus and groupthink that he found common in peer conversations. The result, in Sal's case, was to value indirect interactions with strangers and with online information that enabled him to apply his own information literacy skills when outside the classroom: scrolling through page after page of Reddit returns and listening in on the conversations of people around him was preferable to feeling bombarded by others' biases. In Micah's case, indirect contact was also at the forefront of out-of-school learning. Access to online commons spaces enabled him to work with his buddy on a self-motivated learning project and his interactions in the Technology Commons suggest that he was interested in sharing his knowledge with people he didn't know well. Literacy educators and researchers should be thinking more about how these background interactions are formed and managed, as we continue to research how students engage more direct communication with peers, mentors, and others.

Social Potential in Tension with Social Exclusion

As the opening epigraph from Turkle highlighted, navigating social potential across multiple platforms often means appearing disengaged. This is particularly true when individuals attune to indirect, background social contact ahead of direct interactions. When social potential is distributed across multiple platforms and monitoring becomes just as important as contributing, it is easy to begin to imagine why students reading and writing in shared social places can appear isolated. The binary of alone/together, however, is misleading in its dismissal of the very real stakes associated with presence in online, participatory spaces. The roles and identities that students engage online are no less real and often just as high-stakes (and potentially risky and challenging) as the ones they inhabit in their life lived face to face. It is no longer useful to position online participation as a meaningless escape from the confines of physical presence: to do so is to undervalue the effects that online presence can have on learning, employment, and social relationships. Given Rainie and Wellman's emphasis on the steps individuals must take to coordinate relationships and construct social networks that will matter to their work, civic, and personal lives, it is no wonder that so many students appear glued to their phones. Those who do not take steps to understand the unfolding social potential around them or to contribute in meaningful ways may also be avoiding potential interactions with positive implications for their personal lives, careers, and civic lives. To focus only on any one social platform, whether the immediate face-to-face context or another channel for communication, is always a risk: it is a shutting down of possibilities incoming from other domains.

In response to the dominant refrain from scholars such as Turkle, it is important to emphasize that ambient sociability does not mean that students are solitary, and the interactions that take place as a result of this context also may not be motivated by an interest in avoiding opportunities for contact. Rather, ambient sociability means that keeping up with cultivating the potential for contact also always means the risk of being inundated with social interactions—so much so that some form of potential exchange is always relegated to the background or reserve. This might be the ubiquitous Facebook feed or SMS text barrage entering through one's mobile phone that fades to the background during a collaborative work session or conversation, or it might be the in-person buzz of conversation that temporarily becomes the background when one directs focus to a computer screen. In both cases, it is necessary to move back and forth from one to the other and to adjust attention constantly (Stone, 2007). Even when attention is directed entirely toward a mobile device screen, social potential is divided among a collection of mundane texts from social outlets. Incoming messages shift continually and how to direct attention is not obvious. As a result, what may appear to be "social isolation" from the outside may actually be the mechanisms through which individuals deal with social abundance, enacting the attention structures that they have developed for moving back and forth among always layered social streams and different forms of engagement expected across social platforms. At the same time, it is important to maintain a sense of the problems and challenges that ambient sociability poses for students in everyday life: "FOMO" or fear of missing out on life shared on screen is a powerful material that many students carry through their experiences with mobile devices.

Conclusion: Rethinking the Sociability of Transient Literacies in Action

This chapter has focused on some of the social platforms, arrangements, and practices that are central to networked mobile composing to which students adapt and adjust as a transient literacy practice. These literacies are meaningful not only because they affect composing in the moment but also because they continually invent the social environments that surround networked mobile device use. Both within and outside classrooms, these social interactions are frequently invoked as evidence of the social isolation of mobile device users; however, educators and researchers have reason to challenge some of these assumptions.

As educators, we may find that students who have become habituated into network-centric social models may perceive direct, focused conversation as antithetical to the shuttling social movement across platforms that is central to how they must cultivate social potential. With faces downturned to device screens, a resistance to direct conversation may be inevitable. As educators and writing studies scholars responding to this moment, it is important to remember that actively managing social interactions is central to transient literacy practices. When using networked, mobile devices, the social surrounding comprised of both people and information is not an aspect of literacy practice that can be assumed but instead one that students must continually participate in co-constructing. The act of assembling social influence means making difficult choices about how to orient oneself toward other people and information, and this is a risk that plays out across students' choices about participation in both online and offline spaces.

Locating oneself in an environment with high social potential is always risky, and this is the case for both online communities and local shared spaces. The dynamics of place, mobility, and technological mediation that intersect in the ambient sociability of shared spaces like cafés, coffee houses, and libraries heightens attention to less explicitly organized social influences that resonate: the social potential that exists around us but that it is our own responsibility to seek out. Rather than assuming that the only generative social actions are those that stem from direct connection with a given community of practice, ambient sociability implies a "nomadic thinking" (Creswell, 2006) in which resonances that influence may come from outside a community's accepted boundaries. We can see that students such as Sal and Micah interact across physically proximal and virtual places to which they connected through mobile devices. Sal and Micah's examples illustrate how social interactions with peers—distant and co-present, direct and ephemeral—are not only mediated by mobile devices and networked software but also by lived experiences in these kinds of places. Of course, these resonances can be distracting—in both the embodied and intellectual sense of the "noise" they create for writers, as well as for the common places that we share with others. In Chapter 5, I continue this discussion by focusing on composers' co-production of attention with their mobile devices and surroundings.

Chapter 5: Attention as a Thing Composed

> What if direction, as the way we face as well as move, is organized rather than casual?
>
> –Sara Ahmed, 2006, p. 15

Although millennials have been blamed for ruining everything from bar soap to the auto industry, the years between 2005 and 2015 saw the population of people born between 1981 and 1996 blamed most for lack of attention. With the ubiquity of personal computing devices happening alongside the rise of social media and the shift of the internet toward user-generated content models, attention practices were unquestionably changing. The result was pervasive cultural confusion: do ideals of attention exist for which we should strive? Do technologies harm these ideals? These tensions could be observed in public media accounts, which often depicted the under-35 generation as the walking, talking, texting embodiments of attachment to mobile devices. Take, for example, a late 2015 example in *BBC Online* entitled "A Generation of Cyber-slackers" (Alsop, 2015). The piece opened by describing Alexandra Douwes, a 26–year-old entrepreneur who had recently taken steps to detach herself from the habit of constantly checking her cell phone. Alexandra explained that she had difficulty trying to avoid constantly looking at her messages and social networks. As she put it, "it fe[lt] unproductive to do otherwise." The article positioned Douwes as a kind of unicorn: an elusive member of the "cyber-slacking" generation who managed to beat the odds by breaking her constant phone habits. Others, either unlucky or less trained, remained affected by how continual mobile phone use was "making it difficult for young people to concentrate and stick with demanding assignments at school and work" (Alsop, 2015, para. 7).

Distraction is often positioned as a cognitive state to which people are "hard-wired" due to the use of technologies, and that wiring is often discussed generationally, usually unfairly. A broad interdisciplinary literature has challenged the myth of the digital native. For instance, contributors to Michael Thomas' (2011) *Deconstructing Digital Natives* covered domains ranging from multimodal texts to internet searching to networked participation while questioning the appropriateness of assuming digital fluency based on generation. If public media examples illustrate tensions around how to interpret attention in landscapes impacted by mobile devices, digital studies scholarship also bears out many different takes on the subject. As Howard Rheingold (2012) explained, the distraction associated with using mobile technologies can be alternately positioned as a neurological problem resulting from the neuroplasticity of brain cells (Carr, 2011); a social problem arising from the anxiety of needing to be "always on" and available to other people (Baron, 2008); an "adaptive behavior" of continuous partial attention through which employees try to gain a competitive economic advantage by "constantly scanning for opportunities and staying on top of contacts, events, and activities in an effort to miss nothing" (Stone, 2007, p. 28); and, a textual problem difficult to avoid in the convergent materiality of digital interfaces, whose conflicting fields and components invite split attention (Jackson, 2009). These differences matter because they position attention as stemming from divergent institutions or interfaces, which influence whether we understand attention as a neurological condition, social anxiety, required performance in a knowledge economy, or an inevitable part of navigating the current media landscape.

The ambiguities related to what we mean when we use the term "attention" are compounded because literacy and humanities researchers and teachers are often removed from the research on attention as a neuroscientific phenomenon. Scientific approaches can position attention as a black box to researchers and educators in the humanities (Nass, 2010; Ophir et al., 2009). By contrast, *distraction* is often associated with observable embodied interactions and gestures rather than with cognitive function: the tendency to glance down at one's phone repeatedly, to return habitually to social media sites, or to focus on online interactions at the expense of face-to-face ones. As a result, the so-called cyberslackers of Alexandra Douwes' generation are simultaneously labeled by their embodiments and reduced to their brains, but not at all easily understood.

In the prior chapter, I argued that the experience of networked mobile device use can be associated with ambient sociability, by which I mean a context in which some form of social potential is continually relegated to the background of focus. In this chapter, I analyze attention as an outcome and contributor to composing in contexts where ambient sociability is at play. To do so, I emphasize how attention can be understood as a product composed during the process of interacting with networked mobile surroundings. To put it another way, attention may be bracketed through a neuroscientific lens, an economic lens, or a behavioral lens, but also through a material/rhetorical lens that positions it as invented through interactions. To understand attention in this way is to imagine it as produced in collaborations that involve both people and materials. This stance toward attention opens it up to the expertise of rhetoric and composition and digital literacy scholars. It enables us to take this easily generalized phenomenon and re-specify it as something that humans participate in with the people and materials that surround them. This way of understanding attention makes it possible to challenge the assumption that distraction is the causal result of a particular technology based on a reading of specific cases.

To begin an example of that work in this chapter, I first further set the scene by taking up the recent interest in how mobile devices affect attention dynamics in classroom spaces. However, although classroom-based models are relevant to understanding how students are attending (or not) to *some* materials that matter to composing in *some* contexts, the vast majority of writing practices take place in environments where norms and expectations for attention are less tightly controlled. While ambient sociability is experienced across these locations, mobile surroundings differ and thus shape the materials that participate in constructing attention. To provide examples, the chapter traces two instances of composing attention, using examples to draw out vocabulary for how attention is composed in interactions with surroundings.

Learning from Classroom Device Debates

Positioning attention as a crucial underlying aspect of twenty-first century digital literacy competence, Howard Rheingold built on the now-familiar concept of the attention economy (Lanham, 2006; Lankshear & Knobel, 2003), which captured the market-like dynamics surrounding attention in cultures whose technological development resulted in round-the-clock information access. As Richard Lanham's (2006) *Economics of Attention* emphasized, attention has become a "scarce resource" sought and cultivated due to the multiplying choices people have for expression, information, and interaction across modes and media. Positioning attention as a resource that circulates within markets has been a useful conceptual lens for navigating the emerging dynamics of university classrooms, where many instructors find that attention is a scarce resource. As I described in Chapter 1, networked mobile devices impact environments by creating conditions through which unrelated materials interact. When students carry networked computers into classrooms, materials within proximity of students' perception multiply exponentially. The supply of materials to which one might attend multiplies as the digital reserve surrounds us. Mobile devices bring invisible clouds of information front and center in classroom environments, dispersing the number and kinds of materials that compete for focus.

Instructors often find it difficult to ignore the presence of the digital reserve during classroom instruction because it positions their voice as one competing in a marketplace of sights, sounds, words, and images. As a result of this dynamic, educators disagree about how to adjust and have debated their options publicly, which has resulted in fruitful and generative conversations about the limits and possibilities for attention in classrooms. For the past 10 years, negotiating how to address classrooms of students with heads turned toward smartphones or hiding behind laptops has become a defining part of developing contemporary composing pedagogies, an issue routinely addressed when supporting new teaching assistants for instance. Clay Shirky (2014) invigorated a conversation about laptops in classrooms by publishing a blog entry that explained how he had asked his students to stop using mobile devices during class. This was an unanticipated response, given that Shirky is otherwise understood to be a technology supporter or even enthusiast. The complexity and thoughtfulness of Shirky's posting set off a wave of replies from across academics and public intellectuals. To name a few, digital humanities scholar Dave Parry (2014) admitted to making similar decisions for similar reasons; *The Shallows* author Nicholas Carr (2014) took the opportunity of Shirky's post to echo his longstanding refrain that mobile devices lead to destabilized classrooms and reduced learning; and Steven Krause (2014), a digital writing scholar and educator, suggested that teachers should respond to the impact of mobile device distractions by changing their methods. Krause suggested that instructors lean less heavily on lectures, "be more interesting," and decenter themselves as classroom focal points (2014).

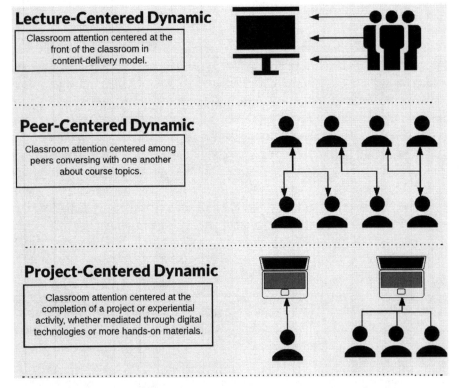

Lecture-Centered Dynamic
Classroom attention centered at the front of the classroom in content-delivery model.

Peer-Centered Dynamic
Classroom attention centered among peers conversing with one another about course topics.

Project-Centered Dynamic
Classroom attention centered at the completion of a project or experiential activity, whether mediated through digital technologies or more hands-on materials.

Figure 5.1. Simplified models of classroom attention orientations.

This public discussion and debate has shaped how many educators understand the intersections of attention, literacy, and mobile devices and offers a useful jumping-off point for any teacher examining the range of possibilities for how well informed, technologically savvy educators are addressing the attention economy in university classrooms. Within the debate and from the position of a market framework, researchers and instructors generally disagree about whether decentering the focus from a central teacher and students toward the wealth of resources (related and unrelated to course content) contained across the physical classroom and the digital reserve affords positive opportunities for learning. My perspective on the debate is somewhat different. For me, the "device debates" illuminate how educators have focused on the dynamics of classroom settings to the detriment of caring about attention outside them.

Behind common stances in classroom device debates often lie assumptions about what kinds of materials should be central in students' perceptions when they participate in classroom learning. For example, as Krause suggests, mobile devices are often framed as problems in classrooms because they interrupt centralized focal objects of the classroom, such as a teacher's body or course lecture slides. Mobile devices in other cases are constructed as moving student focus away from peers in a classroom setting or from shared course texts (i.e., textbooks or reading printouts). By contrast, educators who applaud integrating mobile devices during class time tend to position them as supporting a dynamic of attention that is central to their pedagogical stance, such as the social learning dynamics I discussed in Chapter 4 that ask students to draw on networked mobile devices to connect online while practicing online research or design. Emerging pedagogies (e.g., active learning pedagogies, makerspace pedagogies, or pedagogies of play) often purposefully attempt to distribute and maintain classroom attention in ways that differ from traditional "sage on the stage" models. Across these possibilities, instructors design pedagogies that cultivate particular kinds of attention and, quite naturally, plan and carry out activities that regulate students' attention: moving them toward particular attentional dynamics that they understand to foster learning.

Classroom guidelines and technologies participate in this regulation of attention by enforcing and incentivizing forms of attention that instructors (or programs, or universities) understand as ideal. Syllabi statements banning laptops or mobile phones or calling for restraint in personal device use during classroom moments are just one kind of guideline that acts in this way: participation grades, content quizzes, peer-learning projects and other daily classroom practices function at least in part to orient students toward embodying and living the forms of attention that instructors or programs believe will best lead to their learning. The growing number of educational technologies that enforce attention dynamics in classrooms through surveillance also play a role in maintaining normative models of attention. For example, I have received email advertisements that promised to "reduce distractions" during class by providing a way to keep students from "texting, playing and going into Facebook." The computer application, the email continued, is helpful because it "automatically tracks those using their phones during class (especially the sneaky ones you can't see or don't notice)" (email communication, Flipdapp. co, 2016). While this is a rather extreme measure of maintenance, all course experiences urge students toward particular ways of attending: as if there are imaginary targets toward which instructors aim students through classroom values, standards, people, and technologies. Generally, this is a positive way for instructors to think through the objectives of their classroom presence and goal setting.

In reality, we know that the actual practices of attention inside classrooms never meet instructors' ideals. Students have always stared out windows, passed notes to friends, and daydreamed about lunchtime or what will happen after class. Students are active agents who in Michel De Certeau's (1984) terms tactically react against the strategic norms of official spaces such as classrooms, and often for the better. For example, writing instructors have long recognized that students create their own lively "underlife" that exists parallel to teacher-initiated conversations (Brooke, 1999; Mueller, 2009). This underlife not only connects students socially but can also extend and enrich learning. Attention ideals are at best useful myths that inform the practices, standards, and values of classrooms; however, they are never completely realized in practice.

Attention and Literacy Beyond the Classroom

Although "perfect attention" by the standards of pedagogies will never be achieved in practice, literacy instructors are well served to take attention dynamics seriously in classrooms that are shaped by mobile networked devices, whether this means banning laptops or taking measures such as teaching meditation or other focusing techniques while integrating mobile devices (Rheingold, 2012). The recent changes that mobile devices bring to attention in classroom spaces may be more pervasive, disruptive, and subject to control by profit-motivated marketeers and interface designers than "distractions" of staring out the window or daydreaming. However, even the most "decentered" or "student-centered" classrooms are distinctive environments for attention, where attention is explicitly regulated through guidelines that sanction particular norms. Curricula, educational technologies, and classroom expectations act in Lanham's (2006) terms as situated and local "attention structures": *designed* texts, interfaces, technologies, and other mediators that actively shape how attention is garnered and received in a particular context.

Normative models of attention associated with classrooms, however, are limited in predicting or supporting how attention is performed outside them. Classroom rules, standards, and incentives do not automatically travel with students to regulate their attention in all the other meaningful places of students' lives, particularly in commons spaces. For example, even if a student consistently performs attention to the slides of a course lecture in ways that align with a teacher's expectations, she may not pay attention in the same way when working alone on her laptop computer in the shared space of a coffee shop. The attention produced through the practice of composing with networked mobile devices, then, may differ substantially across environments. In particular, places that lack explicit guidelines for attention or surveillance technologies such as distraction reduction software may lead students to assemble different kinds of materials. Distraction-reducing technologies, of course, are not unique to academic contexts. In 2007, Stone suggested that this issue was already leading to the development of a number of tools and technologies designed to mediate the cognitive overload associated with burgeoning information and the need to continually check for new opportunities. Many of these software packages create incentives for ongoing focus or eliminate the possibility to orient away from a given online task or writing window. To use Paul Prior and Jody Shipka's (2003) terms, students writing outside classrooms work with their own "external aids and actors" and continually make mundane decisions that "shape, stabilize, and direct consciousness in service of the task at hand" (p. 44). Tools that mediate attention are important external aids for contemporary students writing outside of classroom spaces.

Alex Reid (2014) made a related point in response to Shirky's post about laptops in the classroom, arguing that modes of attention assumed in traditional classrooms differ dramatically from those expected in many contemporary workplaces, where employees are less frequently expected to perform in stable hierarchical trajectories. By contrast, Reid argued, today's employees are expected to chart their own course toward advancement through collaboration, risk-taking, and lateral movements. In other words, the importance of carefully constructing attention does not end at the borders of classroom walls; it only begins there. Attention is composed across the range of environments students inhabit temporarily, including on- and off-campus locations (Delcore et al., 2014). While popular discourse and instructors' own attention often focuses on students' multitasking within classrooms (Flanagan, 2014; Weimer, 201;), educators have been less concerned with how students construct attention across the other places that line learning pathways, from hallways to park benches to freeways to libraries to dorm rooms. Ironically, given our constant focus on mobile devices in classrooms, it may be that formal educational spaces are students' least challenging environments for maintaining attention because instructors put so many technologies, standards, and social expectations in place to guide them. If attention is significant to learning and connected to materials across different situated environments, it is important to think beyond classrooms to survey the impact of shifting technologies and information access on how students assign focus. Understanding transient literacies requires educators and researchers to think more carefully about how attention is constructed during hours outside those that instructors observe (and to some degree control). Rather than focusing exclusively on intervening to alleviate distraction in classrooms, educators also must help students understand how attention is intertwined with literacy across environments with different materials, resources, and expectations.

Literacy educators enacting mobile pedagogies, unfortunately, have traditionally applied assumptions about attention that emerge from classrooms to understand composing practices beyond them. Amy Kimme Hea (2009) illustrated that pedagogies that integrate mobile devices often rest on assumptions that students will possess values, responsibilities, and skills that will lead them to use devices in ways that align with university classroom expectations. Students were often expected to take charge of the process of their learning as well as their ability to use devices in the right ways, to stay on task and/ or avoid risky or criminal behavior (Kimme Hea, 2009). Although we often directly observe students struggling with information saturation in our presence, as Kimme Hea describes, instructors also often tacitly proceed as if students will use technologies outside classrooms according to our assumptions about how they are most ideally suited to shape their learning. Students are thus "expected to control their own learning through the internalization of standards" but also to "police themselves in relationship to sanctioned laptop use" (Kimme Hea, 2009, p. 210). It is not realistic to expect that students' practices of attention outside the classroom will derive from norms expected within them. By learning from how students manage attention when composing in contexts of ambient sociability, we can begin to understand the habits and values of individuals using networked mobile devices and how these practices have impacts beyond personal literacy development.

Composing Attention in Two Case Examples

With a few exceptions, little research on composing has extended beyond theorizing composing to trace how attention is practiced in collaboration with the materials in writers' environments. Literacy educators have offered several terms to describe forms of attention that impact reading practices, however.

N. Katherine Hayles' (2008, 2012) well-known concept of "hyperreading," for instance, positioned skimming and scanning as potentially useful emergent practices that contrast with close reading techniques. Daniel Keller's (2013) concept of "foraging" also described a common reading practice in which students appear to stake a haphazard movement through a text but actually read in a non-linear, "gathering" fashion that identifies relevant and useful bits of text more efficiently. Practices such as culture jamming and meme circulation described by new literacy scholars Lankshear and Knobel (2003), remind us that composing practices are also developing from attention dynamics students practice outside traditional classrooms. At the same time, composition scholar Richard Miller has blogged about how ways of thinking aligned with wandering (that appears distracted) may actually be welcome manifestations of a humanistic, creative mind (qtd. in Keller, 2013). In Miller's estimation, some reading, writing, and thinking practices easily elided with non-attention could be central to the open-minded thinking trajectories that many composition scholars hope to encourage.

Examples like these are useful for understanding attention as a dynamic that affects composing practices in information-saturated contexts. However, we need more examples that focus on the detailed processes through which attention is composed. To elaborate, I now present two examples from the Technology Commons. In each case, I first introduce participants' stories along with basic time-use interaction sequences, which reveal preliminary information about the kinds of materials that become participants in composing attention during two different instances of composing with a laptop. I then analyze what these sequences of interaction suggest about how materials moved in and out of students' focus during the time observed. After presenting these interactive series, I turn toward a more detailed discussion of how attention is invented in collaboration with the mobile surround in each case.

Ann's Story

The first example I discuss is a criminal justice student named Ann, who often used the Technology Commons between classes to socialize with her boyfriend and friends. Ann was a white female student who grew up in a small town on Florida's east coast, about an hour's drive away from UCF's campus. She had completed her introductory general education courses at a community college less than thirty minutes away from her home and transferred to UCF after finishing there. During moments between other scheduled campus activities, Ann looked for comfortable places on campus to sit and interact socially for a few moments while also getting short homework assignments completed when possible. When I first approached Ann, she was reclining with sneakers propped

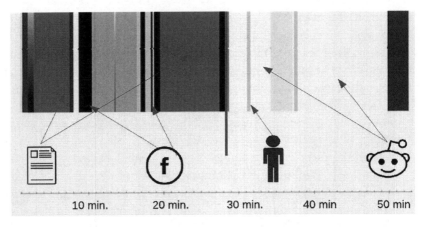

Figure 5.2. Ann's informal study session as a sequence of interactions.

on a coffee table in a secluded area of the Technology Commons: a small nook outside the PC lab that included a large round table and seating for five or six students. As she explained when we chatted later, she didn't understand her time in the Technology Commons that afternoon to be a study or homework session *per se*. She positioned it as mainly for socializing, where she would "go on the internet and talk to people" to relieve stress between classes.

In spite of this "downtime," Ann had made the decision to keep one particularly challenging course, Archeological Sciences, in the back of her mind even while killing time. As we discussed that current course which was a requirement for her criminal justice degree, Ann explained, "So I have completely different habits just for that class. My other classes I can usually like study for a few days and I'm okay. That class I have to study constantly." While Ann was waiting on her boyfriend and friends to arrive, she accessed a course assignment, read an assigned article, checked her course management system for assignment information, all while checking her social media feeds. She described her activity this way: "we had a test maybe in a week and I was checking to see if anybody had posted questions about what they didn't understand. Because I wasn't understanding." Since interacting with friends and maintaining some focus on Archeological Sciences were both important goals, she moved across social media sites where she monitored peers' activity but also positioned Archeological Sciences as a constant presence. As Figure 5.2 suggests, Ann was interacting among many different kinds of materials during the 50 minutes that she agreed to participate in an observation. The darkest black areas represent the time that she spent looking at Facebook, the medium gray shows time that she was reading a PDF document that her instructor had uploaded to the course management system. There are also substantial chunks of time devoted to Reddit, which are visualized in white. When her boyfriend entered the scene of the observation thirty-five minutes in, her attention also changed quite dramatically as she spent more time talking with him and less time with her laptop.

Dean and Carly's Stories

The second case example involves Dean and Carly, who were enrolled in three courses together during the spring 2013 semester. During my observation, they studied and completed homework together in the Technology Commons for a digital imaging course. Dean explained that when they worked together that day they were still "getting a feel for the class and how to study for it." To speed this process along and have some fun in the process, the two had decided to combine their respective strengths and energies toward completing a tutorial together before each taking a required quiz for the course. As Dean explained, "She has a graphic design background and I have a web design background. So between the two, it helped a lot."

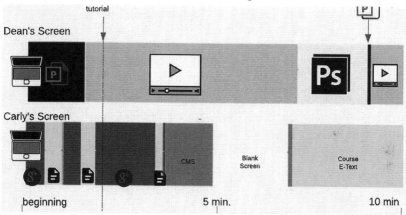

Figure 5.3. Ten minutes of Dean and Carly's study session as a series of interactions.

As Figure 5.3 illustrates, Dean and Carly's sequence had as many twists and turns as Ann's, though the two students largely remained "on task," working together toward a series of more or less shared tasks required for their course. Notably, working together at the same time and side-by-side created an atmosphere in which they shared access to personal technologies. During their study session, they read a class PowerPoint presentation for information and watched related tutorial videos about Photoshop on which they would later be tested. Initially Dean displayed the course PowerPoint presentation on his laptop screen while Carly searched the web to find out whether there were existing notes online that identified key concepts related to the particular functionalities of Photoshop they were studying. When they turned toward the laptop screen to begin watching the tutorial, Carly and Dean shared one set of earbuds. However, Carly simultaneously scrolled through Google search results looking for relevant corresponding information, later pulling up the course management system and e-textbook to cross-reference concepts explained in the video tutorial.

Unlike a textbook, video tutorials did not provide a surface-level method for "skimming" or easily transporting key concepts into notes nor open word processing documents. As they watched a video, then, Dean describes that he and Carly took advantage of the ebook's "extensive search function," to read the chapter at the same time they watched—not linearly, but by skipping to and around key concepts covered in the video. As he put it, "The ebook has a very nice search function. So, we'd try to find it very quickly. So, we'll find a keyword or a key phrase, and then we'll read around it to get context." While watching the video, searching the web, and scanning their course e-textbook for relevant and related material, they also chatted with one another to identify important concepts or to discuss when something was confusing.

The Thick Sequencing of Transient Literacies

What do these two stories suggest about the attention/distraction of students once they leave the normative expectations of classrooms? To answer this question, let's start with a basic description of what materials appear to be in focus for students during their study sessions. In both cases, these sequences are not linear in the sense that neither Ann or Dean and Carly practiced a planned, ordered, series of events designed to accomplish one narrow purpose. Instead of narrowly focused, these sequences could be described as thick or expansive: they wind together threads of interaction from across domains while making forward progress toward a study goal. To further explain, I will now explore the kinds of materials these sequenced literacy interactions bind together. As I argue below, both of these students practice attention in ways that depart from normative models of practiced attention assumed in classrooms in at least two ways.

Thick Sequencing that Combines Multiple Goals

Ann's case involved a student during a relatively "relaxed" time in her schedule that enabled her to multiply the number of goals that she could work toward at the same time. This session was "thick" because it was loaded with interactions and materials that served multiple—and potentially conflict-ing—personal motivations. This way of distributing attention made sense from Ann's perspective in the moment because she was not working toward any particular time constraint that pushed her to finish a given task immi-nently. By contrast, her goal with regards to coursework was simply to keep her mind continually engaged with the class that was most challenging to her. Recall that she felt she needed to study constantly for Archaeological Sci-ences, rather than simply completing her homework and moving along. The more relaxed schedule associated with killing time enabled her to distribute her attention among purposes, so that she could keep in the course in her immediate realm of thought as often as possible. She thus capitalized on what she understood to be down-time in her schedule to bring in materials from the course that she felt required her constant engagement. From her point of view, any time that was "free" in her schedule warranted at least a brief nod to materials from this course, which she felt that she should be studying for constantly.

Clearly, Ann was as devoted to keeping an eye on her friends through social media as she was to keeping her course in her mind. She also spent a great deal of time in perusing Reddit, reading several threads that she said she tends to check daily. Together, then, Ann made use of the variable intensity of moments of time in her schedule in order to thickly organize attention across personal and academic interests. Similar attitudes toward time use were described by many participants in the Gone Wired Café and the Technology Commons, who discussed experiencing literacy- and learning-directed time in varying degrees of intensity, where factors ranging from their current affective state to the nearness of academic deadlines affected their likelihood to intertwine materials associated with multiple literacy goals in short proximity.

Thick Sequencing That Expands the Scene

Dean and Carly's case, like Ann's, involved students working using attention tactics to increase the efficiency of their use of time. However, the "thick-ness" of their sequences worked differently. They too appeared to be enjoying one another's company, but their conversations and direct social interactions were limited to the topic of completing the one literacy task that they were working on together: learning content delivered via a course instructional video and preparing to be quizzed on the content to meet an online course deadline. Their study session was thick with interactions not because they were trying to accomplish different goals but instead because they combined individual attention capacities (and associated materials) in order to expand the scene of their learning. Instead of layering attention toward their goals in personal and professional domains, they layered a range of technologies and interactions into the space of the study session in order to increase the number of resources present to help them absorb and grasp course material. They understood this to be a reasonable and effective way of distributing attention in order to efficiently and effectively meet the demands of the assignment—passing a content quiz—that had been assigned to them.

Dean and Carly's side-by-side laptop screens enabled a way of paying attention that fell outside the norms of what instructors might expect from students working with digital content provided to them in online or hybrid/blended courses. Dean described how mediating attention through the dual laptop setup changed their study practices:

> Two people can search for the same topic in both screens as opposed to being dependent on one screen. Um, what we did for that time is we kinda split up the things. Because obviously everything in the video isn't important—just key concepts. So we watch the video and then tell each other what the key things were. To save a little bit of time there.

When they divided videos, one of them watched the tutorial and "t[ook] pictures of it," and then he or she described the content of the video to the other so that both could read relevant sections from their course text to better understand the highlighted functions. As Dean put it, "I was watching a video; she was watching another video. So, I would pull up all the key concepts of, say, video A and she would have video B. And we would take out all the stuff that wasn't really that important. And then we'd just tell each other the main points." Whether Dean and Carly watched videos together or took screenshots from them to share with one another separately, Dean preferred analyzing the video to simply reading a chapter alone or watching a video linearly because it helped him understand how to prioritize information and highlight key concepts. It was also, from their perspective, possible to do more in a shorter amount of time by working together to expand the scene.

Dean stressed, of course, that the pair did not work together every time a video was assigned because the coordination of schedules required them to figure out how to be in the same place at the same time. That level of coordinated work was not always worth the payoff for a particular video and the effort required to mediating their attention together. Dean admitted, "Normally I just watch the video by myself—it's easier." However, time was of the essence for both students, at least in how they perceived their situation, and working together enabled them to make their time denser without losing individual focus.

Ambient Sociability and Attention

Ann and Dean and Carly's cases have interesting implications regarding the relationship among literacy, mobile devices, and attention outside classrooms. The sequences of interaction that comprise these selections of their practice suggest that students outside the classroom are, indeed, paying attention in ways that many educators would understand to fall outside classroom norms. When they fail to "police themselves" in Kimme Hea's terms by using mobile devices in ways that do not align with normative expectations, instructors may read students' behaviors as motivated by "sneakiness," laziness, or a desire to avoid deep thinking (2009). However, these two stories suggest something different. Both Ann and Dean and Carly purposefully make use of distributed interaction patterns, in ways that are not simply multitasking. As Keller details, neuroscientific studies suggest that multitasking typically leads to worse performance on tasks than would be experienced when working only on one task at a time. Although moments in these sequences of interaction align with descriptions of multitasking identified by researchers such as Gloria Mark and Melissa Niiya (2014), Keller has argued that applying the concept of multitasking to literacy practices requires us to account for the ways in which "not every task" associated with literacy "carries the same cognitive load" (2013, p. 103). That is, complex composing tasks almost always require braiding together many different practices and text types, so that drafting an academic assignment often requires something like constant switching across multiple activities and texts (see e.g., Blythe & Gonzales, 2016). In these examples, although we might think of the students switching among multiple tasks, it is also possible to instead interpret their activity as attempts to make the time available to them more densely filled with useful interactions. Their ultimate purpose was to fill more interactions into a given time in order to accomplish a study goal: Ann was using her laptop to keep a tab devoted to materials from her tough course even when "killing time," and Dean and Carly drew on one another's existing knowledge and technologies to expand their learning scene with more materials designed to help them learn content.

I am purposefully withholding judgment about whether Ann, Dean, or Carly would have been more or less successful if they had performed attention in more "expected" or "sanctioned" ways. That is, I am not suggesting that Ann is more successful in her difficult course because she has found a way to continually attend to it rather than devoting, for example, an uninterrupted hour each day to reading course materials. Neither am I suggesting that Dean and Carly know more about graphic design because they found a way to bring resources from the internet and their course etextbook into immediate proximity with the experience of watching course tutorial videos. Instead, I want to emphasize that students have formed purposeful assemblies from materials around them as ways to navigate the constraints of learning outside the classroom. Rather than working among a flood information that they struggle to control or which threatens to overtake them, these three participants describe themselves as working in purposeful ways to integrate complex materials toward the ends of their goals. Indeed, it may be that these students are still novices in constructing attention structures in collaboration with their surroundings. However, they do not appear overwhelmed by expectations of reciprocity associated with being "always on" and available. In fact, as I will discuss later, Ann appears a bit bored by the available information from her social connections. Although their environments are infused with a great deal of potential incoming information, the thick sequences of attention in these two cases read as more self-imposed and strategic than reactive.

Notably, across both cases these students are driven primarily by the desire to squeeze every available possibility out of time (Wajcman, 2015). Ann, Dean, Carly, and other participants in this research did not want to waste time—when completing coursework, when socializing, nor when learning new material. The ability to manipulate time by making it thick and dense with interaction is partly what these students understand to be the unusual constraints that mobile technologies afford them with respect to composing attention related to academic coursework. Another participant named Max stated it outright while discussing how he attempted to condense study sessions for his calculus class by working with a peer who understood the materials better than he did: "I hate wasting time thinking about like, all right, why can't I figure this out?" Rather than "spinning his wheels" on his own, Max wanted to get to a point of understanding faster and thus partnered with his friend Luna who had more experience with Calculus. Like Max, many of the students I encountered during this research were increasingly (and perhaps counterintuitively) driven to expand the materiality of scenes around them because of an intense desire for temporal efficiency, even in moments that might appear unproductive. That is, their networks of proximal materials tended to spiral outward as they attempted to fit more into available moments of time. Within this task fragmentation, students described making active choices about literacy tasks that required high individual concentration and those that could be completed in the presence of others with whom they are socializing. For example, Luna worked in particular campus locations when her work is not pressing: "it's time of day and like, whether I actually like really need to get things done . . . or if I can socialize." The Technology Commons, for her, was a place that invited a social element that separated it from more spartan locations on campus that invited more quiet study. As a result, students across the situated case examples in the Technology Commons and the Gone Wired Café staged personal settings for transient literacies to bring maximum potential and flexibility.

How Proximities Shape Attention

To take a step back now from these sequences of interaction, we can ask questions about *why* these sequences developed in the ways that they did. In scenarios where large amounts of information are available through mobile devices and networks, why do given students orient toward certain materials and not others? What makes Ann likely to use her laptop to integrate her coursework into her downtime? Why do Dean and Carly combine technologies together in order to come up with a new way of moving through assigned course material? The attention that is constructed during composing has roots in its participating materials. Much in the same way that students' traditional written products such as essays are informed by their histories, student's attentional performances take shape as a result of how they have previously interacted with worlds around them, including by the ways in which repeated locational movements have become sedimented into familiar ways of moving. These ways of moving shape the materials likely to surround them when they travel through places that matter to them.

Ways of paying attention outside classroom spaces follow from and continually reconstruct experiences: those bodily habits, boundaries, and pathways that become repertoires. To understand how attention is composed in information-saturated landscapes, educators need to know more about how people build proximities to environments and materials. For an example relevant to the current discussion, Ann emphasized that she habitually found herself traveling across the same social media feeds in the same way, even as they became increasingly boring and therefore annoying to her. Much in the same way that she plotted familiar pathways through social media landmarks, she also used the Technology Commons frequently as a "regular" because of comfort and convenience. Ann even began spending her less scheduled time in the Technology Commons because it was located on a pathway that she frequently took across campus. Recalling her first time stopping into the center, Ann recalled that she noticed the workspace shortly after it opened when walking along a usual route with her sister. Discussing the first time she entered, Ann said, "Me and her were walking by, and we said, 'Oh, what's this?' And we went inside and we were like, 'Wow, this is really cool.' So we just started sitting in there. And now I sit in there. Again and again." Across my research, I found that students used the Technology Commons as a result of one or two scenarios: either they were using it for the first time at the request of a friend, or they used it repeatedly as a result of creating a habit that put the center on the pathways that they usually took across campus. These students who used Technology Commons frequently understood it to be on their daily trajectories: it shared a perceived proximity to pathways, materials, values, and people on their horizons.

At the level of scope of their movements across campus, proximities shaped what places were likely to be salient to students participating in this research: their pathways across campus and across the cities in which they lived building a likelihood that a particular location would become meaningful to them. These locations, in turn, influenced what materials would become available and shape the interactions of transient literacies in action in a given space and time. However, individuals' proximities and pathways also functioned at smaller levels of scope: at the granular level of sequencing where we are more likely to discuss attention.

Proximities and Materials: A Detailed Example

Perhaps another example would be useful for returning to how proximities work hand-in-hand with attention, particularly as it intersects with networked technologies and digital reserves. To stick with Ann's study/social session that afternoon, it is possible to see how the university course management system and interfaces to which it was networked directly affected which materials rose to and fell from her focus. For example, when attempting to access the materials related to her difficult Archeological Sciences course, Ann accessed the university's central web portal, which offered access to the university course management system, along with other online resources. She waited for the relatively (and typically) long load time for the portal to open. However, this site was a temporary stop, a place accessed in order to go somewhere else. From the front portal, she clicked on the link that opened the university-supported course management system (running the Canvas platform) where many instructors host online courses or the online components of mediated or face-to-face courses. The front page of this second portal listed recent activity across courses in which she was enrolled, including updates made by instructors or contributions made by other students. Ann glanced at this page briefly and ran her cursor over the link to a discussion board that was displayed there, clicking on the "Assignments" tab at the top of the page. "Assignments" was where she would find links to the online course material from across classes—but most importantly today for Archeological Sciences.

When the "Assignments" page opened, Ann then clicked on the first assignment at the top of her page. Opening it took her to a case study assignment from archeological sciences called "Case 4: Detection & Recovery of Children." She paused on this screen, which contained a prominent link to a

PDF file and a set of bullet points describing the significance of the reading. She moved her cursor rather quickly to click the link to the PDF file that was in the center of the screen. And waited. Her cursor changed back and forth from the customary arrow to the brightly colored pinwheel that Mac users know means that the computer is processing (and often overprocessing). The gray progress bar on the URL line of her browser crept forward. Ann was clearly annoyed by the wait. She took a drink of her smoothie and put the cap back on—still no PDF. She smoothed her hair and crossed her arms, staring ahead at the idle screen. Still no PDF. She looked to the table at her right and began reading her printed notes. She didn't notice when the PDF, a chapter from a book that had been scanned and loaded into the course management system, finally appeared on the screen. By then, she had become invested in her print course notes in a spiral notebook, and she flipped the page to continue reading. A few minutes later, she looked up and jumped a bit when she realized the PDF document had opened. Because it was a chapter scanned from a book and uploaded, the PDF file was a series of two side-by-side pages from the chapter, and the opened file displayed the first series of pages, which presented the title, authors, and a brief conceptual table of contents for the chapter.

These are insignificant minutiae of Ann's day, to which she did not likely give much thought and to which literacy researchers would often not pay much attention. However, these familiar and transparent pathways, in this case for accessing course material, not only shape attention in the moment but also inform how she is likely to move through the world in the future. Ann did not take time to think about why she clicked on certain links in order to access her PDF readings; these movements were merely operations. However, this short operation of accessing and beginning to read a PDF file from her course management system was meaningful, to echo the chapter epigraph, for illustrating how the mundane ways that "we face as well as move" can be understood as "organized rather than casual" (Ahmed, 2006; p. 15). In turn, even short temporal gaps—when the PDF was loading or the course management system failed to open quickly—were meaningful to the materials that entered the scene. During these lapses in time, Ann was driven to fill her moments with as many materials as possible and tended not to sit and wait just staring at the computer screen. She chose to engage in another activity rather than simply "wasting" time. These breakdowns in the flow of time opened the door for the "thick sequencing" of time that I have already described. Over time, Ann had become accustomed to turning toward particular materials over and over again. Mark Nunes (2006) has called this a "drift logic," in which movements in online space lead to wandering outside intended places rather than a logic of efficiency of movement. These actions seemed natural, so much so that she barely recognized that she was making them. However, her actions were also greatly impacted by the nearby materials that lined her pathways, making proximities an important facet of attention. Proceeding forward from this materially rich understanding of attention requires shifting toward ways of valuing attention as a construct that is not only affected by brains but also by bodies.

Building Proximities as an Extension of Mindfulness

I have emphasized Ann's example and the relationship of proximities to attention because this intersection represents a new issue for digital literacies instructors and researchers to consider. A common approach to supporting attention is to emphasize mindfulness. In *Net Smart*, for instance, Howard Rheingold (2012) discusses making students aware of attention by helping them become more conscious of their choices during moments in which they have the choice of whether or not to react to—or interact with—a given stimulus. To use his language: "I can suggest a simple, powerful idea: you can learn to be aware of how you shift your attention when your phone buzzes or your laptop screen beckons" (2012, p. 36). He continues by announcing that "introducing a little mindfulness where previously there had been none can be insidiously irrevocable" (2012, p. 36). Mindfulness, as positioned by Rheingold, brings conscious awareness to attention choices that have become tacit or transparent. This means not checking a cell phone or social media feed merely because it has become an automatic behavioral response but rather because it is a purposeful, desired action given one's purposes and circumstances.

Mindfulness provides a useful framework to issues of attention and mobile device use by teaching people who have grown up with smartphones and laptops to shift to more consciously monitoring their existing habits and personal repertoires during moments of use. However, if we think of mindfulness in dialogue with the examples presented thus far in this chapter, shifting to a more conscious and aware use of technologies would only shift so much about how attention was invented in each instance. Ann, Dean, and Carly were not "unaware" of their technology interactions. Instead, they were "oriented" in particular ways to their technologies, which affected the kinds of interactions they were likely to have. We might recall the example in Chapter 2, for instance, in which Kim is likely to check her email during a composing session because she has created a desktop notification alert that sends a small banner across her screen when she receives an incoming email. In these situations, the phenomenological experience of materials in one's surroundings matter to attention.

As I explained in Chapter 3, Sara Ahmed in *Queer Phenomenology* uses the term orientations to describe the tendencies, built over time and through experience, through which bodies relate to space, time, people, and materials

(2006). Orientations influence what materials are in the immediate surroundings and describe one way that discursive (constructed through encounters with cultures, institutions, and designs) and material (constructed in matter) realms are experienced together in human movements. Mobile composers experience complicated orientations that have been shaped by prior experiences. The rhythms, pacing, and intensities that emerge from institutions, experiences, communication technologies, patterns of consumption, participation in workplaces, and a range of other life experiences people encounter in everyday practice shape their pathways and expectations of how time should be conceptualized and managed (Glennie & Thrift, 1996; Sharma, 2014). Richard Ling (2004), for example, described how temporalities associated with using watches and clocks vary significantly from those associated with mobile devices. In turn, people oriented toward one or the other devices tend to organize their approach to time differently.

Orientations and proximities are useful lenses for thinking through the shape that attention takes, especially concerning the thick sequencing of interactions. By teaching students not only to practice mindfulness but also to read and potentially reconstruct proximities and orientations, digital literacy instructors have the opportunity to help students become more aware of the designed nature of materials that weigh on their perceptive capacities and to become purposeful about cultivating their nearness to or distance from them. This way of thinking about intention and purpose repositions the attention that matters to literacy as more than an internal phenomenon shaped by conscious control. Instead, our embodied movements matter, as they put us into particular positions with reference to the agential environments and materials through which we move. Understanding the constructedness of embodied movements is important, for instance, for addressing the very real concerns that Shirky and others have suggested are associated with how often social technologies are designed to capture and maintain attention for marketing purposes.

To compose and to live attention differently, students will need to organize new proximities, which in turn shape alternatives for how, what, and when materials enter salience. These alternative proximities and orientations may mean constructing new surroundings that reduce the need for the "constant checking" or the continuous partial attention (Stone, 2007) that keeps students glued to mobile phones. However, helping students construct alternative orientations will also mean helping students extend beyond the normative expectations of attention commonly habitualized through classrooms with lecturing teachers and/or PowerPoint slides at the front of the room. Ann, Dean, and Carly may suggest that many students are already pushing far beyond those norms of attention in their transient literacy practices.

Ignoring the range of students' attempted attention innovations may leave educators out of touch with the realities of their lived experience, but it may also leave educators out of touch with the changing realities of attention outside the relatively unusual dynamics of classrooms.

Conclusion: Attention and Lived Composing Practices

Attention, from the perspective developed in this chapter, is active, embodied, performed, and mediated. It is composed. Its compositions are shaped by designs external to the brain and performed in dialogue with them, emerging in relationship to environments, materialities, and infrastructures. Because it is in part a product of how we orient to materials around us, attention is central to networked mobile composing. Because the number of potential materials to be taken up is always greater than what can be noticed, studying attention provides a means for understanding students' naturalized values as lived through their orientations to materials and the places that gather them. Ann, Dean, and Carly's cases emphasize thick sequencing, as students make use of many materials, and sometimes multiple goals, in order to expand the potential of their time. This thickness is characteristic of other students in the study as well, suggesting that a feeling of overwhelm at the amount to be accomplished is a central tension of life with mobile devices. Individuals are continually staging environments and allowing proximities that they establish to shape what comes into the action and what fades into the background.

In spite of this thickness, "distraction" does not quite capture the complexity of the staging and braiding that enables the sequences of interactions I observed through research. Rather than the result of a simple generational divide or changing hard wiring of the brain, these thick sequences exist at complex intersections of materials. People carry in some of these materials, and some of them exist as a part of the public commons that is available in the places they have decided to dwell. Importantly, when these materials are braided together into the thick sequences of transient literacies, the practices themselves are agentive in creating habits that affect future attention practices.

These constructed proximities over time become orientations that are individually unique, while still deeply culturally and ideologically inflected. How people move depends upon how they are situated but also to the meaning that they have assigned to situations. What we find in our focus is individualized, even while affected by social forces. That means that some regulars and sporadic visitors find the Technology Commons difficult for establishing deep focus and concentration, while others seek it out for respite. That also means that social media can be easily regulated for some students and overly burdensome for others.

Chapter 6: Conclusion— Reorienting to the Realities of Mobile Composing

> I am struck by how transient are the images of myself as a writer when compared to the seemingly immutable picture of the author limned by the scene in the garret.
>
> –Linda Brodkey, 1984, p. 396

Student practices like those I have traced in this book challenge educators to reposition ourselves beyond the vantage point typically afforded to university instructors: to pay attention to and care about the unfamiliar pathways that students take through even the simplest writing tasks. Most students chart their own course through writing assignments, inventing their own processes of composing just as much as their own products. Those processes are heavily influenced by the materials that surround students—those that have been taken up into their habitual routines for writing, as well as those that they encounter as the result of making decisions about where and when to write.

Electronic mobile composing devices do not create this situation. By contrast, composing has long been transient and transitory; pens and pencils and notebooks supported writing along life's pathways long before smartphones and laptops were integrated into many people's everyday lives. However, the presence of networked devices expands the surroundings composers can easily reach in transient locations. In addition to co-present people and materials, composers have proximity to the expanse of the internet. Mixing this abundant information into the social and material context of local places has direct effects on composing, in part by shaping agencies such as sociability and attention that are constructed by interacting materials.

Rather than focusing attention only on screens or on movements through space, understanding composing under these conditions requires looking across geographical and informational orientations to the multiple materials that anchor composing choices. I argue that doing so will require us to interrogate normative models of both attention and sociability as they intersect with composing processes and conditions. Instead of positioning interactions among co-present people as a "general good," we will need to see them instead as "means to aid particular kinds of work" (Heerwagen et al., 2004, p. 525). Furthermore, we will need to look beyond the concepts of "distraction" and "multitasking" in order to develop new language for describing the practices of writing with and in the presence of burgeoning information. We will need to think about when and how strategic detachment from mobile devices can support moments of relative "social quiet" for contemplation, as well as understanding when abundant sociability can expand the potential for composing connections. Users of networked mobile technologies are invited into new forms of collaboration that will benefit from strategic reflection and habit-building.

With the goal of supporting future research and teaching practices, this concluding chapter connects what I have learned about composing with networked mobile technologies to a broader framework for composing. After reviewing key insights from research participants, I momentarily step back from the focus on mobile networked technologies by arguing for a conception of composing based in bodily rather than cognitive intention, where embodiment is understood as contingent and interconnected with time, space, and technology and where movement, location, and positioning matter to composing experience. I argue that this way of approaching composing demands that we look beyond the classroom, decentering school environments from the central place we often assume they have in composing practice or indeed composing learning. I introduce this idea in order to argue for a model of composing learning or development that is more aware of bodily habit and routine across contexts. From this perspective, writing learning becomes more than a cognitive practice of metacognition or a social practice of apprenticeship. In addition to social and cognitive dimensions, composing learning has a physical, spatial dimension that relates directly to how composers develop relations of familiarity and habit with places, materials, and information. These relationships become participants in composing, such that learning to write differently often means explicitly changing habits of movement, location, and proximity. While Nedra Reynolds (2004) and Terese Monberg (2009) have made similar arguments about writing development, I want to reposition the spatial proximities that matter to learning as always existing as hybrid spaces experienced across multiple social and informational domains. The information domains that accompany mobile device use can no longer be positioned as distractions from the real movements that take place in physical space, but instead should be understood as integrated with physical materials in composing practice.

To illustrate, I weave my ideas about composing with a final research narrative about a student named Ray. Ray, an African-American male health sciences major, used campus social spaces for gaming as well as writing for his composition course. I anchor this concluding chapter to *Transient Literacies in Action* with Ray's case because I ended my analysis convinced that Ray's activity in the Technology Commons epitomizes the complexities and contradictions of habits, routines, sociability, attention, and interactions among information domains and resources that are enmeshed in transient literacies. Those of us who encounter students in higher education institutions often glimpse only a limited view of these practices that can be clouded by our positions of power in classroom settings and assumptions about when and what kinds of sociability and attention are appropriate to writing learning. After reading Ray's experience of movement across university spaces, the chapter draws on this narrative to broaden the scene of where transient literacies matter. I conclude with a closer look at how transient literacies intersect with contemporary academic, workplace, and community literacy domains.

The Conditions of Networked Mobile Composing

To begin, I want to review some key insights from research participants. First, and most simply, paying close attention to networked mobile composing reveals the ways in which composing relies upon dynamic, shared resources experienced across physical and online environments. Composing with a laptop is always a cross-domain experience. It means moving within densely interconnected physical and information space, and it means invoking personal repertoires alongside materials, attitudes, and values that emerge from elsewhere. This is a relatively simple idea on the surface; however, the way that we discuss composing tasks and situations frequently highlights the material dimension of composing that describes where and how writing will eventually circulate. For example, we tend to think of social media posts as "digital writing" or as research papers as "academic writing," failing to account for the way that social media posts are composed in physical places that are impacted by how attention has been redirected to online spaces through phones or laptops or how research papers are composed with technologies that place their production in close proximity to online information and platforms. These kinds of categorizations are useful, but obscure the realities of the conditions of their production.

Participants in this research situated a range of "academic" and "digital" genres into hybrid spaces, though they frequently discussed physical and online spaces as separate rather than interconnected. Take, for example, Kim in Chapter 3 who chose Gone Wired as a workspace for academic composing purposefully as an alternative to her home and campus office because of its ambiance, as well as its ability to create temporary privacy. She had an intuitive sense of what each physical place offered and could position herself in ways that enabled positive interactions. Things became more complicated for Kim and others, however, as they began to position shared social spaces as layered with information spaces. Planning composing as an activity invoking both online and offline materials was more complicated for the students in this study. Ed, for instance, noted that he came to Gone Wired to study but frequently found himself surfing the internet instead.

Students also struggled to find ways to work across physical and online environments when composing as groups. For example, recall that the business students Charlotte, Owen, and Gabriel discussed in Chapter 2 had a difficult time bringing their multiple individual habits and assumptions into alignment when composing a business plan together. As we know from Amanda Bemer, Ryan Moeller, and Cheryl Ball (2009), students composing in flexible shared social places of the university often do not configure their environments in ways that might best support their needs. This case study suggested that they likewise may be less well prepared to reconfigure the interpersonal dynamics of collaboration, as layered in physical and information spaces. As I argue through their case, students are often unprepared for how bringing the wide-ranging materials of composing into alignment requires methods of negotiation that are more complex than a frame for collaboration based in shared presence or simply "showing up in the same place."

If my research reveals that online and physical information realms are complexly interconnected in composing, an implication of this idea is that "presence" in composing is also complicated. Presence, by which I mean the condition of being in a place, cannot be defined only by co-location in physical space when we experience life across online and physical spaces. The participants in this study reveal the ways in which being in a place for writing is a complex exercise of negotiating multiple social channels. While writing with laptops, participants such as Micah and Sal in Chapter 4 gesture to how presence continually shifts as composers sense and monitor physical and online places simultaneously. Recall that an important part of Sal and Micah's basic negotiations in Chapter 4 when using mobile devices involved practices to prioritize when to foreground each of the multiple, overlapping social platforms that existed around them simultaneously. Ann, discussed in Chapter 5, demonstrates how this passive social contact made coursework present during moments when she was socializing. Thus, "presence" looks different when we carry networked mobile devices: the same ties that scholars such as Sherry Turkle (2011) identified as responsible for social disconnection and isolation in face-to-face presence are simultaneously creating the potential for online connection.

Participants in this study further illustrate how the experience of being in time compounds for composers alongside the experience of being in space. Participants in the research were consumed by strategies to manipulate time by making it thick and dense with interaction. Much in the same way that social learning theories emphasize what Colin Lankshear and Michel Knobel (2011) called "innovation and productiveness," the students in this book use layered spaces in time to expand the scene of their learning. Rather than thinking in linear paths, they were constantly looking for ways to get there faster by expanding the horizon of possibility in a moment. For example, in Chapter 5, I discussed how Ann, Dean, and Carly sought to make time "thicker" by multiplying the channels and potential resources that participated in their composing in a given moment. The presence and potential of mobile technologies enabled ways of orienting to coursework that would be unlikely to happen without them: the continual monitoring of class content for Ann, and the expansion of a learning scene through the dual laptop setup for Dean and Carly. As these spatial and temporal practices become second nature, composers may find themselves overwhelmed by layering more materials or interactions than can be fully engaged. In addition to cultivating social potential, networked mobile device users also need to be prepared to make overt decisions about when to disengage from one or more of the multiple channels through which they interact with others. For students in this research, planning to disengage from people they knew or from co-present others appeared to be easier than disengaging from online contacts.

Resituating Composing Learning Through a Focus on Bodily Intention

These lessons about the temporal, spatial, and informational experience have implications for composing that extend beyond an interest in networked mobile devices. Participants' practices emphasize how what writers do when they compose is a matter that depends upon material participants in dialogue with their own orientations and tendencies. Composing movements are often habitual—the ways that we move can be carefully calculated, but often emerge from more pragmatic lived realities connected to convenience, access, schedules, comfort, and perceptions and realities of acceptance. While this issue has been of interest to writing researchers and educators as it relates to how to keep attention in the classroom when students use mobile devices, we have not done enough to think outside that context to the problem (and opportunity) of understanding composing's materiality outside of it. As dimensions of materiality beyond the classroom become entangled in composing, we are seeing arrangements that create new interpersonal and attentional contexts. At the same time, people are constantly adjusting and changing as they move through the world with technologies, developing with and alongside them.

These conditions point to the need for a conception of writing learning that is more engaged with how experiences of navigating information-rich

spaces leave legacies of prior experience and tendency written onto composing bodies. Because people's composing processes are continually in a slow
process of becoming with technologies and the infrastructures that support
them, we need ways to understand the slow bodily learning that participates
alongside cognitive changes and social apprenticeship in how composers
develop. This necessarily will mean decentering the classroom as central to
our inquiries into writing development. Classrooms are sometimes meaningful and memorable to our becoming as writers, but they represent only slivers
in the expanses of experience that add up to inform a moment of action in
the present. Caring about composing from this perspective means that we
need a better understanding of how composers become with technologies,
as devices, platforms, and their social positioning likewise change and enable
new possibilities. In short, I am arguing for an approach to composing that
situates composers as more fully embodied, where embodiment is not separate from space, time, and technology. To explain what I mean, I now turn to a
final narrative from a research participant named Ray, emphasizing a process
of material apprenticeship in his transient literacy practices where his movement in information-rich spaces outside the classroom provide a metaphor
for the act of becoming with technology-rich environments.

Ray's Story: Habits of Movement, and Building Transient Literacies

Ray squinted through thin, silver-rimmed glasses as he leaned back and
adjusted positions in the chair he had been sitting in for hours. His battle was
set to begin. Crossing one leg over the other, he waited for the opening screen
that would soon display the text, "Injustice: Gods Among Us," over the top
of a city skyline, gray streets set off by purple sky.[10] As the title screen trailed
away, two arch-enemies entered the screen: Superman and Lex Luthor. This
clash, just one confrontation in a long history between the two characters,
transpired on a flat panel display screen supported by an X-box game system in the Technology Commons. Normally the screens set into the walls of
the learning commons displayed weather conditions, hours of operation, and
brief instructional programming; however, on this day space administrators
had connected an X-Box game system to this screen. According to a yellow
post-it note affixed to the console, the game system was open for public use

---

10   Injustice: Gods Among Us is a video game developed by NetherRealm Studios and
copyrighted by Warner Brother Entertainment Inc. Released by the creators of Mortal
Kombat, this "fighting game" used legendary DC Comics characters like Batman and Wonder
Woman to populate battle scenes. Players could maneuver a character through the game's
storyline or play a battle mode that entailed one-on-one fights between characters in "arenas"
or story environments.

until 3 p.m., when the Commons reached peak usage hours. And, so at noon on a Tuesday, Ray sat in a small chair usually paired with the café-style tables across the room. Someone had placed the chair in front of the display screen about three feet away—close enough for the relatively short cable on his wired personal game controller to reach the game system. Although the room was full of other students, Ray was playing Injustice alone, his focus intense on the screen as he gripped the game controller.

Ray typically played video games alone, located among other students dotted on couches and café tables across the large room. These were other students mostly tuned into collaborative projects or their own technologies. While he sometimes met people in the Technology Commons who wanted to join him, Ray shared that his participation in gaming was less motivated by any desire to interact socially and more connected to his love for the game: for his desire to *practice*, in the sense that the term means enacting an activity repeatedly with the goal of honing an ability or craft. At first I was unsure about whether to include activities like Ray's in my analysis. After all, Ray was not using a laptop. However, gamers were a ubiquitous presence in the Technology Commons whenever space administrators hooked up the X-Box and left it connected for students to use during open hours. The gamers' presence also invoked tensions I have referenced throughout this book: Was this an appropriate use of a shared university commons space, one that university and space administrators should support? Or just a waste of time?

Cultivating Habits of Movement

I decided to look more closely at what Ray was doing while he played Injustice through the lens of my interest in transient literacies. I'm not a game studies scholar and do not have much experience playing video games, so my observation came from the perspective of an outsider. However, what I noticed immediately was the game involved routine sequences of interaction that involved engaging with materials in the game world to build the potential for new forms of movement. While Injustice was far from a "learning game," it engaged Ray in what James Paul Gee (2003) in *What Video Games Have to Teach Us About Learning and Literacy* referred to as the "active learning" of gameplay.

Let me explain. The gist of Injustice is that it is a fighting game in which users battle an opponent by controlling a character or avatar of their choice. To locate fights, players also choose an arena in which to conduct their battles, a meaningful task because different environments for fighting create the possibility of interacting with different possible materials gathered in the varied places. Each arena contained a different set of "interactables" or materials in a scene that could be manipulated to one's advantage (e.g., cars, robots, and a plane rudder in the Metropolis arena) and thus shaped the possibilities for how to gain advantage in a given battle. Furthermore, each environment also included different "stage transitions" that moved a battle from one place to another internal to the environment.

Watching Ray for over an hour of gameplay was interesting because he often replayed battles in which he had previously failed, now armed with new knowledge about the possible interactions of the environment. If Ray lost a battle within a particular environment, he would enter the game scenario again with the new memory of how the skills and materials in this particular arrangement might intersect in practice the next time. Of course, things were not exactly the same when he entered an environment for a second time, but there were certainly overlapping dimensions of the experience that could inform what he understood about sequencing interactions. For example, when he re-played a battle among Wonder Woman and Solomon Grundy for the second time, Ray did not precisely retread the steps of his prior fight. Instead of maneuvering to the right side of the Hall of Justice and using the stage transition to relocate characters, he pushed Wonder Woman to the left toward two statues that could be used as props. This time he won, which meant he'd proceed on to a different battle next time.

Intuitively, Ray went about orienting his avatar to each battle's arena's chosen environment by moving in ways that enabled him to continually test each form of knowledge, to sometimes succeed and sometimes fail, and then to return to the scene again with a clearer sense of the potential for materials, movements, and interactions. Ray picked up new knowledge about each battle setting and environment through practice and, in so doing, began to orient to each environment in new ways. He honed his movements (through an avatar in this case) through training as he repeated sequences of interaction with small differences (Hawhee, 2004). When he became bored, succeeded repeatedly, or found himself continually failing, he changed up the combination and tried out something else.

In the same way that I learned something about how students negotiate face-to-face interactions with strangers by paying attention to their social media use, I found myself reflecting on how the knowledge that students develop about places and materials of composing could be described in terms that are similar to the way that Ray proceeded through the game. Ray negotiated the potential of constructed material objects and architectures, invoking and mobilizing their potential as just one part of what it meant to play. Kurt Squire's (2007) learning heuristics for fighter games helped me understand more about the kinds of practical skill building that are associated with becoming an expert at this kind of game: someone who practices the game as an art rather than as a "buttonmasher." While I admit to reading this activity through my own uninitiated lenses, I began to see in Ray's game play an illustration of how we build the practical knowledges of navigation and location that I have described in this book as transient literacies.

Learning to Move

By enacting the repeated strategy for gameplay that I have just described, Ray *learned to move* within the game through an intricate but implicit trial and error system. By continually interacting in similar but slightly different ways, he built many kinds of knowledge that helped him begin to predict the sorts of interactions that were likely to take place when he engaged elements of the game. As he played, he was first building knowledge about the capacity of the avatar he had chosen. Each character was associated with different strengths and weaknesses and playing within a particular embodiment meant taking on the material constraints of that avatar. Likewise, all opponents in the fight were embodied differently and also worked within their individual constraints. Turning outward, Ray was also gaining a knowledge of what materials each environment offered that could be taken up and used by those in the fight. He was learning about the arrangement of the setting and its rooms, the interactables that were included within them, and where to find them. In order to be an expert fighter, one needed to understand the capacity of those materials relative to the strengths and constraints of one's own avatar and the opponent's. Interacting with those materials also sometimes changed the environment itself in meaningful ways, and so it was important to understand how those reactions might alter the fight. Finally, Ray learned how to position one's avatar within the time and space of the setting in order to access interactions, as well as to avoid potential danger.

It is possible that I have stretched the metaphor of Ray's gameplay too far, but my point is not to reflect on Injustice as a game. Instead, I would like to shift to a more speculative mode in order to suggest that we think about students' acquisition of transient literacies through a model that works a bit like Ray's gameplay. That is, students often develop routines of spatial and informational navigation and location through informal trial and error. In this model, they internalize the capacity of places and their materials as they intersect with their own strengths and weaknesses, picking up bits of knowledge about where they can plug in laptops or whether they can find the quiet sections in a large, open room. This learning is rarely articulated, but instead is picked up implicitly. Students develop and carry embodied knowledge about the relationship between their own practices, the capacity of environments and materials, and specific ways of positioning themselves that lead to interactions with materials that support their goals.

Of course, there are significant differences between the stakes of the trial-and-error approach to learning that Ray enacts to build embodied knowledge as he plays a fighter game and the realities of learning about the capacity of materials, environments, and one's own resources as a composer. For one, the video game allows for failure in ways that composing choices often do not. When Ray realizes that a given strategy is not working in the game, he loses a battle and starts that game over. However, when students fail to gain access to needed materials or mobilize materials that do not perform in expected ways, the stakes associated with failure in writing are much higher. As the previous chapters have illustrated, different kinds of danger are associated with testing out the capacity of ourselves and our surroundings when composing. For students who work with(in) the mediated attentional, social, and spatial dynamics this book describes, strategies for planning and orchestrating practices cannot be positioned an avoidable "add-on" to the important cognitive work of literacy. Without these coordinative practices that might easily be dismissed as lower-level skills (i.e., "time management," or "getting organized"), students cannot achieve literacy practices.

Furthermore, the metaphor is limited in a different way. Game players often do not rely on their embodied movements alone to build a practical knowledge of how to move through a game space. Instead, they conduct meta-play moves: they read guides, they talk to friends, they watch others, they check Wikis. In short, they enter into a vast online and physical information expanse that enables them to get new perspective on the possibilities of gameplay. In other words, their movements do not have to be isolated from alternative co-existing experiences and perspectives that can alter their own understandings in ways that create interventions into habits and routines. We are not stuck in habits forever. Composers learn through bodily habit and intention, but also need the opportunity to gain alternative perspectives on their orientations and proximities—to learn what other people do, to understand alternative technological platforms, to get outside their prior experience of the game.

Getting Outside the Game

This is where we can turn back to the embodied material approaches that I cited in Chapter 3. Recall that Paula Moya (2002) argued that interpretation of experience can become an object that participates in our ongoing becoming, shaping who we are and how we operate. In addition to learning transient literacies through a trial and error experience of interaction with places and technologies, composers can also get outside the game so to speak, through reflections on their own orientations and/or experiences with alternative positionings. In classroom learning, study projects that ask students to explicitly focus on mapping their use of time, space, or materials create the possibility for making interpretations of experience agentive objects in our ongoing development as composers. Outside the classroom, our networked mobile devices can help with these self studies. Both Apple and Android mobile phones, for instance, offer time tracking capabilities that can help composers better understand their use of their phone in general and applications in particular. Furthermore, the vast range of available productivity software can push composers into new kinds of habits and orientations to their technological platforms in ways that encourage reflection. As we talk through these ways of interpreting experience and potentially ask students to use them in classes, it is important not to resort to normative conceptions of how time should be spent while writing. Instead, these tools should be positioned as ways to gain new perspective on experience. Furthermore, it is important to talk with students about the data, privacy, and surveillance implications of these tools.

As for Ray's ability to get outside the game, I learned much from our conversation about his transient literacies outside the game and, in particular, his movement through campus spaces. In particular, his academic writing coursework was mediated across a range of shared university social environments that were likely invisible from the perspective of his instructor and that were both physical and online at once. At the level of his movement through campus, completing his academic writing coursework enacted an uptake of multiple shared social environments and materialities afforded by the university: not only the university library where he put fingers to laptop keys but also the Technology Commons where he prepared himself to focus. The environments and materialities that mattered to his composition course extended beyond those we might expect from the vantage point of an instructor (i.e., in his case, the library). During the summer I met him, Ray set up shop in the Technology Commons three or four times a week for a couple of hours at a time to play video games like Injustice. He was enrolled in two courses during that summer session and understood his video game moments (or hours) in the Technology Commons as directly related to what would come next in his day: heading over to the library next door to do homework on his laptop. In particular, Ray said he used the Technology Commons for "relaxation" directly after his two-hour-a-day, five-day-a-week, six-week summer first-year composition course. He had made a habit of stopping in the Technology Commons after his class. He would play on the X-Box when available, or socialize on his laptop when it was not. Afterward, he would head to the library to complete the work due for the next day. On the day I had videoed him, he said that he had "just wanted to take a little break before I started working on my essay." Places like the Technology Commons were important to his routines for completing academic coursework even if no visible materials connected to his essays were present there. Although he did not elaborate about why and I did not push him on the point, Ray told me that he did not keep a game system in his campus dorm room. The Technology Commons served as a location where he could play within limits imposed by the commons rules and the general public accountability associated with shared and not owned resources. He also mentioned that his current summer course was his second attempt at first-year composition, and that he felt that he would be more successful this time around.

Ray had just finished his first year as a student at UCF. Had his current orientations developed out of a trial and error of his first year spent attempting to navigate the demands of coursework in different ways? Had he initially kept a game console in his dorm room? Had he initially struggled with how to integrate academic coursework with the interests and the activities that felt most comfortable and "relaxing" (in his words) to him? What did it look like when Ray used his laptop now for writing his essays for first year composition? Had he similarly cultivated habits of mind and body that enabled him to focus when moving within the space of the device screen? If so, could we have better supported his experience in transitioning to university-level academic writing? And what can we better do to support students of color like Ray who may face invisible barriers to entry to some academic spaces? How do we better support students whose bodies orient differently from the norms assumed by contemporary space designers?

Intervening in the mundane ways of operating that are developed and ingrained through personal orientations is rather unusual territory for composing pedagogies. As I've already suggested, instructors can engage with transient literacies by helping students better understand the important role that materials play in their own composing habits and repertoires, with the understanding that learning outside the classroom affects what happens within it. This kind of engagement takes the step of helping students alter their own personal settings and repertoires for transient literacies through processes that ask them to think more deeply and consciously about the kinds of knowledge like those listed above, as well as to practice the kind of ongoing negotiation and adjustment that Ray illustrates.

While engaging with students' personal repertoires is important for literacy educators and researchers, this is not the only important site for intervention. If we broaden the lens, another way to change Ray's performance would be to take on the role of game designer (or space designer) and to change the kinds of materials he can access and how they function. Thus, it is also important to think about transient literacies from the perspective of space design. The impacts of learning spaces were long underresearched (Temple,

2008); however, increased attention to the changing learning needs and social demands of contemporary students has meant a burgeoning transdisciplinary literature on learning space design, as well as increased interest on how places beyond the classroom impact composing (Carpenter et al., 2015; Kim & Carpenter, 2017). Literacy and writing researchers and educators increasingly have a responsibility to become involved with campus, workplace, and community space design choices, as the arrangement and elements of these places participate directly in composing learning.

A related implication of these realities is that literacy educators must pay closer attention to how places, and the materials, technologies, and information that gather in them, become associated with values and subtle "standards" of use that impact students' literacy practices (Lampland & Star, 2009; Star & Ruhleder, 1996). While this project was limited in that it did not explicitly focus on LGBTQ people, disabled people or people of color, it did allow students to disclose identity categories if they desired and these aspects of personhood did impact what spaces were available, useful, or usable to them. The standards that develop in places create unexpected divides—particularly for students who lack access to the latest mobile technologies or to knowledge needed to effectively negotiate the so-called freedoms enabled by the potential for movement. The designers who arrange literacy environments and/or who imbue materials with potential for interaction play an important role in shaping the potential for how transient literacies take place. Thus, supporting transient literacies also involves working directly to design better environments and materials for supporting mobile work, learning, and organizing, as well as better environments and materials for learning about how to practice transient literacies. As we design spaces for work and learning, creating designs that help enact more awareness and better trajectories will require designers to address some common challenges for the design and use of social places.

Adjusting Our Frames of Reference

I have argued that caring about transient literacies means decentering the classroom as the center of our composing worlds. Thus, I want to move forward by discussing a larger set of domains for transient literacies. The intertwining of physical and information space in composing practice is not just an issue for composition classrooms. As mobile networked technologies such as laptops complexify composing, composers will need to create processes for composing in contexts where practices will always be in tension with other "modes of ordering" that conflict with their goals (Knox et al., 2008; Law 1994; Law & Mol 2002). Transient literacies will be important to students across the domains of academic, workplace, and community life. For this reason, it is important to understand how the experiences of effectively negotiating spaces and information are crucial across university, workplace, and civic spaces.

University Space Design and Use

Academic writing educators, researchers, and administrators increasingly must pay attention to varied environments where academic literacies take place: not only classrooms but also in the offline and online social locations where students dwell. As students traverse the university, physical and virtual classrooms anchor student social networks held together by course rosters, but the writing required to participate in classrooms takes place beyond them in dorm rooms, apartment buildings, common areas, student unions, libraries, and other flexible, temporary workspaces. Though we know that students use these common places in a variety of ways, relatively little research has focused on how students move across the university through shared, technologically rich common spaces for completing school tasks (Rossitto & Eklundh, 2007). Increasingly, the strategy for contemporary academic institutions, libraries, and university writing programs has been to decrease investment in hard-wired desktop computer labs and increase the investment in "BYOT," or bring your own technology labs (Hochman & Palmquist, 2009; Miller-Cochran & Gierdowski, 2013). Furthermore, as universities have become more aware that students seek flexible space for the informal learning that accompanies coursework (and that such spaces are important for university financial concerns related to student recruitment and retention), many have advocated for student commons areas or learning spaces that have been designed to be occupied temporarily for study, projects, and extracurricular activities (Temple, 2008). Many university libraries, in particular, have been redesigned as information commons centers where students work individually and collectively while located with others (Forrest & Halbert, 2009). Other relevant campus design trends include a move toward active learning classrooms, where traditional lecture halls are transformed into decentered spaces that lack front lecterns and support active student reading, writing, and speaking during courses (Oblinger, 2005).

These university environments invite students to use mobile technologies for literacy practice and by definition require students to organize mobile literacy environments that will support their goals. In so doing, they also invite the movement across online and offline spaces that is central to students' uses of these devices. To support students who practice academic writing in these spaces, educators need to become more aware of their opportunities and challenges. Furthermore, designers and administrators of such spaces need more insight into actual practices within them that extend beyond student satisfaction surveys. Research has already shown that responses to these remediations range from ignoring them to actively taking advantage of one or more of their affordances, while downplaying others (Bilandzic & Foth, 2014). Transient literacies require better investment in ambient social media, signage, and other resources that lower barriers to collaboration among peers and increase the chances that students will connect with resources (Hemmig et al., 2012). Given the influence of environments, materials, and infrastructures on literacy practices, the design of and experiences of social places should become the direct concern of academic writing educators and administrators, not just library and university facilities committees.

As the previous sections suggest, transient literacies redirect academic writing teachers, researchers, and administrators to how literacy is shaped by the materials, locations, and technologies that are accessible to students, given their unique social and cultural positioning. Teaching students academic composing means cultivating a new sensitivity to and investment in the environments that surround students when they produce academic coursework outside the classroom. Paying more attention to embodied habits or bodily intentions, as well as their constructions and constraints, should rank alongside the new focus on issues such as the importance of "dispositions" on literacy learning (Yancey et al., 2014). The possibilities for how students experience place depend upon what is accessible to individuals as they approach them (i.e., based on race, gender, sexuality, employment status, abilities, and so forth), as well as how they have oriented to the places of their literate lives. Furthermore, possibilities for places shift and change as locations are shaped and reshaped by the social networks and institutions that assign them meaning.

In addition to thinking more about where students complete academic writing and what technologies support them, it will be important to consider how students access social resources that shape composing in online spaces, as well as how they disconnect from social spaces when they are dangerous, lead to fractured thinking, or surface-level engagement with tasks. Many students are learning these skills through practice and without explicit training, and in doing so, are also shifting the way that they interact with other students. As Charles Crook and Gemma Mitchell (2012) describe, many students seek opportunities to complete coursework alone in atmospheres where other students are also working separately. The need to find "blank space" fuels many individuals' movements into commons spaces; however, the same ideas apply to interactions in online spaces. To simply identify students as "distracted" by online spaces can downplay how important these social dimensions are to students' experiences.

The particular tools and assignments that can support students in this way could vary significantly. For example, like many instructors, I have designed and taught a first-year writing class that is organized around places of the university. In this course, students read about the impact of place on a range of practices and then conduct original research within the place that focuses on describing the impact of materials in that place on the literacy interactions there. If I were teaching this course again, I would not only ask students to focus on articulating the social interactions, meaningful materialities, and hidden infrastructures associated with campus places but also focus on how the assemblies of online places work hand-in-hand with these places in everyday experience. My goal would be to hone students' attention not only to developing a knowledge of places and their capacities, but also to thinking in more complex ways about the intersections between online and physical space.

Workplace Design and Use

While it might seem strange to think of college students in this way, many students share something important in common with professional and technical communicators: a lack of official sanctioned place for completing composing tasks that are essential to their roles. Professional and technical communication educators, researchers, and administrators need to understand transient literacies, as more and more professional writing takes place outside traditional office environments, on the move or in redesigned social open offices that require actively cultivating temporary foundations to ground literacy practices. Dave's case in Chapter 2 highlights how many professionals bear a burden of assembling the social contexts that will ultimately lead to their career advancement or sustainment. In his case, this means both cultivating social potential by maintaining contacts with those who will potentially read and sponsor his writing (see Pigg, 2014a for a more detailed discussion) and cultivating enough privacy and social distance from others to arrange a production setting that means that achieving writing is possible. Both of these moves are coordinative, existing often invisibly alongside the important work of composing the texts that will eventually be taken up as the valued products of his knowledge work. Workplace researchers have long understood that professionals do not only work in personal offices anymore (Büscher, 2014; Costas, 2013; Czarniawska, 2014; Fealstead et al., 2005), but we need more focus not only on how these professionals navigate their lack of office space but also with how they use online spaces in tandem to anchor their careers.

To elaborate, whether resulting from self-employment, the opportunity to telecommute, or the spatial reorganization of offices, many professionals organize their productivity in shared places that layer disparate social inter-actions, technological and communication infrastructures, and rhetorical demands. For telecommuters and other mobile workers, the locational coor-dination of completing work practices will be an ongoing struggle in coming years. As research participants who took part in Clay Spinuzzi's (2012) study of co-working suggested, coffee shops may not be the most conducive loca-tion for professionals to maintain this balance, particularly for knowledge workers who live in urban areas and can financially invest in the co-work-ing environments he describes. Furthermore, while the cubicle may still be the prototypical in-office workspace, organizations are redesigning offices to support and provoke new kinds of movement. Across recent innovations in office design, places increasingly must support worker flexibility by pro-viding temporary dwellings for a user population whose needs shift with the task to which they are attending at the moment. Thousands of organiza-tions are thus realizing changes to physical office space that were planned, predicted, and theorized with the first signs of large-scale ubiquitous com-puting.[11] In 1999, Norbert A. Streitz and his colleagues worked from a frame-work in the field of Computer Supported Collaborative Work (CSCW) to describe the impact of having desktop computers become the primary (and often the only) information source in an office space. In order to relieve some of the problems of centralizing all information in this way, Streitz et al. sug-gested augmenting physical space so that it provides more spatial flexibility and mobility, while offering technological configurations that "go beyond desktops" (1999, p. 122).

Google's offices may be the most famous example. The 1.1–million-square-foot GooglePlex in Mountain View, California, has no private offices and combines a mix of semi-private and communal workspaces with cafés, court-yards, and green roofs (Goldberger, 2013). In a similar vein, the *Washington Post* online (2013) documented the new Washington, D.C., offices of Accen-ture, a consulting, technology, and outsourcing firm that designed new offices "with the millennial worker in mind." Accenture uses *hot desking* or *hoteling*. Employees reserve temporary office spaces that fit temporary needs; their available choices range from large conference rooms to smaller collaboration suites with café tables. When working "alone," Accenture's employees might sit on opposite sides of a long conference-style table wearing headphones and attending to separate projects. According to the managing director of the firm's Washington-area office, Accenture settled on this flexible, social office space as a result of the demands of "20-something workers."

---

11   Office Snapshots, available at http://officesnapshots.com, offers an archive of these emerging office space designs. The archive offers a glimpse into how offices are responding to the needs of mobile, distributed work.

Both examples align with a broader movement toward designing collaborative workplaces to support organizational team processes, while offering the potential for more personal flexibility. Scholarship in ubiquitous computing from the 1990s imagined that workplaces of the future would come stocked full of technologies built into the environment (such as smart desks and smart walls). While research and design to augment workspace continues, personal mobile devices largely support professional writing that takes place across hotdesks, open offices, and remote workspaces. The public health crisis of 2020, for example, shifted the use of mobile workspaces from a situation experienced by few to one that was suddenly the reality for workers who had long depended on offices to structure their workflows and practices. Mobile devices enable individuals to transform settings typically associated with one kind of activity into one that's appropriate for others—even when those places do not intuitively support their use (e.g., Laurier's 2004 example of "doing office work" while driving). As many new converts to working at home have experienced, redesigning a workspace around mobile technologies also implies new demands on employees. For example, Accenture's office does not include desk phones because "employees are set up to do all of their phone communication over the Web." The reconfigurations also mean that employees must actively seek privacy when they need to devote focused attention to tasks without interruption. Although offices are trending to emphasize collaboration, open office setups in which colleagues work side-by-side in large, undivided rooms can be detrimental to worker productivity and satisfaction. Large-scale survey research ($N = 10,500$) commissioned by the design firm Steelcase found that 98 percent of the most highly satisfied surveyed workers were able to concentrate easily in their workspaces and 95 percent could find distraction-free places to work with teams; however, 31 percent of workers overall had to leave their offices to find adequate space to complete work tasks (Congdon et al., 2014). While the movement in office design has been toward designing toward access to other people, design for collaboration also has had the unintended effect of pushing workers and their work outside the office.

Professional and technical communicators have the opportunity to contribute knowledge about the demands of networked mobile composing that can shape the design and administration of workspaces. Furthermore, students preparing to enter contemporary workplaces need to understand these dynamics and to prepare for composing within them after graduation. Within organizational office design, John Peponis et al. (2007) argued that workplace design for knowledge-intensive work must support users' access to two kinds of cognitive resources: people with diverse expertise and needs and the "material inscriptions" that are constructed, circulated, and accessed as part of knowledge work. They suggest that users of space need to be able to intuitively interpret the relationships among space designs and work processes, and these relate to co-presence, co-awareness, and interaction patterns. Two models are often used to attempt to support this access: 1) a flow model in which offices mirror the flow of communication and information associated with a task or 2) a "serendipitous communication model" in which informal spaces for inter-action are highlighted in ways that encourage individuals to interact without plans. Peponis et al. advocate strongly for the first of these two choices; that is, tailoring spatial designs to activities rather than expecting that informal space will in of itself generate the kinds of communication necessary.

With this in mind, professional writing courses at the undergraduate level are another important site for having students think through how the kinds of materials that become participants in their composing will be central to the possibilities for what and how they read, write, think, and communicate. As a grounding for professional writing pedagogy, teaching future professionals to prepare to compose with environments that continually change represents a full turn from professional and technical communication pedagogies based on a twentieth century industrial production model, which needed students prepared to enter and fit into highly organized and controlled hierarchies where they responded to knowable situations and executed predetermined protocols (Henry, 2000; Spinuzzi, 2015). In this context, the closed and unam-biguous network that Jim Henry called the "hermetic environment of a class-room" provided a spatial academic training ground that disciplined students for the grammar and correctness that mattered most to success. The para-digms for success associated with twenty-first century knowledge work differ significantly from this emphasis on correctness, and coordination is central to creating the conditions through which successful workplace writing can take place.

Although social workspaces are a matter of choice for some, they are a matter of necessity for others, particularly during moments of public health crisis or for technical and professional writers who work in contract posi-tions and seek modular, flexible space to support multiple projects and tasks (Hart-Davidson, 2013; Spinuzzi, 2012). Between telecommuting, non-traditional offices, and independent careers, it is important that future profes-sional writers understand the importance of transient literacies to everyday professional and technical writing practices that students are likely to expe-rience at some point in their careers. As more professionals become respon-sible for coordinating their methods and practices, the domain of personal knowledge management may also become increasingly important. Personal knowledge management focuses on "helping individuals to be more effective in personal, organizational, and social environments" (Pauleen, 2009, p. 221). Frequently, personal knowledge management is associated with effectively using technological resources to facilitate productivity, which increasingly means individual and organizational attention management (Davenport & Völpel, 2001). However, personal knowledge management also includes life-long and social learning, as well as an interest in "the development of skills and attitudes that lead to more effective cognition, communication, collabo-ration, creativity, problem solving, lifelong learning, social networking, lead-ership, and the like" (Pauleen 2009, p. 222). These are the kinds of skills that will increasingly create a foundation for effective writing on the job. Having students map relevant networks and resources rather than focusing merely on the reproduction of genres introduces coordination in powerful ways for students, who can simultaneously become better connected to the materials that support workplace literacies in fields that matter to them.

Community Space Design and Use

Finally, transient literacies directly impact community literacies. Mobile device use directly impacts civic and public spaces, which are increasingly commercial, personal, and atomized (Welch, 2008). Cafés, coffee shops, bookstores, and other kinds of socially shared spaces long associated with conversation and community gathering are often becoming more private and are inhabited for relatively long periods of time for personal or professional reasons. Thus, coffeehouses and other locations that may not be explicitly designed as workspaces are often mobilized for professional or academic activities because they can support moving people, mobile technologies, and their interactions. Community literacy educators, researchers, and admin-istrators need to understand transient literacies in order to better support community exchange, given the shifting realities of how contemporary young people integrate civic and community concerns into their saturated lives and inhabit community environments that have shifted due to the impact of net-worked devices. These shifts are more complex than many of us have under-stood, as cell phones and internet networks support new positive forms of public and community interaction (Hampton et al., 2015; Jennings & Zeitner, 2003) but also have negative effects as well (Purdy, 2017).

On the one hand, it is not surprising that cafés, coffeehouses, and other traditional community locations often become crowded with readers, writers, and collaborators who are also workers or students: individuals huddled over laptops taking advantage of clean space, wireless networks, and available sup-plies of caffeine. The rise of telecommuting and *remote homeworking*, which I have already mentioned, has enabled workers to make use of such spaces while conducting their business by logging into organizational networks from remote locations of their choice (Fealstead et al., 2005; Halford 2005). Remote employees using coffeehouses for work have become so ubiquitous that mass media publications have begun to promote cafés as central to productivity and efficiency. For example, Conor Friedersdorf's (2011) "Working Best in Coffee Shops" in the Atlantic not only links coffeehouses with the relatively recent rise of internet-based telecommuting via the web but also describes how coffeehouses offer writers a sense of deadline (they do close, after all) while also exposing them to being monitored by others in public. With others holding you accountable, it seems more important to "look busy," Friedersdorf suggests. Wesley Verhoeve's (2013) "Why You Should Work from a Coffee Shop, Even When You Have an Office" in the popular online business publication *Fast Company* cites a lack of distractions and the community that develops around coffeehouses as stimuli for creativity. For those who would rather not leave home to experience what makes coffeehouses so useful, mobile device applications such as Coffitivity and Hipstersound even transport the environmental factors of cafés into personal workspaces. These mobile apps simulate the ambient sounds of cafés in order to help individuals supplement any workspace with the perfect level of audio intensity, or what they call "enough noise to work."

Students are taking over coffeehouses for writing, as well. In addition to my own prior research in this area (Pigg, 2014a, 2014b), Katie Zabrowski and Nathaniel Rivers (2015) use multimodal autoethnography to depict coffeehouses as respites that stimulate academic thinking. As they state, "writers are nomads in search of a place, and coffeehouses are an oasis for such weary travelers." Michael J. Faris (2014) further describes the appeal of coffeehouses for academic writing in a narrative for the *College Composition and Communication* special issue on "Locations of Writing." He argues that coffeehouses "offer something that the isolation of an office cannot: a lively, social atmosphere with ambient sounds, movements around that serve not to distract but to help me focus, and my own ability to move" (2014, p. 22). Drawing on the social mapping service, FourSquare, Faris mapped his recent (impressive) composing practices across coffee shops spanning two countries and at least six U.S. states. Even when coffee shops have "regulars" who visit them often, they are continually inhabited by new people who become actors in continually changing scenes.

Transient literacies require new ways of encouraging civic and public dialogue in these shifting environments. Coffeehouses are different places in the morning, when patrons stop in to grab a quick cup of coffee (Laurier, 2008), than during evening hours, when others stop by to spend a few hours catching up with friends after work. Of course, cafés and coffeehouses differ from sanctioned offices or university social places because their informal hot desking system is grounded by a different economic imperative. Cafés generally do not have strong economic motivation to support individuals' productivity; these businesses succeed financially only insofar as they can support themselves through the "rent" they collect from individuals who buy their goods when they claim space within them. However, plenty of cafés and patrons are willing to comply with this unofficial contract. Thus, locations that are not officially institutionalized as domains of work become sites for workspace because they allow autonomy for individuals to enter, stay for a while, and use the place to their own ends. However, the freedom to take up new spaces for literacy, whether as a student or a professional, leads to challenges, as neighborhood spots once positioned as anchors for face-to-face conversation are increasingly re-envisioned as places for personal work or leisure.

For a small way of inviting students to think through these issues, I supported students in a rhetoric and civic engagement class in conducting research to trace, map, and visualize the places of the university that support civic rhetorical action. To frame this class-wide investigation, students read about contemporary challenges to public space and organizing, as well as the fears that civic engagement is declining among younger populations. This assignment challenged students to articulate the kinds of materials associated with supporting contemporary civic life so that they could identify relevant places on campus where these materials might be found. Students then proceeded to visit relevant places associated with civic engagement, to define how they were meaningful. Their final step was to share and map these places on a public online shared networked map that would articulate these linkages and connections.

In spite of how we address these issues, it is clear that community and civic literacy practices will be affected by the changes to place and sociability associated with transient literacies. The question of how to keep places more conducive to civic and community concerns, while also enabling people to use the social potential of networked mobile technologies will be increasingly important to civic and community literacy. Already, scholars such as Nathaniel A. Rivers' (2016) have argued for using geocaching and other locative media interactions as a means for engaging students in the complex relations among public rhetoric and place, and writing and literacy scholars will need to continue to teach ways to help students become more aware of how environments are intertwined with public and community literacies. Alongside this issue, community literacies will continue to contend with the challenges of organizing affiliations in contexts where personal desires drive many people's turn to common places. Sociologist John Urry (2007) linked mobility to emerging "interspaces" where "groups come together, involving the use of phones, mobiles, laptops, SMS messaging, wireless communications and so on, often to make arrangements on the move" (p. 12). The social interactions that characterize the community commons are taking different forms, and often laptops are supporting face-to-face contact. Keith N. Hampton, Oren Livio, and Lauren Sessions Goulet (2010), for example, stressed that Wi-Fi users in public parks often use their laptops intentionally for active participation in the public sphere. In order to both create new places that support face-to-face contact among community members and to help people make new social connections, community literacy researchers, educators, and administrators will need to directly address these blurred boundaries.

Conclusion: New Collaborations

While new environments are being continually designed to support mobile technologies, the presence of shared social space oriented to mobile technologies does not guarantee accessibility or usefulness, much less collaboration, increased participation, or decentralization. However, just as clearly, the presence of a cell phone also automatically does not mean students' inattention or the inability to focus. Throughout the preceding chapters, *Transient Literacies in Action* has explored how students orchestrate literacy practices in educational and extracurricular landscapes affected by networked, technologies that move with them. The analysis has suggested that in order to understand the practices associated with these technologies, we must look beyond devices and their users into the complexly mediated mobile surround that shifts and is shifted by mobile practices. These environments matter. For example, it is qualitatively meaningful that students like those portrayed in the opening scenes of *Digital Nation* are using laptops (often for Facebook and online shopping, according to their professors) in classrooms, which shifts the building blocks for literacy in those environments in ways that affect the attention, sociability, and resource needs of the students composing with them. As soon as the students in the film open up those laptops, they are faced with negotiating potential from across social spheres, which might include information deemed interesting, amusing, or that has been programmed to appear in the scene based on prior choices. The environments cultivated around them are temporary and depend upon ongoing interactions that both construct and change the materials around them. These changing environments have implications for how students interact with academic, professional, and civic contexts.

While I was writing this book, my next-door neighbor opened a new coffee shop in a nearby part of town that was experiencing revival. Its location reminded me of the Gone Wired Café. He and his partner had rented a commercial space that had been vacant for some time along a well-traveled north-south corridor. I asked him whether he was seeing much mobile work there. "Everyone wants to work," he told me, obviously disappointed. "They're all mad that we don't have Wi-Fi. But just because it's a pretty space, doesn't mean it's for your work" (personal communication, 2015). Only a few months after the café opened, he was still avoiding adding the Wi-Fi network, trying to preserve a hub for leisure and conversation. But he already realized his business was affected by the common use of cafés as a workspace. He navigated the design of the space realizing that both the livelihood and ambiance of his café depended upon it.

His experience resonated with what I have learned about how many of us position third places that traditionally have been so important to community life. On the one hand, we want them to be pure and free from the intrusions of our technologies, but on the other hand, to exclude the social potential that is enabled by those devices means another kind of void, in which we lack access to the tools that many of us use to get involved with and learn about our communities. To be sure, there are real problems associated with how people and information are blurred when so much social contact is mediated by mobile composing and its technologies. Even my own use of the term "materials" to include both people and technologies as participants or building blocks in literacy practices has the effect of blurring the differences among relationships with people and those with devices. As both human and textual social resources are increasingly blurred with and experienced as "information," it becomes easy to dehumanize people—to treat them as objects of information. For example, in Chapter 5, Micah and Sal often treated people around them almost identically to their technological feeds: an issue and potential problem that I want to suggest is actually more complex than mere "alone togetherness." John Seely Brown and Paul Duguid (2000) associated this attitude with what they call an infocentric approach to information design: the problem of conceiving of relational work merely as "information handling." When the importance of social interaction is underemphasized, the long-term success of projects can suffer. As they suggest, desks are useful for more than propping up laptops, offices create learning environments through social proximity, and work patterns are difficult to disrupt once in place. The environments around information processing tools shape capacity to use these tools. In this case, the attitudes that led to a difficulty in collaborating on a team writing task (Chapter 5) may arise from similarly blurred boundaries among people and information.

Across contexts for literacy practice, researchers and educators will increasingly need to account for how the digital reserves that follow us through life are more than backdrops behind the "real" activity of literacy. Social media and other online information platforms actively participate in literate action; they co-constitute it. Many students bring a seemingly infinite collection of virtual places into connection as they read, write, and collaborate. These places are accessible whenever they carry the appropriately charged handheld or wearable computing device in a place that offers connection to one of many types of wireless networking connections. It can be easier to imagine contemporary students exist on a completely different plane from their instructors, with different tendencies and maybe even different brains. The more challenging but richer way forward will be to perceive, care, and engage with composing habits and environments differently, knowing that none of us can predict the changes that we all face as we practice literacy in contingent worlds. Certainly, navigating the public health crises of 2020 has been a reminder that at any moment we may have to reform habits that support attention and sociability in composing in response to events beyond our control.

With the movement from the cubicle to the coffee shop and from the classroom to the commons, everything depends upon what happens to materials when and where they interact. Importantly, different bodies interact with places and the materials within them differently. There is no generalized distracted, isolated, or indifferent student body, just as there is no ideally and perfectly-positioned student consumer, fully packaged with the correct BYOT (bring-your-own-technologies) spirit and tools. The realities are much more complex. Ray and the other students I have chronicled represent new faces of academic, professional, and community literacies today. Luckily, we have every opportunity to learn with them.

References

Ackerman, J. & Oates, S. (1996). Image, text, and power in architectural design and workplace writing. In A. H. Duin & C. J. Hansen (Eds.), *Nonacademic writing: Social theory and technology* (pp. 81–121). Lawrence Erlbaum.

Adler-Kassner, L. & Wardle, E. (2015). *Naming what we know: Threshold concepts of writing studies.* Utah State University Press.

Ahmed, S. (2004). *The cultural politics of emotion.* Routledge.

Ahmed, S. (2006). *Queer phenomenology: Orientations, objects, others.* Duke University Press.

Alexis, C. (2016). The material culture of writing: Objects, habitats, and identities in practice. In S. Barnett & C. Boyle (Eds.), *Rhetoric through everyday things* (pp. 83–95). University of Alabama Press.

Allen, F. R. (2011). The knowledge commons: Reasserting the library as the heart of campus. *College and Research Library News, 72*(8), 468–492. https://doi.org/10 .5860/crln.72.8.8619.

Alsop, R. (2015). A generation of cyberslackers. *BBC Generation Work.* http://www .bbc.com/capital/story/20150408-a-generation-of-cyberslackers.

Alvermann, D. E. & Moore, D. W. (2011). Questioning the separation of in-school from out-of-school contexts for literacy learning: An interview with Donna E. Alvermann. *Journal of Adolescent and Adult Literacy, 55*(2), 156–158. https://doi .org/10.1002/jaal.00019.

Anzaldúa, G. (1999). *Borderlands/La Frontera: The new mestiza.* Aunt Lute Press.

Anzaldúa, G. E. (2002). Now let us shift . . . The path of conocimiento . . . inner work, public acts. In G. E. Anzaldúa & A. Keating (Eds.), *This bridge we call home: Radical visions for transformation* (pp. 540–578). Routledge.

Atkinson, P. (1988). Ethnomethodology: A critical review. *American Review of Sociology, 14,* 441–465. https://doi.org/10.1146/annurev.soc.14.1.441.

Augé, M. (1995). *Non-places: Introduction to an anthropology of supermodernity.* Verso Books.

Bailey, R. & Tierney, B. (2002). Information commons redux: Concept, evolution and transcending the tragedy of the commons. *The Journal of Academic Librarianship, 28*(5), 277–286. https://doi.org/10.1016/s0099-1333(02)00319-1.

Bandura, A. (1977). *Social learning theory.* Prentice Hall.

Barad, K. (2007). *Meeting the universe halfway: Quantum physics and the entanglement of matter and meaning.* Duke University Press.

Baron, N. S. (2008). *Always on: Language in an online and mobile world.* Oxford University Press.

Barone, M. (2020). Millennials choose the path of least resistance. *National Review.* http://www.nationalreview.com/article/375008/disconnected-generation-michael -barone (Reprinted from Millennials choose the path of least resistance, 2014, April 4, *The Washington Examiner*).

Barton, D. & Hamilton, M. (1998). *Local literacies: Reading and writing in one community*. Routledge.

Bazerman, C. (2013a). *A rhetoric of literate action: Literate action*, vol. 1. The WAC Clearinghouse; Parlor Press. https://wac.colostate.edu/books/perspectives/literate action-v1/.

Bazerman, C. (2013b). *A rhetoric of literate action: Literate action*, vol. 2. The WAC Clearinghouse; Parlor Press. https://wac.colostate.edu/books/perspectives/literate action-v2/.

Beaton, C. (2017). Why millennials are lonely. *Forbes under 30 column*. https://www.forbes.com/sites/carolinebeaton/2017/02/09/why-millennials-are-lonely/#9750 c897c351.

Bemer, A. M., Moeller, R. M. & Ball, C. E. (2009). Designing collaborative learning spaces where material culture meets mobile writing processes. *Programmatic Perspectives, 1*(2), 139–166. https://cptsc.org/wp-content/uploads/2018/04/vol1-2.pdf.

Benhabib, S. (1992). Models of public space: Hannah Arendt, the liberal tradition, and Jurgen Habermas. In C. Calhoun (Ed.), *Habermas and the public sphere* (pp. 73–98). MIT Press.

Bilandzic, M. & Foth, M. (2014). Learning beyond books—Strategies for ambient media to improve libraries and collaboration spaces as interfaces for social learning. *Multimedia Tools and Applications, 71*, 777–795. https://doi.org/10.1007/s110 42-013-1432-x.

Blyler, N. R. & Thralls, C. (Ed.). (1993). *Professional communication: The social perspective*. Sage.

Blythe, S. & Gonzales, L. (2016). Coordination and transfer across the metagenre of secondary research. *College Composition and Communication, 67*(4), 607–633.

Bolter, J. D. (2001). *Writing space: Computers, hypertext, and the remediation of print* (2nd ed.). Lawrence Erlbaum.

Bowker, G. C., Star, S. L. (2000). *Sorting things out: Classification and its consequences*. MIT Press.

boyd, d. (2010). Social network sites as networked publics: Affordances, dynamics, and implications. In Z. Papacharissi (Ed.), *Networked self: Identity, community, and culture on social network sites* (pp. 39–58). Routledge.

Brandt, D. (1992). The cognitive as the social: An ethnomethodological approach to writing process research. *Written Communication 9*(3), 315–355. https://doi.org/10 .1177/0741088392009003001.

Brandt, D. & Clinton, K. (2002). Limits of the local: Expanding perspectives on literacy as a social practice. *Journal of Literary Research 34*(3), 337–356. https://doi.org /10.1207/s15548430jlr3403_4.

Brodkey, L. (1984). Modernism and the scenes(s) of writing. *College English, 49*(4), 396–418. https://doi.org/10.2307/377850.

Brooke, C. G. (2009). *Lingua fracta*. Hampton Press.

Brooke, R. (1999, 1988). Underlife and writing instruction. In L. Ede (Ed.), *On writing research: The Braddock essays, 1975–1998* (pp. 229–241). Bedford St. Martin's.

Brown, J. S. & Duguid, P. 2000. *The social life of information*. Harvard Business School Press.

Brueggemann, B. J., Feldmeier White, L., Dunn, P. A., Heifferon, B. A. & Cheu, J. (2001). Becoming visible: Lessons in disability. *College Composition and Communication, 52*(3), 368–398. https://doi.org/10.2307/358624.

Bruffee, K. (1984). Collaborative learning and the "conversation of mankind." *College English, 46*(7), 635–652. https://doi.org/10.2307/376924.

Burnett, R. E., Cooper, A. & Wellhausen, C. A. (2013). What do technical communicators need to know about collaboration? In J. Johnson-Eilola & S. Selber (Eds.), *Solving problems in technical communication* (pp. 454–478). University of Chicago Press.

Büscher, M. (2014). Nomadic work: Romance and reality. A response to Barbara Czarniawska's "Nomadic work as life-story plot." *Computer Supported Collaborative Work, 23*, 223–238. https://doi.org/10.1007/s10606-013-9194-6.

Canagarajah, A. S. (2013). *Translingual practice: Global Englishes and cosmopolitan relations.* Routledge.

Carpenter, R., Selfe, R., Apostel, S. & Apostel, K. (Eds.). (2015). *Sustainable learning spaces: Design, infrastructure, and technology.* Computers and Composition Digital Press. http://ccdigitalpress.org/sustainable.

Carr, N. (2011). *The shallows: What the internet is doing to our brains.* W. W. Norton.

Casey, E. (1996). How to get from space to place in a fairly short stretch of time: phenomenological prolegomena. In S. Feld & K. Basso (Eds.), *Senses of Place* (pp. 13–52). School of American Research Press.

Casey, E. (2009). *Getting back into place: Toward a renewed understanding of the place-world* (2nd ed.). Indiana University Press.

Congdon, C., Flynn, D. & Redman, M. (2014, September 30). Balancing "we" and "me". *Harvard Business Review, 92*(10), 50–57.

Cooper, M. (1986). The ecology of writing. *College English, 48*(4), 364–375. https://doi.org/10.2307/377264.

Cope, B. & Kalantzis, M. (Eds.). (2000). *Multiliteracies: Literacy learning and the design of social futures.* Routledge.

Costas, J. (2013). Problematizing mobility: A metaphor of stickiness, non-places, and the kinetic elite. *Organization Studies, 34*(10), 1467–1485. https://doi.org/10.1177/0170840613495324.

Cowan, B. (2005). *The social life of coffee: The emergence of the British coffeehouse.* Yale University Press.

Cresswell, T. (2006). *On the move: Mobility in the modern western world.* Routledge.

Crook, C. & Mitchell, G. (2012). Ambience in social learning: Student engagement with new designs for learning spaces. *Cambridge Journal of Education, 42*(2), 121–139. https://doi.org/10.1080/0305764x.2012.676627.

Czarniawska, B. (2014). Nomadic work as life-story plot. *The Journal of Collaborative Computing and Work Practices, 23*(2), 205–221. https://doi.org/10.1007/s10606-013-9189-3.

Davenport, T. H. & Vopel, S. C. (2001). The rise of knowledge towards attention management. *Journal of Knowledge Management, 5*(3), 212–221. https://doi.org/10.1108/13673270110400816.

Davidson, C. N. (2011). *Now you see it: How the brain science of attention will transform the way we live, work, and learn.* Viking.

de Certeau, M. (1984). *The practice of everyday life*. Translated by Steven Rendall. University of California Press.

Delcore, H. D., Teniente-Matson, C. & Mullooly, J. (2014, August 11). The continuum of student IT use in campus apaces: A qualitative study. *EDUCAUSE Review*. http://www.educause.edu/ero/article/continuum-student-it-use-campus-spaces -qualitative-study.

de Souza e Silva, A. (2006). Interfaces of hybrid spaces. In A. Kavoori & N. Arceneaux (Eds.), *The cell phone reader: Essays in social transformation* (pp. 19–44). Peter Lang.

de Souza e Silva, A & Frith, J. (2012). *Mobile interfaces in public spaces: Locational privacy, control, and urban sociability*. Routledge.

DeVoss, D. N., Cushman, E. & Grabill, J. T. (2005). Infrastructure and composing: The when of new-media writing. *College Composition and Communication, 57*(1), 14–44.

Dias, P., Freedman, A., Medway, P. & Paré, A.. (1999). *Worlds apart: Acting and writing in academic and workplace contexts*. Lawrence Erlbaum.

Dickinson, G. (2002). Joe's rhetoric: Finding authenticity at Starbucks. *Rhetoric Society Quarterly, 32*(4), 5–27. https://doi.org/10.1080/02773940209391238.

Diehl, A., Grabill, J. T., Hart Davidson, W. & Iyer, V. (2008). Grassroots: Supporting the knowledge work of everyday life. *Technical Communication Quarterly, 17*(4), 413–434. https://doi.org/10.1080/10572250802324937.

Dobrin, S. I. & Weisser, C. R. (2002). Breaking ground in ecocomposition: Exploring relationships between discourse and environment. *College English, 64*(5), 566–589. https://doi.org/10.2307/3250754.

Dretzin, R. & Rushkoff, D. (2010). *Digital Nation*. FRONTLINE. https://www.pbs .org/wgbh/frontline/film/digitalnation/.

Drucker, P. F. (1999). Knowledge-worker productivity: The biggest challenge. *California Management Review, 41*(2), 79–94. https://doi.org/10.2307/41165987.

Duggan, M. (2013). Cell phone activities 2013. *Pew research center's internet and American life project*, September 19. https://www.pewresearch.org/internet/2013 /09/19/cell-phone-activities-2013/.

Eagleton, T. (1984). *The function of criticism*. Verso Books.

Ehret, C. & Hollett, T. (2014). Embodied composition in real virtualities: Adolescents' literacy practices and felt experiences moving with digital, mobile devices in school. *Research in the Teaching of English, 48*, 428–452.

Ellis, M. (2002). The devil's ordinary. *Cabinet, 8*. http://www.cabinetmagazine.org /issues/8/coffeehouse.php.

Ellis, M. (2004). *The coffee house: A cultural history*. Weidenfeld

Erickson, I., Jarrahi, M. H., Thomson, L. L. & Sawyer, S. (2014). More than nomads: Mobility, knowledge work, and infrastructure. EGOS Colloquium. http://www .jarrahi.com/publications/EGOS_Erickson_Subtheme52.pdf.

Eyman, D. (2015). *Digital rhetoric: Theory, method, practice*. University of Michigan Press.

Faris, M. J. (2014). Coffeehouse writing in a networked culture. *College Composition and Communication, 66*(1), 21–24.

Faris, M. J. & Selber, S. (2013). iPads in the technical communication classroom: An empirical study of technology integration and use. *Technical Communication Quarterly, 27*, 359–407. https://doi.org/10.1177/1050651913490942.

Fealstead, A., Jewson, N., Walters, S. (2005). The shifting locations of work: New statistical evidence on the spaces and place of employment. *Work, Employment and Society, 19*(2), 415–431. https://doi.org/10.1177/0950017005053186.

Fife, J. (2017). Composing focus: Shaping temporal, social, media, social media, and environments. *Composition Forum 35.* http://compositionforum.com/issue/35/composing-focus.php.

Fishman, T. & Yancey, K. B. (2009). Learning unplugged. In A. C. Kimme Hea (Ed.), *Going wireless: A critical exploration of wireless and mobile technologies for composition teachers and researchers* (pp. 35–49). Hampton Press.

Flanagan, M. (2014, June 6). The Classroom as arcade. *Inside Higher Ed.* https://www.insidehighered.com/views/2014/06/06/technology-classroom-distraction-students-essay.

Flower, L. & Hayes, J. R. (1981). A cognitive process theory of writing. *College Composition and Communication, 32*(4), 365–387.

Fonner, K. L. &, Roloff, M. L. (2012). Testing the connectivity paradox: Linking teleworkers' communication media use to social presence, stress from interruptions, and organizational identification. *Communication Monographs, 79*(2), 205–31. https://doi.org/10.1080/03637751.2012.673000.

Forrest, C. & Halbert, M. (Eds.). (2009). *A field guide to the information commons.* Scarecrow Press.

Fox, S. (2013). 51% of U.S. adults bank online. *Pew Research Center's Internet and American Life Project.* http://www.pewinternet.org/2013/08/07/51-of-u-s-adults-bank-online/.

Fraser, N. (1992). Rethinking the public sphere: A contribution to the critique of actually existing democracy. In C. Calhoun (Ed.), *Habermas and the public sphere* (pp. 109–142). MIT Press.

Friedersdorf, C. (2011, April 15). Working best at coffee shops. *Atlantic.* http://www.theatlantic.com/business/archive/2011/04/working-best-at-coffee-shops/237372/.

Frith, J. (2015). *Smartphones as locative media.* Polity Press.

Garfinkel, H. (1967). *Studies in Ethnomethodology.* Prentice Hall.

Garsten, C. (2008). *Workplace vagabonds: Career and community in changing worlds of work.* Palgrave Macmillan.

Gee, J. P. & Hayes, E. R. (2010). *Women and gaming: The SIMS and 21st century learning.* Palgrave Macmillan.

Geisler, C. (2004). When management becomes personal: An activity-theoretic analysis of palm technologies. In C. Bazerman & D. Russell (Eds.), *Writing selves/writing societies: Research from activity perspectives* (pp. 125–158). The WAC Clearinghouse; Mind, Culture, and Activity. https://wac.colostate.edu/books/perspectives/selves-societies/.

Gere, A. R. (1994). Kitchen tables and rented rooms: The extracurriculum of composition. *College Composition and Communication, 45*(1), 75–92.

Gergen, K. J. (2002). The challenge of absent presence. In J. E. Katz and M. Aakhus (Eds.), *Perpetual contact: Mobile communication, private talk, public performance* (pp. 227–241). Cambridge University Press.

Gillen, J. & Merchant, Gu. (2013). Contact calls: Twitter as a dialogic social and linguistic practice. *Language Sciences, 35*, 47–58. https://doi.org/10.1016/j.langsci .2012.04.015.

Glennie, P. & Thrift, N. (1996). Reworking E. P. Thompson's "Time, work-discipline, and industrial capitalism." *Time and Society, 5*(3), 275–299. https://doi.org/10.1177 /0961463X96005003001.

Godbee, B. (2012). Toward explaining the transformative power of talk about, around, and for writing. *Research in the Teaching of English, 47*(2), 171–197.

Goldberger, P. (2013, February 22). Exclusive preview: Google's new built-from-scratch GooglePlex. *Vanity Fair.* http://www.vanityfair.com/online/daily/2013/02 /exclusive-preview-googleplex.

Goswami, D. & Odell, L. (Eds.). (1986). *Writing in nonacademic settings.* Guilford.

Gordon, E. & de Souza e Silva, A. (2011). *Net locality: Why location matters in a networked world.* Blackwell.

Grabill, J. T. (1998). Utopic visions, the technopoor, and public access: Writing technologies in a community literacy program. *Computers and Composition, 15*(3), 297–315. https://doi.org/10.1016/s8755-4615(98)90003-2.

Graff, H. J. (1979). *The literacy myth: Cultural integration and social structure in the nineteenth century.* Transaction Publishers.

Grego, R. C. & Thompson, N. S. (2008). *Teaching/writing in thirdspaces: The studio approach.* Southern Illinois University Press.

Haas, C. (1996). *Writing technology: Studies on the materiality of literacy.* Lawrence Erlbaum.

Haas, C. & Witte, S. P. (2001). Writing as an embodied practice: The case of engineering standards." *Journal of Business and Technical Communication, 15*(4), 413–457. https://doi.org/10.1177/105065190101500402.

Habermas, J. (1989). *The structural transformation of the public sphere: An inquiry into a category of bourgeois society.* (T. Burger & F. Lawrence, Trans.). MIT Press. (Original work published 1962)

Halford, S. (2005). Hybrid workspace: Re-spatialization of work, organization, and management. *New Technology, Work, and Employment, 20*(1), 19–32. https://doi .org/10.1111/j.1468-005X.2005.00141.X.

Hampton, K. N., Goulet, L. S. & Albanesius, G. (2015). Change in the social life of urban public spaces: The rise of mobile phones and women, and the decline of aloneness over 30 years. *Urban Studies, 52*(8), 1489–1504. https://doi.org/10.1177 /0042098014534905.

Hampton, K. N. & Gupta, N. (2008). Community and social interaction in the wireless city: Wi-Fi use in public and semi-public spaces. *New Media and Society, 10*(6), 831–850. https://doi.org/10.1177/1461444808096247.

Hampton, K.N., Livio, O. & Goulet, L. S. (2010). The social life of wireless urban spaces: Internet use, social networks, and the public realm. *Journal of Communication, 60*, 701–722. https://doi.org/10.1111/j.1460-2466.2010.01510.X.

Haraway, D. J. (1991). *Simians, cyborgs, and women: The reinvention of nature.* Routledge.

Hart-Davidson, W. (2013). What are the work patterns of technical communication? In J. Johnson-Eilola & S. Selber (Eds.), *Solving Problems in Technical Communication* (pp. 50–74). University of Chicago Press.

Hart-Davidson, W., Bernhardt, G., McLeod, M., Rife, M. & Grabill, J. (2008). Coming to content management: Inventing infrastructure for organizational knowledge work. *Technical Communication Quarterly, 17*(1), 10–34. https://doi.org/10.1080/10572250701588608.

Hawhee, D. (2004). *Bodily arts: Rhetoric and athletics in ancient Greece.* University of Texas Press.

Hawk, B., Rieder, D. M. & Oviedo, O. (Eds.). (2007). *Small tech: The culture of digital tools.* University of Minnesota Press.

Hayles, N. K. (2008). Hyper and deep attention: The generational divide in cognitive modes. *Profession, 2007,* 187–199. https://doi.org/10.1632/prof.2007.2007.1.187.

Hayles, N. K. (2012). *How we think: Digital media and contemporary technogenesis.* University of Chicago Press.

Heath, S. B. (1983). *Ways with words: Language, life, and work in communities and classrooms.* Cambridge University Press.

Heerwagen, J. H., Kampschroer, K., Powell, K. M. & Loftness, V. (2004). Collaborative knowledge work environments. *Building Research and Information, 32*(6), 510–528. https://doi.org/10.1080/09613210412331313025.

Hemmig, W., Johnstone, B. T. & Montet, M. (2012). Create a sense of place for the mobile learner. *Journal of Library and Information Services in Distance Learning, 6,* 312–322. https://doi.org/10.1080/1533290x.2012.705175.

Henry, J. (2000). *Writing workplace cultures: An archaeology of professional writing.* Southern Illinois University Press.

Hesford, W. (2006). Global turns and cautions in rhetoric and composition studies. *PMLA, 121*(3), 787–801. https://doi.org/10.1632/003081206x142887.

Hindmarsh, J. (2009). Work and the moving image: Past, present, and future. *Sociology, 43*(5), 990–996. https://doi.org/10.1177/0038038509340723.

Hindmarsh, J. & Heath C. (2007). Video-based studies of work practice. *Sociology Compass, 1*(1), 156–173. https://doi.org/10.1111/j.1751-9020.2007.00012.x.

Hochman, W. & Palmquist, M. (2009). From desktop to laptop: Making transitions to wireless learning in writing classrooms. In A. C. Kimme Hea (Ed.), *Going wireless: A critical exploration of wireless and mobile technologies for composition teachers and researchers* (pp. 109–131). Hampton Press.

Hollet, T. & Ehret, C. (2017). Relational methodologies for mobile literacies: Intra-action, rhythm, and atmosphere. In C. Burnett et al. (Eds.), *The case of the iPad* (pp. 227–244). Springer.

Husserl, E. (1970). *The crisis of European sciences and transcendental phenomenology.* (D. Carr, Trans.). Northwestern University Press. (Original work published 1936)

Ito, M. (2009). Introduction. In K. Varnelis (Ed.), *Networked Publics* (pp. 1–14). MIT Press.

Ito, M., Baumer, S., Bittanti, M., boyd, d., Cody, R., Herr-Stephenson, B., Horst, H. A., Lange, P. G., Mahendran, D., Martínez, K. Z., Pascoe, C. J., Perkel, D., Robinson, L., Sims, C. & Tripp, L. (2010). *Hanging out, messing around, and geeking out*. MIT Press.

Jackson, A. Y. & Mazzei, L. A. (2012). *Thinking with theory in qualitative research*. Routledge.

Jackson, M. (2009). *Distracted: The erosion of attention and the coming dark age*. Prometheus Books.

Jennings, M. K. & Zeitner, V. (2003). Internet use and civic engagement: A longitudinal analysis. *The Public Opinion Quarterly, 67*(3), 311–334. https://doi.org/10.1086/376947.

Johnson-Eilola, J. (2005). *Datacloud: Toward a new theory of online work*. Hampton Press.

Kaptelinin, V. & Nardi, B. A. (2006). *Acting with technology: Activity theory and interaction design*. MIT Press.

Katz, J. E. (2006). *Magic in the air: Mobile communication and the transformation of social life*. Transaction.

Keller, D. (2013). *Chasing literacy: Reading and writing in an age of acceleration*. Utah State University Press.

Kerschbaum, S. L. (2014). *Toward a new rhetoric of difference*. National Council of Teachers of English.

Kim, M. & Carpeter, R. (Eds.). (2017). *Writing studio pedagogy: Space, place, and rhetoric in collaborative environments*. Rowman & Littlefield.

Kimme Hea, A. (Ed.). (2009). *Going wireless: A critical exploration of wireless and mobile technologies for composition teachers and researchers*. Hampton Press.

Knights, D. & Willmott, H. (1989). Power and subjectivity at work: From degradation to subjugation in social relations. *Sociology, 23*(4), 535–558. https://doi.org/10.1177/0038038589023004003.

Knox, H., O'Doherty, D., Vurdubakis, T. & Westrup, C. (2008). Enacting airports: Space, movement and modes of ordering. *Organization, 15*(6), 869–888. https://doi.org/10.1177/1350508408095818.

Krause, S. (2014). Enough with the no laptops in classrooms already. stevendkrause.com. http://stevendkrause.com/2014/09/20/enough-with-the-no-laptops-in-classrooms-already/.

Lampland, M. & Star, S. L. (Eds.). (2009). *Standards and their stories: How quantifying, classifying, and formalizing practices shape everyday life*. Cornell University Press.

Lanham, R. A. (2006). *The economics of attention: Style and substance in the age of information*. University of Chicago Press.

Lankshear, C. & Knobel, M. (2011). *New literacies: Everyday practices and social learning*. Open University Press. (Orignial work published 2003)

Laurier, E. (2004). Doing office work on the motorway. *Theory, Culture, and Society, 21* (4/5), 261–77. https://doi.org/10.1177/0263276404046070.

Laurier, E. (2008). How breakfast happens in a café. *Time and Society, 17*(1), 119–134.

Lave, J. (1988). *Cognition in practice: Mind, mathematics, and culture in everyday life.* Cambridge University Press.

Law, J. (1994). *Organizing Modernity.* Blackwell.

Law, J. & Mol, A. (Eds.). (2002). *Complexities: Social studies of knowledge practices.* Duke University Press.

Leander, K. & Boldt, G. (2012). Rereading "A pedagogy of multiliteracies": Bodies, texts, and emergence. *Journal of Literacy Research, 45*(1), 22–46. https://doi.org /10.1177/1086296x12468587.

LeFevre, K. B. (1987). *Invention as a social act.* Southern Illinois University Press.

Lessig, L. (2001). *The future of ideas: The fate of the commons in a connected world.* Vintage Books.

Levinson, P. (2006). The little big blender: How the cellphone integrates the digital and the physical, everywhere. In A. Kavoori & N. Arceneaux (Eds.), *The cell phone reader: Essays in social transformation* (pp. 9–18). Peter Lang.

Lewis, L. (Ed). (2015). *Strategic discourse: The politics of (new) literacy crises.* Computers and Composition Digital Press. https://ccdigitalpress.org/strategic.

Lindquist, J. (2002). *A place to stand: Politics and persuasion in a working-class bar.* University of Oxford Press.

Ling, R. (2004). *The mobile connection: The cell phone's impact on society.* Morgan Kaufmann.

Ling, R. & Yttri, B. (2002). Hyper-coordination via mobiles in Norway. In J. Katz & M. Aakhus (Eds.), *Perpetual contact: Mobile communication, private talk, public performance* (pp. 139–169). Cambridge University Press.

Lorimer Leonard, R. (2013). Traveling literacies: Multilingual writing on the move. *Research in the Teaching of English, 48*(1), 13–39.

Lorimer Leonard, R. (2017). *Writing on the move: Migrant women and the value of literacy.* University of Pittsburgh Press.

Lynch, M. (1993). *Scientific practice and ordinary action: Ethnomethodology and social studies of science.* Cambridge University Press.

Lynch, M. (1999). Silence in context: Ethnomethodology and social theory. *Human Studies, 12,* 211–233. https://doi.org/10.1023/a:1005440501638.

McDowell, L. (1999). *Gender, identity, and place: Understanding feminist geographies.* Polity.

McKee, H. & DeVoss, D. (Eds.) (2007). *Digital writing research: Technologies, methodologies, ethical issues.* Hampton Press.

MacMillan, J. (2013, August 28). An office built with the millennial worker in mind. *Washington Post Online.* https://www.washingtonpost.com/business/capitalbusi ness/an-office-built-with-the-millennial-worker-in-mind/2013/08/29/9b6d70a6 -10b8-11e3-8cdd-bcdc09410972_gallery.html.

Mapes, A. C. & Kimme Hea, A. C. (2018). Devices and desires: A complicated narrative of mobile writing and device-driven ecologies. In J. Alexander & J. Rhodes (Eds.), *The Routledge handbook of digital writing and rhetoric.* Routledge.

Mark, G. & Su, N. M. (2010). Making infrastructure visible for nomadic work. *Pervasive and Mobile Computing, 6*(3), 312–323. https://doi.org/10.1016/j.pmcj.2009 .12.004.

Mark, G., Wang, Y. & Niiya, M. (2014). Stress and multitasking in everyday college life: An empirical study of online activity. In *Proceedings of the SIGCHI conference on human factors in computing systems* (CHI '14) (pp. 41–50). Association for Computing Machinery. https://doi.org/10.1145/2556288.2557361.

Massey, D. (1994). *Space, place, and gender.* University of Minnesota Press.

Mauk, J. (2003). Location, location, location: The "real" (e)states of being, writing, and thinking in composition. *College English, 65*(4), 368–388. https://doi.org/10.2307/3594240.

McCullough, M. (2013). *Ambient commons: Attention in the age of embodied information.* MIT Press.

McGonigal, J. (2011). *Reality is broken: Why games make us better and how they can change the world.* Penguin Books.

McNely, B., Spinuzzi, C. & Teston, C. (2015). Contemporary research methodologies in technical communication. *Technical Communication Quarterly, 24*(1), 1–13. https://doi.org/10.1080/10572252.2015.975958.

Merchant, G. (2012). Mobile practices in everyday life: Popular digital technologies and schooling revisited. *British Journal of Educational Technology, 43*(5), 770–782. https://doi.org/10.1111/j.1467-8535.2012.01352.x.

Meyrowitz, J. (1985). *No sense of place: The impact of electronic media on social behavior.* Oxford University Press.

Micciche, L. R. (2014). Writing material. *College English, 76*(6), 488–505.

Miller-Cochran, S. & Gierdowski, D. (2013). Making peace with the rising costs of writing technologies: Flexible classroom design as a sustainable solution. *Computers and Composition, 30*, 50–60. https://doi.org/10.1016/j.compcom.2012.12.002.

Mirtz, R. (2010). From information to learning: Pedagogies of space and the notion of the commons. *College and Undergraduate Libraries, 17*, 248–59. https://doi.org/10.1080/10691316.2010.487446.

Moeller, R. (2004). Wi-Fi rhetoric: Driving mobile technologies. *Kairos, 9*(1). http://kairos.technorhetoric.net/9.1/coverweb/moeller/introduction.html.

Monberg, T. G. (2009). Writing home or writing as the community: Toward a theory of recursive spatial movement for students of color in service-learning courses. *Reflections, 8*(3), 21–51.

Moore, J. L., Rosinksi, P., Peeples,T., Pigg, S., Rife, M. C., Brunk-Chavez, B., Lackey, D., Rumsey, Su. K., Tasaka, R., Curran, P. & Grabill, J. T. (2016). Revisualizing composition: How first-year writers use composing technologies. *Computers and Composition, 39*, 1–13. https://doi.org/10.1016/j.compcom.2015.11.001.

Moraga, C. & Anzaldúa, G. (Eds.). (1981). *This bridge called my back: Writings by radical women of color.* Persephone Press.

Moran, C. (1999). Access: The A-word in technology studies. In G. E. Hawisher & C. L. Selfe (Eds.), *Passions, pedagogies, and 21st century technologies* (pp. 205–220). Utah State University Press.

Moya, P. M. L. (2002). *Learning from experience: Minority identities, multicultural struggles.* University of California Press.

Mueller, D. N. (2009). Digital underlife in the networked writing classroom. *Computers and Composition, 26*, 240–250. https://doi.org/10.1016/j.compcom.2009.08.001.

Naas, C. (2010, Summer). Thinking about multitasking: It's what journalists need to do. *Nieman Reports.*

Nardi, B. A. (1996). Studying context: A comparison of activity theory, situated action models, and distributed cognition. In B. A. Nardi (Ed.), *Context and consciousness: activity theory and human-computer interaction* (pp. 69–102). MIT Press.

Nardi, B. & O'Day, V. L. (1999). *Information ecologies: Using technology with heart.* MIT Press.

Nordquist, B. (2017). *Literacy and mobility: Complexity, uncertainty, and agency.* Routledge.

Nunes, M. (2006). *The cyberspaces of everyday life.* University of Minnesota Press.

Oblinger, D. (2005, January 1). Leading the transition from classrooms to learning spaces. *EDUCAUSE Review.* https://er.educause.edu/articles/2005/1/leading-the -transition-from-classrooms-to-learning-spaces.

Oldenburg, R. (1999). *The great good place: Cafes, coffee shops, bookstores, bars, hair salons, and other hangouts at the heart of a community.* Perseus Book Group.

Olinger, A. (2014). On the instability of disciplinary style: Common and conflicting metaphors and practices in text, talk, and gesture. *Research in the Teaching of English, 48*(4), 453–478.

Ophir, E., Nass, C., Wagner, A. D. & Posner, M. I. (2009). Cognitive control in media multitaskers. *Proceedings of the National Academy of Sciences of the United States, 106*(37), 15583–15587.

Owens, D. (2001). *Composition and sustainability: Teaching for a threatened generation.* National Council of Teachers of English.

Pariser, E. (2011). *The filter bubble: How the new personalized web is changing what we read and how we think.* Penguin.

Parry, D. (2011, April 7). Mobile perspectives: On teaching mobile literacy. *EDUCAUSE Review.* http://www.educause.edu/ero/article/mobile-perspectives -teaching-mobile-literacy.

Pauleen, D. (2009). Personal knowledge management: Putting the "person" back into the knowledge equation. *Online Information Review, 33*(2), 221–224. https:// doi.org/10.1108/14684520910951177.

Pegrum, M. (2014). *Mobile learning: Languages, literacies, and cultures.* Palgrave Macmillan.

Peponis, J., Bafna, S., Bajaj, R., Bromberg, J., Congdon, C., Rashid, M., Warmels, S., Zhang, Y. & Zimring, C. (2007). Designing space to support knowledge work. *Environment and Behavior, 39,* 815–840. https://doi.org/10.1177/0013916506297216.

Pigg, S. (2014a). Coordinating constant invention: Social media's role in distributed work. *Technical Communication Quarterly, 23,* 67–87. https://doi.org/10.1080/1057 2252.2013.796545.

Pigg, S. (2014b). Emplacing mobile composing habits: A study of academic writing in networked social spaces. *College Composition and Communication, 66*(2), 250–275.

Pigg, S. (2015). Distracted by digital literacy: Unruly bodies and the schooling of literacy. In L. Lewis (Ed.), *Strategic discourse: The politics of (new) literacy crises.* Computers and Composition Digital Press. https://ccdigitalpress.org/strategic.

Pigg, S., Grabill, J. T., Brunk-Chavez, B., Moore, J., Rosinski, P. & Curran, P. (2014). Ubiquitous writing, technologies, and the social practice of literacies of coordination. *Written Communication, 31*(1), 91–117. https://doi.org/10.1177/07410883135 14023.

Price, M. (2007). Accessing disability: A nondisabled student works the hyphen. *College Composition and Communication, 59*(1), 53–76.

Prior, P. (1998). *Writing/disciplinarity: A sociohistoric account of literate activity in the academy.* Lawrence Erlbaum.

Prior, P. A. (2014). Combining phenomenological and sociological frameworks for studying literate practice: Some implications of Deborah Brandt's methodological trajectory. In J. Duffy, J. N. Christoph, E. Goldblatt, N. Graff, R. S. Nowacek & B. Trabold. (Eds.), *Literacy, economy, and power: Writing and research after literacy in American life.* Southern Illinois University Press.

Prior, P. A. & Hengst, J. A. (Eds.). (2010). *Exploring semiotic remediation as discourse practice.* Palgrave Macmillan.

Prior, P. & Shipka, J. (2003). Chronotopic laminations: Tracing the contours of literate activity. In C. Bazerman & D. R. Russell (Eds.), *Writing selves/writing societies: Research from activity perspectives* (pp. 180–238). The WAC Clearinghouse; Mind, Culture, and Activity. https://wac.colostate.edu/books/perspectives/selves -societies/.

Puig de la Bellacasa, M. (2012). "Nothing comes without its world": Thinking with care. *Sociological Review, 60*(2), 197–216. https://doi.org/10.1111/j.1467-954x.2012 .02070.x.

Purdy, S. J. (2017). Internet use and civic engagement: A structural equation approach. *Computers in Human Behavior, 17*, 318–326. https://doi.org/10.1016/j .chb.2017.02.011.

Putnam, R. D. (2000). *Bowling alone: The collapse and revival of American community.* Simon and Schuster.

Rainie, L. & Wellman, B. (2012). *Networked: The new social operating system.* MIT Press.

Reid, A. (2014). Laptops, pedagogies, and assemblies of attention. digitaldigs.com. https://profalexreid.com/2014/09/24/ laptops-pedagogies-and-assemblages-of-attention/

Reynolds, N. (2004). *Geographies of writing: Inhabiting places and encountering difference.* Southern Illinois University Press.

Rheingold, H. (2012). *Net smart: How to thrive online.* MIT Press.

Rice, J. (2012). *Digital Detroit: Rhetoric and space in the age of the network.* Southern Illinois University Press.

Rickert, T. (2013). *Ambient rhetoric: The attunements of rhetorical being.* University of Pittsburgh Press.

Rivers, N. A. (2016). Geocomposition in public rhetoric and writing pedagogy. *College Composition and Communication, 67*(4), 576–606.

Rossitto, C. & Eklundh, K. S. (2007, August). Managing work at several places. In *14th European conference on cognitive ergonomics Invent! Explore!* (ECCE '07) (pp. 45–51). Association for Computing Machinery. https://dl.acm.org/doi/abs /10.1145/1362550.1362562.

Royster, J. J. & Kirsch, G. E. (2012). *Feminist rhetorical practices: New horizons for rhetoric, composition, and literacy studies.* Southern Illinois University Press.

Rule, H. (2018). Writing's rooms. *College Composition and Communication, 69*(3), 402–432.

Sauer, B. A. (2003). *The rhetoric of risk: Technical documentation in hazardous environments.* Lawrence Erlbaum.

Sayers, J. (2009). Flat whites: How and why people work in cafés. *New Zealand Journal of Employment Relations, 34*(2), 77–86.

Schneider, B. (2002). Theorizing structure and agency in workplace writing: An ethnomethodological approach. *Journal of Business and Technical Communication, 16*(2), 170–195. https://doi.org/10.1177/1050651902016002002 .

Scribner, S. & Cole, M. (2001). Unpackaging literacy. In E. Cushman, E. R. Kintgen, B. M. Kroll & M. Rose (Eds.), *Literacy: A critical sourcebook* (pp. 123–137). Bedford/St. Martin's.

Selber, S. A. (2004). *Multiliteracies for a digital age.* Southern Illinois University Press.

Selfe, C. L. (1999). Technology and literacy: A story about the perils of not paying attention. *College Composition and Communication, 50*(3), 411–436. https://doi .org/10.2307/358859.

Sewell, G. & Wilkinson, B. (1992). Someone to watch over me: Surveillance, discipline, and the just-in-time labour process. *Sociology, 26*(2), 271–289. https://doi .org/10.1177/0038038592026002009.

Sharma, S. (2014). *In the meantime: Temporality and cultural politics.* Duke University Press.

Sheridan, D. M. & Inman, J. A. (Eds.). (2010). *Multiliteracy centers: Writing center work, new media, and multimodal rhetoric.* Hampton Press.

Shipka, J. (2011). *Toward a composition made whole.* University of Pittsburgh Press.

Shipka, J. (2016). Transmodality in/and processes of making: Changing dispositions and practice. *College English, 78*(3), 250–257.

Shirky, C. (2014). Why I just asked my students to put their laptops away. *Medium.* https://medium.com/@cshirky/why-i-just-asked-my-students-to-put-their -laptops-away-7f5f7c50f368.

Simon, B. (2009). Consuming third place: Starbucks and the ilusion of public space. In M. Orvel & J. L. Meikle (Eds.), *Public space and the ideology of place in American culture* (pp. 243–261). Rodopi.

Slattery, S. (2005). Understanding technical writing as textual coordination: An argument for the value of writers' skill with information technology. *Technical Communication, 52*, 353–60.

Slattery, S. (2007). Undistributing work through writing: How technical writers manage texts in complex information environments. *Technical Communication Quarterly, 16*, 311–325. https://doi.org/10.1080/10572250701291046.

Sokolowski, R. (2000). *Introduction to phenomenology.* Cambridge University Press.

Spillers, H. (2003). *Black, white, and in color: Essays on American literature and culture*. University of Chicago Press.

Spinuzzi, C. (2003). *Tracing genres through organizations: A sociocultural approach to information design*. MIT Press.

Spinuzzi, C. (2007). Guest editor's introduction: Technical communication in the age of distributed work. *Technical Communication Quarterly, 16*, 265–77. https://doi.org/10.1080/10572250701290998.

Spinuzzi, C. (2012). Working alone together: Coworking as emergent collaborative activity. *Journal of Business and Technical Communication, 26*, 399–441. https://doi.org/10.1177/1050651912444070.

Spinuzzi, C. (2015). *All edge: Inside the new workplace networks*. University of Chicago Press.

Squire, K. (2007). *Beyond fun: Serious games and media*. Carnegie Mellon ETC Press. https://press.etc.cmu.edu/index.php/product/beyond-fun-serious-games-and-media/

Stallybrass, P. & White, A. (1986). *The politics and poetics of transgression*. Cornell University Press.

Star, S. L. & Ruhleder, K. (1996). Steps toward an ecology infrastructure: Design and access for large information systems. *Information Systems Research, 7*(1), 111–134. https://doi.org/10.1287/isre.7.1.111.

Starbucks.com. (2020). Company information. https://www.starbucks.com/about-us/company-information.

Stone, L. (2007, February). Living with continuous partial attention. The HBR breakthrough ideas for 2007. *Harvard Business Review*. https://hbr.org/2007/02/the-hbr-list-breakthrough-ideas-for-2007.

Stornaiuolo, A., Smith, A. & Phillips, N. C. (2017). Developing a transliteracies framework for a connected world. *Journal of Literacy Research, 49*(1), 68–91. https://doi.org/10.1177/1086296x16683419.

Streitz, N. A., Geisler, Jorg, H., Torsten, K., Shin'ichi, T., Reischl Muller, W., Rexroth P. & Steinmetz, R. (1999). I-LAND: An interactive landscape for creativity and innovation. In *Proceedings of the ACM conference on human factors in computing systems* (CHI '99) (pp. 120–127). Association for Computing Machinery. https://dl.acm.org/doi/10.1145/302979.303010.

Suchman, L. A. (2007). *Human-machine reconfigurations: Plans and situated actions* (2nd ed.). Cambridge University Press.

Sun, H. (2012). *Cross-cultural technology design: Creating culture-sensitive technology for local users*. Oxford University Press.

Swarts, J. (2007a). Mobility and composition: The architecture of coherence in non-places. *Technical Communication Quarterly, 16*(3), 279–309. https://doi.org/10.1080/10572250701291020.

Swarts, J. (2007b). *Together with technology: Writing review, enculturation, and technological mediation*. Baywood Press.

Swarts, J. & Kim, L. (2007). Guest editors' introduction: New technological spaces. *Technical Communication Quarterly, 18*, 211–123. https://doi.org/10.1080/10572250902941986.

Syverson, M. A. (1999). *The wealth of reality: An ecology of composition*. Southern Illinois University Press.

Takayoshi, P. (2016). Methodological challenges to researching composing processes in a new literacy context. *Literacy in Composition Studies, 4*(1), 1–23. https://doi .org/10.21623/1.4.1.2.

Temple, P. (2008). Learning spaces in higher education: an under-researched topic. *London Review of Education, 6*(3), 229–241.

Thomas, M. (Ed.). (2011). *Deconstructing digital natives: Young people, technology, and the new literacies*. Routledge.

Trimbur, J. (1991). Literacy and the discourse of crisis. In R. Bullock, J. Trimbur & C. Schuster (Ed.), *The politics of writing instruction: Postsecondary*. Heinemann.

Turkle, S. (2011). *Alone together: Why we expect more from technology and less from each other*. Basic Books.

Urry, J. (2007). *Mobilities*. Polity.

Van Ittersum, D. (2009). Distributing memory: Rhetorical work in digital environments. *Technical Communication Quarterly, 18*, 259–280. https://doi.org/10.1080 /10572250902942026.

Varnelis, K. (Ed.) (2008). *Networked publics*. MIT Press.

Varnelis, K. & Friedburg, A. (2008). Place: The networking of public space. In K. Varnelis (Ed)., *Networked Publics* (pp. 15–42). MIT Press.

Verhoeve, W. (2013, January 25). Why you should work from a coffee shop, even when you have an office. *Fast Company*. http://www.fastcompany.com/3005011 /why-you-should-work-coffee-shop-even-when-you-have-office.

Virilio, P. (1986). *Speed and politics: An essay on dromology* (M. Polizzotti, Trans.). Semiotext(e). (Original work published 1977)

Virilio, P. (2012). *The great accelerator*. Polity Press.

Wajcman, J. (2015). *Pressed for time: The acceleration of life in digital capitalism*. University of Chicago Press.

Wargo, J. M. (2015). Spatial stories with nomadic narrators: Affect, snapchat, and feeling embodiment in youth mobile composing. *Journal of Language and Literacy Education, 11*(1), 47–64.

Warner, M. (2002). *Publics and counterpublics*. Zone Books.

Weimer, M. (2014, January 8). The age of distraction: Getting students to put away their phones and focus on learning. *Faculty Focus*. http://www.facultyfocus.com /articles/teaching-professor-blog/the-age-of-distraction-getting-students-to-put -away-their-phones-and-focus-on-learning/.

Weisser, C. R. & Dobrin, S. I. (Eds.). (2001). *Ecocomposition: Theoretical and pedagogical approaches*. State University of New York Press.

Welch, N. (2008). *Living room: Teaching public writing in a privatized world*. Boynton/Cook.

Wellman, B. (2001). Physical place and cyberplace: The rise of personalized networking. *International Journal of Urban and Regional Research, 25*(2), 227–252. https://doi.org/10.1111/1468-2427.00309.

Whittemore, S. (2008). Metadata and memory: Lessons from the canon of memoria for the design of content management systems. *Technical Communication Quarterly, 17*(1), 88–109. https://doi.org/10.1080/10572250701590893.

Williams, P. (1992). *The alchemy of race and rights.* Harvard University Press.

Wilson, J. C. & Lewiecki-Wilson, C. (Eds). (2001). *Embodied rhetorics: Disability and language in culture.* Southern Illinois University Press.

Wise, J. M. (2012). Attention and assemblage in the clickable world. In J. Packer & S. B. Crofts Wiley. (Eds.). *Communication matters: Materialist approaches to media, mobility, and networks (pp.* 159–172). Routledge.

Wolff, B. (2006). Laptop use in university common spaces. *Educause Quarterly, 1,* 74–76.

Wood, A. F. (2009). *City ubiquitous: Communication and the rise of omnitopia.* Hampton Press.

Woolf, V. (1929). *A room of one's own.* Harcourt.

Wysocki, A. F. & Johnson-Eilola, J. (1999). Blinded by the letter: Why are we using literacy as a metaphor for everything else? In G. E. Hawisher & C. L. Selfe (Eds.), *Passions, pedagogies, and 21st century technologies (pp.* 349–368). Utah State University Press.

Wysocki, A. (2004). *Writing new media: Theory and applications for expanding the teaching of composition.* Utah State University Press.

Yancey, K. B., Robertson, L. & Taczak, K. (2014). *Writing across contexts: Transfer, composition, and sites of writing.* Utah State University Press.

Yancey, K. B. & McElroy, S. J. (2017). Assembling composition: An Introduction. In K. B. Yancey & S. J. McElroy (Eds.), *Assembling Composition* (pp. 3–25). Southern Illinois University Press.

Young, I. M. (1980). Throwing like a girl: A phenomenology of feminine body comportment motility and spatiality. *Human Studies, 3*(2), 137–156. https://doi.org/10.1007/bf02331805.

Zabrowski, K. & Rivers, N. (2015). The place(s) of mentorship and collaboration. *The Journal of Interactive Technology and Pedagogy, 7.* http://jitp.commons.gc.cuny.edu/the-places-of-mentorship-and-collaboration/.

Zappavigna, M. (2011). Ambient affiliation: A linguistic perspective on Twitter. *New Media and Society,13*(5), 788–806. https://doi.org/10.1177/1461444810385097.

Appendix

The research reported in this book comes from two case studies that were approved by the institutional review boards at the universities where I was affiliated during the research. Both case studies used similar data collection, coding, and analysis, which had two goals:

1. Better understanding the places and operations of transient literacy *in situ* by observing and video recording individuals and groups spending time using networked mobile devices in shared social places, and
2. Contextualizing the use of these materials and purpose of these interactions through qualitative interviews, including general questions about space use, technologies, and social contacts for composing practice as well as specific questions related to the specifics of their time spent during prior observations.

Choosing Sites and Participants

I chose these two sites because of familiarity, as well as because they represented different relationships to transient literacies. The Technology Commons was a designed environment for temporary university learning, while the Gone Wired Café had no official relationship to mobile work. Different demographic groups also tended to use each space. My choices for recruiting individual participants differed to some degree in each site. At the Gone Wired Café, I approached four individuals who I saw observed working routinely over a number of weeks in the café. My cases thus focus exclusively on individuals who had incorporated the coffeehouse into their work routines, and three of the four cases were graduate or professional students (Ed and Kathryn [Chapter 1], Kim [Chapter 3]) with in addition to one working professional (Dave [Chapter 2]). In the Technology Commons, I recruited individual participants to fit with patterns of place, technology use, and social positioning that I observed frequently over several weeks, while also attempting to choose a diverse set of cases in terms of gender and race. This meant that several case participants were not routine or regular users of the center.

Data Collection

My data collection methods were similar in both sites. Both involved an initial observation phase. During six weeks in 2009, I conducted participant observation within the Gone Wired Café for five days a week at varied times of the day. During participant observation, I observed the café's macro activity, noting prevalent technologies and software, observing when the café contained the most people writing, and determining where individuals who wrote often located themselves. I sat at different locations of the café, recorded observations, and composed several hundreds of pages of handwritten field notes, which I later synthesized in typed research memos. During six weeks in 2012, I worked with a research assistant to conduct similar observational research in the Technology Commons. During this observation, we made use a more systematic observational approach—the "sweep method" (Given & Leckie, 2003)—which allowed the two data gatherers to observe in similar ways. The sweep method, in particular, enabled us to account for the number of people, technologies, and social arrangements that were present in the learning center at particular moments of time for several weeks. Using a shared analytical tool, we "swept" each zone of the Technology Commons, and we both also collected handwritten or typed narrative field notes about spatial use during participant observation, which we synthesized into typed research memos. The goal of this phase of research was to serve as a preliminary guide for familiarizing myself with each place, its materials, and its users before turning toward more specific cases. This phase was invaluable in later analysis of both video and interview data.

Following the observation phase, I recruited individuals in both sites willing to participate in case research. I found most individuals to be surprisingly open and willing to share their routines and their time with me. As I told those who agreed to talk with me, I regularly work in public places, sometimes for writing extended prose but more often for taking care of other symbolic tasks (checking email, transcribing interviews, discussing writing with others or some time to look at social media) and I almost always do that work with virtual and material resources for information and social support. Gone Wired and the Technology Commons attract writers who find these spaces to be useful or comfortable, even if temporarily, when others would not. Thus, it is important to remember that this research traces those who already choose these locations for their work. Each case study participant was engaged in multiple writing projects, routinely communicated with people geographically removed from his or her current physical location, and used social media either moderately or extensively during time spent working.

After identifying participants and obtaining consent, I filmed a work or leisure session participants conducted at the café or social learning space. My decision to videotape and analyze participants' practice was motivated by situated action research. The goal in videotaping was to access both on-screen and off-screen practices. I disturbed individuals as little as possible and positioned the external video camera positioned to capture a view of their laptop or other computing device screens, the artifacts present on their tables, and their bodies within the space (from behind). This enabled me to observe and analyze how individuals encountered and manipulated various physical and virtual objects within their workspaces at multiple levels of scope, to capture tacit practices that potentially would be overlooked in retrospective self-reports, and to record conversations and immediate social encounters.

After analyzing work sessions, I contacted case participants to schedule at least one and sometimes more semistructured, stimulated recall interviews. Four videotaped participants from the Technology Commons did not respond to interview requests and thus were only included in analysis of observations. During interviews, questions addressed habits for organizing work space and time across locations, practices and motivations for working in the particular site, as well as specific details related to operations I analyzed in video recordings. These questions expanded the story of the interactive sequences that participants exhibited in their work and leisure sessions by contextualizing their micro movements within their personal perceptions, which helped to highlight what I would later identify as both proximities and orientations.

Data Preparation, Coding, and Analysis

For participants at both sites, I transcribed interviews, fieldnotes, and the dialogue of filmed work and leisure sessions when applicable. For textual data, I segmented conversational data by conversational turns and fieldnotes by sentences. For embodied data in video format, I watched video sessions closely and repeatedly and segmented the actions of work sessions into sequences, noting the amount of time spent in each action. I entered these data into a relational database for further coding procedures.

I practiced two kinds of coding. The first was a thematic coding of both textual and embodied data. During this analysis, I categorized materials taken up during the action of literacy, as well as forms of interaction among materials. These categorizations led me to the dimensions of interaction and materiality presented in this book. Second, along with analysis for themes, I also time-mapped work sessions to trace sequences of interaction. For the purposes of this analysis, I drew on Slattery's (2005, 2007) analysis of central mediating artifacts or resources that held participants' attention during unfolding action as a way to make Lucy Suchman's interactional approach more tangible. I used these coded work sessions to create visualizations of writing activity at the micro level. These visualizations identified patterns of use for networked technologies such as microblogs (i.e., Twitter), social networking sites (i.e., Facebook, LinkedIn), blogs, and email as well as other material resources like word processing programs, phones, and other external technologies.